THE BOX

by

CLIVE PARKER-SHARP

Published 2012 by Strand Publishing UK Ltd.
Golden Cross House, 8 Duncannon Street, Strand
London WC2N 4JF

E-mail address: info@strandpublishing.co.uk
Internet address: www.strandpublishing.co.uk

Paperback ISBN 978-1-907340-15-4

STRAND NON-FICTION

Dedicated to Ethel & Peter Parker

With thanks to
Dennis Russell who helped on anecdotal information,
and supplying photographs, and without whose support,
almost nothing could happen!

With thanks also to
Mandy Parker-Sharp for further research and editing.

CONTENTS

THOMAS - PHASE 1, ENGLAND

THOMAS'S TRIP TO ENGLAND

Linen and lace fluttered in the air. Thomas pulled out a fresh white hanky to join in the flurry and, as he did so, he customarily felt the small bible that he always carried in his inside jacket pocket. Engines stirred below, the steamer churned the water in the dock and they disembarked. He felt no trepidation he waved and waved. No one was seeing him off but he was buoyed up by the celebrations on the crowded deck. Thomas cut quite a figure; tall, gentlemanly, ebony skin, curly hair, smartly dressed, exuding a natural confidence concomitant to his African dynasty. The SS Sekondi set sail. Some passengers lingered leaning against the rails to watch the long pull away from the shore, the inevitable miniaturising of the dock and people. A haze was forming above the distant coast, the afternoon's heat left behind. Thomas eventually took his leave, an attendant showing him to his first class quarters.

'Wednesday 9ᵗʰ October 1901 - Mainly English & American fellow travellers. Departure joyous, infectious. Crew boy delivered up my luggage. Thankful it is safely on-board. Reminded me of Benjamin, father's houseboy. The good book is close to me - God speed Sekondi.'

The transatlantic liner was headed for Sierra Leone where passengers would transfer to the larger SS Sokoua calling at Las Palmas on the 19th, then on to England, a two-week voyage. Thomas expected to return to the port of Dixcove on the Gold Coast of Africa after the few weeks spent in Britain promoting the timber and mineral deposits held in the swathes of land he owned in West Africa. In his cabin he methodically laid out the news clippings of Dr Alexander Dowie expounding on his 'Divine Healing' claims. The bureau was barely big enough for his collection about the Zion religious order. He re-arranged them by date, the beech grain completely covered.

Thomas Brem-Wilson early 1900s

THE BOX – Nina's Story

You couldn't really call it a box by the time it came into my possession. You couldn't even really call it a 'possession'. It was something that had been lying or knocking around for as long as I could remember. Dusty, battered, obviously once regal and expensive, the jewels it had been studded with had long since fallen off, or more likely pulled off and sold. Once richly embossed with designs of animals and jungle scenes, the carvings in the solid leather were mostly worn down, some barely visible. I cherished it. It had no meaningful use, only a memento of a vibrant family. Arranging the contents of clippings, contracts, documents and diaries evoked the past, my imagination plugging the gaps. Spiriting up what had gone was a pipe dream and others had tried and failed. An excited chill would tingle the hairs on my neck.

I was at my Dad, Philip Brem-Wilson's house in Bromley when he finally told me:

"Nina, you may as well have this now, it's no use to me."

He knew I'd always had my eye on it and it was between my brother Jason and me. We'd both leafed through it dozens of times over the years, but I think my Dad knew that I would try to muster something from the exotic keepsake.

The Box had been the business case of my Grandfather, Thomas Brem-Wilson, and had been amongst his possessions when he died in 1929 – probably something he always carried with him, stuffed full of paperwork and maps, leases for land, rubber plantations, timber concessions and gold mining rights dating back to 1890. There were numerous diaries, his diaries and a motley collection of IOUs – he had lent out plenty of money in his time.

Amongst the records one was headed Indenture. It referred to a piece of land called Tuasi, purchased for *One Hundred and Fifty pounds on 25th April 1898 at 3pm*. It had the fingerprint of Chief Kofi Amuku at the bottom. Land measurements were included *15,000 fathoms more or*

9

less by 15,000 also more or less. It sounded huge – nearly the size of England. It was found to be about two and a half square miles. A big leap from my twenty-foot back yard, having lived most of my life in a two bedroom flat. It had five boundaries *Bezzie Creek, Princess Rd, Akofo Rd, Border Ansah and Intiti Baka mine.*

An accompanying map showed the boundaries and the different types of trees were marked. Also in the 1896-1897 prospector's reports you could see much of the land bordered abandoned mining sites. Results of two to three ounces of gold per ton had been filed - an insight into a real life treasure trail in a far off land.

Thomas was born in 1865 when the Gold Coast was part of the Commonwealth and adhered to British Rule. The majority of the African population lived a subsistence lifestyle in homemade mud huts growing food and fishing for their own needs, women doing most of the work. Villagers travelled around by foot and anyone who could afford it by bicycle. Small ferries were used to get from one coastal village to the next.

Thomas was part of the African elite, prosperity accumulated from deals made with local Chiefs where land freeholds were bought up. A Chief's responsibility was to protect the land ensuring it passed down the line but they often found a cash offer too tempting and sold off the rights. He and his brother Joshua and sister Nancy all had an excellent education. Thomas became Headmaster of Cape Coast College for a short while, and Joshua a surveyor, his skills proving invaluable to their expanding empire. Following Pentecostalism, and a devout Christian, Thomas would preach at the church in Dixcove on Sundays. Nancy married into the Salvation Army based in Sekondi near Dixcove, her husband the staunch follower James Cromwell. Thomas took several wives, which was not unusual for a man of his social status, since a house had to be provided for each one to raise their separate family. Marrying my Grandmother Esther, a Music Hall actress, they had children Phillip, Danny and Raymond. Phillip got together with Nellie and gave birth to me Nina Brem-Wilson and my brother Jason.

' *Two days on... enjoying sea air;*

9 am. Breakfast in room, tea, toast... make notes in diary, bible reading, (will perhaps attend silver service in the dining room later in the journey, but must pursue my studies)

10 am. Stroll on deck, although not completely accustomed to motions of the Sekondi, gaining my 'sea legs'.'

Thomas attracted interest as a suave coloured gentleman in first class. They would have expected him to travel in second but his blue cashmere Persian lamb collar coat and highly polished leather boots would have been even more out of place in steerage. He was elegant and, striding with his gold-topped cane, caught the eye of the ladies, halting frequently to admire his reflection in the concave windows that separated the lounges from the deck, ensuring his hair was swept back and pomade smoothed. There was a little damp in the air from the swell hitting the hull so when he passed an empty deckchair he hoisted his leg up onto the arm to wipe off his boots with a handkerchief. Thomas liked his appearance to be just right, his image was God's work.

"Good Morning," was his introduction, grinning charismatically, stopping to make small talk, sometimes lifting his walking stick up and tapping his forelock with the gold cap, especially to any females. No one could miss the solid gold elephant figure topping the cane.

On day three a note was delivered to Thomas. He was still taking breakfast at nine when there was a tap at the door. He threw his serviette down on the small wooden pull-out table that doubled as a writing desk and which had housed his Zion compendium. The cabin was not the largest of First Class, but was still First Class and, as such, was comfortable - with a main room, a small bathroom and bedroom, wood-lined, finished with a laminate of dark African teak. The bible remained open at the page Thomas had been studying, the binding

11

worn away, pages nearly coming apart. He slid into his leather slippers, affixed his robe grabbing a few pennies from the table, answering as a second bout of knocking started. A small African cabin boy in an oversized bleached uniform with a navy bow-tie thrust a silver tray forward with a card.

"Sir, deeleviry."

He had been told what to say and it did not come out quite right voiced with an African tongue. Thomas looked down and grinned, taking the card, ruffling the boy's hair, pressing the coins into his palm.

"Tak tu Sir," came the lad.

He skated off down the corridor, almost skipping, ready for the next errand, lack of shoes now apparent, trousers dancing over the bare feet. The poor used cowry shells as Gold Coast currency; the English pennies would be a tidy sum. The card was white, it had been printed using the ship's own press, in gold writing, the Shipping Company logo in the top corner. He slowly walked back to his seat, turning it over several times, his dark fingers against the faultless card feeling the quality. He picked up his tea, continuing the rotations, looking at his nails slightly pink and lighter than his hands, then gazing out of the porthole, still turning the card and taking sips. Putting them down next to the bible, he went to wash and dress. Only when completely prepared and turned out in his morning suit did Thomas study it properly. He spoke out loud as if he had an audience.

'THE FIRST MAIN EVENT OF THE VOYAGE BY SPECIAL
INVITATION OF CAPTAIN SENCHERY
A PRIVATE DINNER DANCE IN THE CONCERT ROOMS
FRIDAY 11TH OCTOBER 1901, 7 O'CLOCK
SELECTED FIRST CLASS GUESTS ONLY
EVENING WEAR, RSVP, THE BURSAR.'

Thomas put the card on the table, took a pen and scribbled on the back, murmuring the words, as if he had to speak them for them to become real. 'Accepted with thanks, Thomas Brem-Wilson, cabin 663.'

He pulled the bell cord for the cabin boy and shut the door behind him, sliding the card between the door and the frame for the boy to see, and left for his morning walk.

Thomas arrived at the dance on the dot, punctuality next to Godliness. He made his entrance and necks craned. He wore a tuxedo with contrasting red bow tie against a crisp pleated shirt. He was dashing to say the least, demanding attention. Six enormous glittering chandeliers swaying gently with the motion of the ship highlighted the room's opulence. The Maitre D whispered to ask his name then formally proclaimed:

"Thomas Brem-Wilson."

A bus boy in a ceremonial seaman's regalia with epaulettes and flat cap guided each guest to their table place. Thomas strode across the room, one hand in his jacket pocket, one instinctively the upper inside. He had forgotten the bible and faltered.

"Sir. Can I get you anything?" asked the boy. Thomas hesitated momentarily feeling in each pocket.

"No, no, go ahead." he replied, following the escort to the table. He glanced toward the string quartet playing on the stage as his seat was pulled out for him.

"It's not the main dance band darling, it's a prelude, super isn't it… I'm Helen de Bouvoir."

To his immediate right, a mature attractive lady held out her hand, and Thomas shook it, with a little too much masculinity as he was somewhat taken off-guard by the introduction, and still anxious about the bible he had left in the cabin - taking a breath.

"May I introduce myself, Thomas Brem-Wilson, businessman."

Waiters hovered, spotless service coats, the pristine linen table-cloths almost shimmered with rainbow shards, flickering from the crystal cut wine glasses standing at the ready. The silver cutlery chinked and the first courses left the kitchens - pheasant, soups, and meats in aspic. The tables were spacious, making conversation with the guests opposite a little difficult, but Thomas tried.

"Good evening, good evening, madam, sir." He went round the table nodding, "I'm Thomas Brem-Wilson, how are you?"

'Most of the male passengers were retired – elderly, portly, not the dancing types... They were accompanied by women partners who seemed younger... attractive! Relaxed in the finest eveningwear'.

There may have been some scheming in the seating plan and, considering the age and demeanour of some of the other guests it was lucky for Thomas as his seating partner was outgoing and charming. She was wearing a wonderfully well-fitted sapphire, sequined evening gown that emphasised her fulsome bosom and pale revealed cleavage. Her hair was a smart fashionable bob and, as Thomas engaged her in small talk through dinner, she leaned in to hear his conversation, the smell of his hair cream mingling with her perfume, expensive and French, producing an intoxicating mixture, and with the assistance of the wine they became immersed. Helen's tone was well spoken pure English, but throaty and a little husky.

"It has been a grave time, but we're determined to shed the shackles, so to speak… Lucy my daughter, that is. Incidentally, she had an invitation to the Captain's table! Don't ask me why?"

Thomas turned to look in the same direction as Helen. She waved her fan in the air, a small circular motion and caught Lucy's eye, a pretty girl waved back glaring keenly at Thomas, and he reciprocated raising his eyebrows a tad at the eye-catching young lady. Helen guided Thomas back to her conversation by placing her arm behind his chair and arching toward him.

"Lucy and I decided to take a world tour to get over my husband's death. It was a terrible shock for Lucy but I saw it coming, with his indulgences."

Helen lingered on the 'es' of indulgences, her voice lowering in tone at the end, intimating that Thomas would understand what her husband's private pleasures were. Thomas affirmed with a bob of his head as if he had some insight.

"So I've brought Lucy away to freshen the air."

Helen stayed close leaning toward Thomas, which meant she had to

14

make a theatrical type stretch for her flute, impossible for Thomas not to avoid the sight of her cleavage. She took a taste, constantly training her eyes on him. He coughed and uttered:

"Your dress, what material is it? I'm interested in fabrics, to bring back to The Gold Coast for my business."

"Feel it sir."

Helen put her hand under the table taking Thomas's, which had been firmly placed on his leg, and guided it over her thigh and the seam of her dress.

"Satin, and hand sewn sequins, Paris."

She was now looking away to the stage but continuing to guide him. He looked to see if anyone was watching, but everywhere there was noise and distraction.

"Sheer, like a glove, beautiful, Ms Helen."

"Just... Helen, darling."

He could feel her suspenders and the tops of her stockings and pulled away to reach for a drink.

Dinner continued, sweets, cheese, they chatted, ignoring the incident. Helen kept looking down at his hands trying to accidentally touch them whilst fiddling with the cutlery. His nails were manicured and as he spoke he would run one nail under the other, preening himself - a habit and one of several social idiosyncrasies he had acquired over the years. He also tilted his head back then forward, lips faintly pursed, with a little frown when listening. He found it made the interlocutor believe their words to be the most vitally significant ones in the world at that moment in time. He employed another of these small public quirks at dinner, looking into the middle distance as if acknowledging a friend on the other side of the room, to avoid the entreaties of inquisitive table companions - he did not mean to be rude. It allowed him to savour Helen's company. She found an excuse to grip his hand again, which excited Thomas but he remembered the bible and gently patted her hand in a friendly way under the table then let go. Helen was not perturbed. She had had a few glasses of champagne and, as the Ladies' Invitation was announced and the full orchestra struck up, she called on Thomas for a Foxtrot. He steered her to the floor. They stayed there for the next dance and the next, an intimate Waltz. With his hand on her hip he could feel it was tight and trim. Her heart was pumping fast as they circled the floor. They took a rest at Thomas's suggestion on one of the plush gold and red sofas dotted around the dance-floor, which matched the vast drapes of the concert room.

Helen's daughter joined them. She was eighteen - a younger version of the very good looking Helen - in high heels, wearing a silk Chinese style fitted dress intricately hand embroidered with side vents. As she fell into the sofa clutching a long drink, the scarlet lining and the tops of her stockings were revealed. Breathless and already a little bit tipsy she gravitated immediately towards Thomas.

'I met a spinster, very well turned out... and her zealous daughter. I took to their conversation and ebullience, they in turn enjoyed my quips, and I was pleased to enliven their evening... to take their mind off their obviously sad loss... Helen's husband's demise, the reason for the death I never learned, but I did ascertain he was successful and rich. Helen was over-intimate, (and her daughter Lucy - quite bold! may have experienced alcohol for the first time!), but I acted like a gentleman, as I knew she was behaving out-of-character, due to her recent loss. I promised myself that I would retire to my room at a reasonable time, ensuring they had reached their cabin safely'.

"I love being on a boat; the sailors, uniforms, and the Captain is super-duper." Lucy was talking nonsense with an intense adolescent enthusiasm, her dimples flashing.

"I do like your coat," placing her palms on Thomas's jacket lapels.

Helen pushed them away and grasped his hand.

"Our dance I think, Mr Thomas?" tugging him back into the arena.

Lucy took the next opportunity, her favourite tune. Helen having to sit it out, watching jealously as the pair shimmied by. The competition for Thomas's attention continued. He became thirsty with the prolonged activity, the waiters bringing several silver salvers of champagne over, and Helen was ordering the latest cocktails to try out. Both ladies were squiffy and giggly, touching Thomas at every opportunity, his reticence and graciousness making him even more alluring to them. The evening drew to a close, the orchestra playing a schmaltzy English ballad, the Captain saying a few thanks on the stage, Thomas offering an escort.

"Have brandy and coffee in our cabin sweetie, the night's young, we're having so much fun."

Helen encouraged Thomas to head for their quarters.

"I'll accompany you madam, but no more."

"You're such a gentleman." Lucy taking his arm, and Helen grabbed the other not wishing to be outdone.

They left side-by-side and listing somewhat to the bemusement of the remaining guests. After an unsteady ten minute walk through the night air and several corridors, they arrived at cabin 705 - two inebriated women, mother and daughter, and Thomas, standing at the door, Helen fumbling in her clutch bag for the key, hanging on tight to Thomas.

"You won't disappoint us will you Sir, a gentleman wouldn't... I make a divine coffee, just what you need to help you back to your rooms Mr Thomas."

Before he could protest he was through the thick mahogany door into their luxurious, roomy, wood-panelled suite. They entered the reception (off of which were bedrooms, ante rooms, and a bathroom) when Helen gave up her grip, "Lucy, sweetie, make our guest comfortable... I'll freshen up."

Thomas sat on the sofa whilst Lucy prepared drinks. They could not make coffee and it was too late to order, so Thomas settled for a brandy.

I thought I might have made a wrong move as soon as I saw Kofi's luggage piled up on the departure lounge floor of London's Heathrow Airport. That's when it occurred to me that this was no ordinary escape from the humdrum British winter blues. For me 1975 Britain was about working and the market stall I had in Sutton, because really I'd almost never known anything else. Dad had me working the markets from when I was thirteen, freezing in winter, selling potatoes and veg on a corner in Lewisham. I graduated to my own business, a pitch in the then thriving Deptford, South East London market. I made good money (markets prospered then) and with a bit of business 'savvy', I found some exclusive lines or 'parcels' bought from a friend-of-a-friend. They'd started life on a lorry and had somewhere fell off the back of it and ended up on my stall. A cornucopia of Kickers shoes (the latest fashion) Scholl's sandals, to basket-ware and everything in between.

Flat 4a Bromley Hill where the Brem-Wilson family lived.
Nina and father Philip, 1957

18

Brem-Wilson market stall Lewisham 1957, at a bombsite
next to Woolworths

As above, note 'demonstrator' in the background

My partner Jim (I was divorced and now had a boyfriend) had given Kofi specific instructions about the luggage allowance, and I'd missed the numerous bags being jammed into the back of the cab when we left my house in Caterham, Surrey, probably because it was three in the morning. We'd met Kofi Achampon through my cousin William who had employed him in his business selling office furniture. I can't really imagine what use Kofi was to my cousin, as he was annoying me already and we were nowhere near the plane yet. He was quite loud and excitable which really itched a nerve after my early start.

Jim, me, and Will, had decided to take the plunge and go to Africa - a journey and, from this first morning, a road into the unknown. It was the fact that Kofi seemed knowledgeable about the Gold Coast, had family and contacts there and wanted to help, that ultimately compelled us to investigate my Grandfather's dowry. I think maybe if we'd not known Kofi, this whole chapter of my life never would've started. So, we'd done a deal with him that we'd pay for his flights and expenses. In return he'd accommodate us at his father's hotel for two weeks and we'd have use of his car. Ghana, as it's now called, was definitely not a tourist destination. Flights were expensive but we felt we'd be getting an experience, a holiday of sorts, and some insight into the contents of the Box. I was clutching it tensely against my chest. The gregarious Kofi, the luggage hubbub at the check-in, the tiredness and fuss made me nervous and reluctant, definitely not in holiday mode. It wasn't going in the aircraft hold with all of Kofi's stuff, I had a feeling it might disappear into a black hole.

Kofi's father was a political refugee from Ghana, which is how they ended up in England. His father had escaped when the family, who were members of the ousted government, were arrested and shot. Kofi (and us) had to keep a low profile entering as tourists. He was separated from his countless pieces of hand luggage (many stripy bags taped up, with goods for all his relatives) by the KLM[1] staff, excess was paid, and into the hold it went.

Jim, Will and I managed to get some sleep on the eight-hour ordeal. Before landing Kofi went to change his clothes in the toilet and came

---

[1] KLM – Royal Dutch Airlines

out looking like James Brown. We were too surprised and stunned to ask him why. He was dressed to impress or at least he thought so. Satin navy tracksuit with the most enormous medallion you had ever seen replaced his normal baggy jeans and t-shirt that we had come to know him for. His hair had been slicked by gel into a big chocolate curly wet looking pile. I turned to Jim to say something but nothing came out - perhaps it was the jet lag already kicking in. Jim and Will hung back a little as we left the plane but I stuck to Kofi like a fly to pooh, as I had to know what he was up to. As soon as he was down the steps, he fell to the ground, and in a huge gesture, kissed the tarmac. Clearly no hope of us entering Ghana inconspicuously.

The heat really hit. It felt like checking the roast at the oven door. The temperature doubled when we entered the terminal building. Dirty, chaotic, threadbare woollen curtains, and grimy floors. In stark contrast, the ground attendants were immaculate. Airport handlers and security were in starched shirts, dark skirts and trousers. The whole of the airport was in uproar. Any relaxation and rest I'd had on the plane couldn't have prepared me for this. Jim held my arm and Will kept close, tightly grasping our hand baggage and the Box.

Africans wearing every conceivable garb surrounded the regimented airport staff: traditional plain robes, bright and colourful robes depicting the tribes they came from, and some in western attire. We found the baggage area despite the looming anarchy. Much of the shouting was about lost luggage from our airplane. There was a type of carousel that used rollers and two boys, who pushed round the cases when they emerged from behind the rubber flap guards. It reminded me of a Flintstones clip where cave-bound cartoon dinosaurs pull a roundabout, gears rotating a central bar linked to a permanently revolving cake stand in the kitchen up above. It was insane and a culture shock. At last our luggage came out, and even Kofi's, which really was a small miracle.

"Yabadabadoo!"

"What?" said Jim.

"Don't worry, let's keep going."

The last nerve-racking bit was to get through customs, which looked to be manned by soldiers with guns. I was a little uneasy, as

Kofi was the most ostentatious looking man in the building. We let a good few go ahead, putting a bit of space between him and us, pretending to fiddle with our bags and visas, etc. Kofi was through. We joined the queue. We're tourists, tourists, tourists, I repeated under my breath as we approached the armed barricade.

"Drink dear Sir, can I touch your skin, it's so, so, sooo…"

Lucy's voice tailed off as she unsteadily sidled up to Thomas on the sofa intending to hand him his drink. Before Thomas could say a word she kissed him full on the lips and the drink went flying, the tumbler making a loud smash on the wooden floor, bringing Helen dashing in. As soon as Helen saw Lucy embracing Thomas she also made a move for him, her half buttoned gown falling down. It was immediately apparent that Thomas was very aroused by the attention of both mother and daughter. This excited them and they play acted, laughing and hugging, in front of him. Helen had a twinkle in her eye, inebriation and craving for the potent Negro dulling any inhibitions. Discarding her evening gown, breathing deeply, she rubbed her hands over her black lace panties and bodice, watching salaciously as Lucy deliberately undid Thomas's trousers. Lucy grabbed him. Thomas roughly pulled her clinging dress down over her skin white breasts.

"Sir, I can't wait."

Helen moved to his lap taking Thomas in her mouth, Lucy sliding round to French kiss him, her tongue moist, moving across his lips. Thomas first made love to Lucy, her dress still on, tightly pulled up around her young lithe buttocks, the seams of the side vents ripping a little with each thrust. Panting heavily, Thomas reared up to his full height, entering Lucy from behind, sweating profoundly as the alcohol worked its way out of his body, eyes rolling, his hands like granite against the flesh of her hips where he gripped pulling her toward him repeatedly. Helen gently took one of Thomas's hands and placed it on her backside, moving it downwards, writhing with delight against his forearm. She in turn stroked Lucy's thighs, and Lucy climaxed. Thomas withdrew his penis just before he felt a pang of joy, ejaculating onto

Helen's legs, Helen grabbing the member directing it to her black stockings.

"Oh Mr Thomas."

Helen was throaty and smiling. She massaged the semen into her skin, thrusting her breasts forward in her bodice as she did, making a show to Thomas, both hands gliding up and down her glistening legs. As Lucy crumpled on the sofa, having succumbed to the effect of the drink, Helen took Thomas.

"Come to my chamber, I have something special for you."

She carefully directed him through the shards on the floor, to her bedroom. The more experienced woman fascinated Thomas and the lingering thought of both women making love intensified his fervent sexual appetite. Helen gladly yielded to him over-and-over into the night. When she lay sweating and exhausted Thomas slipped away, his head pounding. He flitted through the ship's web, lost. At that early hour cabin boys passed on errands, their uniforms a blur, corridors distorted, only instinct led him to his cabin and he retired. He ordered tea but did not hear the knock at the door and it was left outside. He had gone to sleep straight away, but it became fitful, the encounter zoned in, intermingling with thoughts of his congregational meetings, the African villages cramming his mind.

'A drunken fervour clouds my judgement, zero, lower than the gutter, if only this was the first or last time, but I consistently snub the Lord – my lack of control has come back to torment. Again, I am taken by a grip of madness, the neglected good book burns through my mind like a stigmata, an evil presage to a dark place, where chaos and mayhem devour my ability to take the righteous path. In bed I perspire and shake, nightmares flash in front of my eyes. Native girls dancing round and round add to my torture... young

23

breasts gyrate with the beat lit by a fire flashing across their sweating bodies. They persecute me with sensual intensity, taunting'.

Thomas, feverish, called out.

Every part of me was wet but I wasn't in the shower, I was in the queue to get into Ghana. It was the kind of wet that my body was producing in bucket-loads to compensate for the heat, stickiness, and general uncomfortableness that was Accra Airport Arrivals Terminal.

"Over here."

A gun pointed and the three of us were taken for full body searches. Why it had to be us and not Kofi, I still do not understand? I had a female officer but it did not make it any less intrusive and upsetting. I don't know what I would possibly be smuggling *into* Ghana, but they had us, and we were not going anywhere until it was done.

I thought the ordeal was over once we were through. We gathered up our belongings ready to leave the building. As soon as we reached the exit, bedlam was upon us. It was dimly lit outside but I could see reams of boys jostling to take luggage to waiting taxis. A tall man with a stick was beating them back only for them to be replaced by more 'luggage boys'. I couldn't see the point of the 'man with the stick'. What was he there for - to beat boys? Was he paid? I saw Kofi at the Taxi rank. We held our bags to us as tight as possible. Jim held on to me and we pushed towards the cab, our energy being quickly diminished in the frenzy. Kofi grabbed our bags, threw them in, dispatched the luggage lads, and we were off, Kofi barking instructions to the driver.

We had no concept of where we were or where we were going and Kofi didn't seem to want to share any of this essential information with us. We were relieved to be out of the terminal so we didn't push the point. Almost immediately it was dirt tracks, no motorways, no signs, no lights, through villages, a few roadside houses and bars, almost total darkness, potholes throwing us around, hardly any vehicles, about an hour's driving with little discussion, only Kofi's conversation with the driver, mostly in broken Ghanaian, some Pidgin English. We pulled up outside a hardly discernible building. All I could see was a sign, half fallen off, 'Beauty Hotel', hanging above the front door waiting to land on someone's head. I was uneasy about entering.

A dingy musty smell was the first thing to fill my nostrils, but we were frazzled, and ready to lay our heads anywhere. It had been many years since this was a hotel by the looks of it, peeling paintwork, scruffy walls and curtains. I had a bath, Jim and I sharing the upstairs bathroom with some lukewarm water, although you can't believe I wanted hot water in these temperatures. I looked at myself in the shabby mirror when I got out. I still had a good shape for a fortyish lady, getting a bit 'lived in', but complemented by my dark complexion. I frizzed my hair - my daughter always called it a 'lock-down' hair-do - mostly because it was nearly an Afro, thick and wily, which I bleached at the ends to stop any grey showing. I patted my hair around - the heat wasn't doing it any favours, but I had various lotions and potions to keep it in check. Jim had finished; he never got in a bath, a habit from his upbringing of sharing a small house with a big family with no proper heating or hot water. He always had a stand-up wash with a flannel at the sink, methodically cleaning the whole caboodle. Jim was tall, swarthy, and trim, handsome, with strong arm muscles and chiselled looks, he'd earned his stripes as an Army fitness instructor, specialising in boxing, teaching a number of up-and-coming champions, and he'd always done physical work. He'd been a popular guy with the ladies when I met him and I was lucky to have hooked up with him after my divorce. By the time we were both done a beer had been summoned from somewhere. We went to our room and we fell into almost a coma. What seemed like seconds later I heard an excitable Kofi calling.

"Breakfast Nina!"

I knew straight away it was morning from the cockerels sounding outside and the scuffing of chickens in a yard below. The hotel didn't look so horrendous in daylight, but I didn't want to walk around in

25

bare feet in case I stuck to something. Kofi had got off the prior evening, with us too worn out to question him on our whereabouts and why this plainly wasn't his father's hotel. Now we wanted to know exactly where we were - we were ready for him. Will, Jim, and I, rounded-up in the hall and went down for breakfast only to be greeted in the dining room by a surge of what looked like half of Africa waiting to meet us and, more importantly, to be fed. Everyone was ordering everything on the menu. Two nimble ladies in fresh African regalia nipped in and out of the kitchen with toast, eggs, and tea. Whilst the breakfast confusion ensued, Will got stuck into Kofi.

"… And who's paying for all this as well?!"

Kofi, ever amiable and evasive, started introducing his family, brother Eddy, cousin Gladys and so on. Jim kept on and in the end Kofi admitted:

"It was too late to go to my father's place last night as it is an hour on from here. We will get a taxi there this morning. I'll order one."

And with that, he disappeared, with us mugs left to foot the bill. Luckily the money for breakfast didn't break us, and we set off for the right venue.

Outside for the first time, it was a busy little area on the outskirts of Accra, a few shops, a bit rundown, single story buildings with prerequisite tin roofs. There were buses, bicycles, and some cars whizzing by, the red grit from the road already mixing with the morning heat to create a haze that sat above the street. They were mainly commuters going to work so we drew little attention. We stared at the completely novel scene around us, at strange little shops with few goods in their windows, the foreign signs, broken English and African words together, sun bleached - Africa was tidy and colourful. A couple of stalls set out selling fish, flies flicked away, a movement clearly practiced a million times by a small old lady joined to a dried grass swatch. The humidity was building and I felt the first sweat of the day drip down my forehead and over my eyebrow. I took a tissue from my bag and wiped it away.

I can't say what I'd imagined. Reclining in a hammock? Fanned by minions? Marvelling at my vast and wondrous lands? Cool drink in my hand? Swathes of wildebeests lolloping on the plains, while I waited for

26

the mining companies to call me with the latest on my gold reserves? The decrepit hotel - I'm not sure where - feeding the multitude, and antiquated plumbing were ink in the ointment. As market workers, we could 'rough it' if needs-be.

We had to be near Tuasi to make a start, and even with the inadequate map we had purchased from the Embassy in London that resembled Mappa Mundi[2], it was obvious we weren't in any position to start what we had come here to do. I wasn't perturbed, though my instinct said Kofi had fleeced us. I hoped the Box wasn't telling me something from Granddad Thomas's grave 'Go Home! Go Home!' Kofi was waiting with a vehicle outside, his now damaged pile of wet-look hair conveyed a hapless sight in the ninety degree heat, an ever more irritating huge grin plastered across his gormless face:

"Nina, Jim, I got your taxi... Nina, Jim...!"

'Spending all my time in cabin... I don't know what day, pouring over the bible trying to come to terms... Only this, writing in my diary has some purgatory effect, removing it from the attaché, each time, gives some minor solace.

14th October 1901 - Jolted from self-immersion being called to take liner change at Sierra Leone, cabin boy doing my packing - managing to avoid other passengers,

---

[2] The Mappa Mundi - is unique in Britain's heritage, an outstanding treasure of the medieval age, which reveals how 13th century scholars interpreted the world in spiritual and geographical terms.

taking meals in the cabin -feigning illness. My shame is, that I strayed from God's word again, a deep blackness in my heart where flesh has overcome and blurred my true belief. A carnal dalliance is one thing, a mistake, but with a mother and daughter together, it must be a <u>slight</u> on the word of God'.

Thomas scribbled furiously, underscoring the word 'slight' obsessively, almost frenetically, the pen held tight in the middle of a fist. A number of notes were delivered to his door by the smartly dressed cabin boy, on a silver dish. Thomas took them cordially, giving him a coin each time but left them unopened on the sideboard, returning to his porthole view, his bible and diary.

'14th October 1901 - I pray for forgiveness, attending the ship's Chaplain, and after days of self induced suffering, decided to summon the courage to go out on deck and observe the docking at Las Palmas, a great deal of hubbub, goods being taken off and on, huge ropes swinging bales and crates onto the deck, and loaded down into the hold... a swarm like ants below'.

They left the Canary Islands shadowing the Spanish and French coasts eventually reaching the Atlantic. A minor episode shook Thomas out of depression - apparently smoke emanating from his mouth. It had become colder, cold enough to produce fog on everyone's breath not seen by Thomas before, it was unusual enough to cheer him up. He took an afternoon amble in the sun inhaling and exhaling deeply to highlight the experience, occasionally making conversation. He met a honeymooning pair arm in arm that recognised him from the Ball. Although a pleasant man, an American, he was disinterested in the small-talk and distracted away by the sea swell hitting the bough, circled by a constant barrage of gulls dipping in for the regular kitchen waste and various ship discharge. He leant his small stocky frame against the rail and puffed on a cigar, observing intently the birds arcing over the waves. The wife was hardly beyond girlhood, a good twenty years her husband's junior, a little awkward, not being able to concentrate her view on one thing as she spoke:

"You haven't been on deck Sir since the Ball, I had noted your absence from the ship's social circle?"

"A terrible sea-sickness overcame me Madam, although, if I'd known such an entrancing creature was concerned for my well-being, my spirits would have been lifted tenfold so as to make a speedier recovery."

She laughed, although Thomas thought it conveyed sorrow rather than levity. The compliment allowed her a brief moment of impulsiveness, touching his arm gently and fixing on his gaze. Thomas could see the husband with his back to them twenty yards away out of the corner of his eye.

"Having seen you at the inaugural Ball I'd hoped for a meaningful encounter as soon as the opportunity arose dear Sir."

She moved closer, both of them backing into a glass alcove that served as the entrance to one of the observation lounges, furnished with padded deckchairs and attended by stewards, out of the wind. They were out of sight of the husband. Thomas could see their reflection; she was side-on to him, a curvaceous bust. Her perfume swirled in the small vestibule, musk.

"Are you married Sir, I notice you travel alone?"

"I am Madam, I'm afraid I have taken more than one wife, the tradition in my country."

"Most exotic Sir... *most* exotic." She craned her neck a little in order to watch her husband, then retracted, her skin untouched by time, clear, delicate, a tiny Adam's apple uncovered above the round lace collar. "Maybe a tradition that should be exported, for I have made a grave mistake," she stumbled on her words continuing, "I feel Sir, I feel that I've made a terrible mistake."

She turned to Thomas her skirt brushing against him. He could

29

taste her scent. Her face was close.

"You gotta get outta that wind." Her husband's voice boomed and Thomas's heart went up into his throat. He quickly stepped back.

"I was just saying to your dear lady wife Sir, a terrible virus struck me down this last week."

"Yeah," came the American's reply, "two folk died in steerage, watta shame, they got it bad, you're lucky buddy."

He took his wife's arm in his and jerked her in the direction of the hull, without a word from her she didn't even glance back. Thomas looked at himself in the salt stained glass. He pulled up his frame, straightening his shoulders so that the image didn't appear unnerved. He continued his walk.

'The lord has spared me. Two deaths on board from a contagion – the lower decks are foul... I am indeed fortunate'.

This wasn't the car promised in the Kofi deal, but it was working and had a driver. Eddy and Kofi were trussed up in the front with him, the three of us in the rear cramped and sweaty. Luggage rammed in the boot, on the roof and tied down with twine fed through the open windows. I held the Box close, it had got me this far alive. It was meant to take an hour to Kofi's hotel. By the second hour, after endless villages, country, bush, small settlements, I pulled Granddad Thomas's little diary from the attaché Box. Opening it and squinting in the sun I read.

'Sunday 20th October, before reaching journey end, a passenger in second class died of fever and was thrown overboard. Monday 21st October, first class passenger died: memorial service at 4 o'clock'.

30

I was suffering in second class, concentrating on the mini-print, when suddenly Jim shouted above the noise of the vehicle:

"Put that away Nina, we're here!"

Heads turned to the left and our attention was immediately drawn to the bombsite that should have been our hotel. It was difficult to comprehend why Kofi had brought us here, to the middle of nowhere, an African thing maybe, to show off a hotel that might one day be built. Four bricks high, a rectangular wall was filled as far as the eye could see with rubble and plastic bottles.

Will got out, paced angrily up and down looking at the site and went berserk manhandling Kofi from the front seat. Jim and I scouted around, but were again speechless.

"Why bring us here?!"

Will had Kofi by the collar up against the car. Kofi waved his arms ludicrously as if some great scheme was going to be beamed in from space and when Will let go he started reprimanding at his brother in dialect, gesticulating madly, as if it was *his* fault. It defied any logic. When we realised that nothing could be done we got in the taxi and went back to the Beauty Hotel resigned and disheartened.

I imagined the newspaper headlines: 'Tourist Misery'...'Holiday Family In Package Nightmare Hell', the article mentioning 'unbuilt hotels', 'lack of plumbing', and 'a deranged tourist guide'. Kofi went into a sulk, which surprised me since we should have been the ones sulking. At Beauty he skulked off under instructions to get us our promised vehicle. A whole day stranded. At least we had cold beer, a cold bath and the two prim African ladies to wait on us. We sat in what was once the veranda of the hotel, overgrown ivy and palms held back by bits of string. For the remainder of the afternoon we discussed a way out.

"I'll go and make some enquires for Taxis to Takoradi, it's a hundred miles, but it's got to be better than being stuck here," Will concluded.

He left in the direction of the roadside stallholders and within twenty minutes Kofi was back promising a car for the following morning. He had probably heard on the African grapevine that we were making alternative plans and was worried he was going to be dumped from the A-team, or he genuinely felt remorse for the day's events. There was a possibility that his brother had told him the hotel was built and that he drove us there in good faith, so we took him at his word this one last time. After about an hour, Will returned. A taxi to Takoradi wasn't as cheap as the breakfast for Kofi's extended family; in fact it was a small mortgage. We decided to wait for Kofi's car the following morning.

'The memorial service was a splendid affair in the Circle Room at the head of the ship. The sight of a hundred or so first class passengers in formal wear, looking out against the bow of the liner cutting into the swell of the Atlantic was quite spectacular. The purser quoted from Matthew 11:28 for the deceased, laid a wreath on the coffin, and sherry and eats were served. Holding up my glass with the others as a toast it did occur to me that nobody there knew the man. I hoped I may go with this sort of respect and ceremony, but not anonymously'.

Helen spotted him and approached, with Lucy in tow. They were immediately excitable, squeezing his hand and asking where he'd been. Helen extended an open invitation for Thomas to visit their quarters, which he diplomatically sidelined, saying how wonderful they both looked. They giggled and flirted. Despite his self-imposed incarceration Thomas was striking in his twill day suit, a cream pleated shirt finished with a ruby red velvet cravat. He mingled, ever the socialite, avoiding Helen and daughter, and this was the last he would see of them. They landed five days later at Plymouth, England, at six-thirty in the evening.

32

'25th October... liner docked. The Bursar recommended I stay at the Duke of Cornwall Hotel in Milbay Road. I took his advice, taking a cab the short ride from the docks, cases to be sent on. I had my day bag with a change of clothes, and leather attaché. The building is impressive, well appointed, with grand decoration and lighting. I ate alone in the dining room and retired weary. My room is comfortable and luxurious, but I have to be woken at six to catch the nine o'clock train to London. My bags have not come - rang for the night porter, booked them to go direct to the terminus... one shilling'.

Thomas was a little surprised on arriving at the station. It was hectic, not dissimilar to those at home, always constantly congested. He had arranged for his ticket with the concierge at the hotel and went straight to his carriage, soaking up the majestic landscape of England in October.

'England is everything I'd expected and more, everything I'd read about and heard, the leaves, colours in abundance, crinkled browns, hues, greens, deep reds, russet, a spectacle flashing by... 'EMPIRE!' villages and towns, spires, houses, streets, ordered, the fields and hedgerows, laid out, enterprise, civilized... England surely is the best country in the world'.

Lodgings had been organised through his African lawyer Mr Renner who had British contacts and once at Victoria Station he hailed a cab

33

to Mayfair, London W1. He really took to it. Thomas loved the hustle and bustle, the taxis and buses, scores of carriages, the ladies, the lamps, taking it in like a gleeful child with a brand new toy.

'The room is small, but quaint, a little seedy and grubby, a bathroom and toilet at the end of the landing... a good price for the area. From the loft-light a spectacular view out over the Kensington rooftops... high & dramatic. Having paid the landlady a deposit, I shall go straight out walking...'

Thomas was enthralled by the shops, city-folk, street stalls - everyone was out.

'At night in Africa, the dark comes down early and it is difficult to get around or do anything useful'.

Darkness descended like a huge lunging blanket from the sky, no nice sunsets, sitting around chatting, having a few chilled cocktails and chewing the fat. Maybe it was the time of year or some special nighttime drama to add to our woes. The second night I still wasn't ready for it. The lack of light outside drew us in to eat in the drab little dining room. The food was good, the prim pair doing a splendid job. We couldn't complain, something like chicken, but we weren't asking or looking too closely in case it put us off.

I sat reciting parts of the diary, again squinting at the small Victorian print, Jim and Will talking over me.

'Arrived London. Lodged 24 Duke of Portland Street. Paid for 2nd class 21 shillings, cab and guide a quarter

shilling, Hotel 11 shillings, Bike 6 shillings, cabs 6 shillings 7 pence, House 30 shillings, telephone 2 shillings and 4 pence'.

"Who do you think he was calling, that seems quite expensive for 1901 doesn't it...Jim?!" But both were ignoring me.

It was difficult to read, difficult to understand, so much money going out, pages and pages of land being bought up in Africa, Chiefs paid, someone dying from smallpox. It was a world apart, yet I was here, not far from the same place. Maybe he had been on this very spot nearly a hundred years before.

We retired. I lay in the heat doubly hot now I intended to sleep. The first night's 'coma' had segued into a second night of 'insomnia', half nightmares flashing in and out of my head, lying in a bed outside, exposed, in a rubble and plastic rubbish dump, surrounded by four walls of half built hotel. Jim thrashed around, an arm, a leg, and jab, jab, jab, the mosquito net constantly sticking to my face. Kofi's face beamed down at me, his mouth tremoring, a constant jibber-jabber, I was racing, and every time I succeeded in escaping, Kofi got in front of me and I was back where I started, in the rubbish tip, his smile engulfing me. I eventually dropped off. I must have done, as the first noise I heard was the scuffing again. There was a loud squawk, a sort of click, followed by a choking sound. I pushed away the net, went to the window, and low and behold one of the 'prims' was strangling a chicken. It suddenly dawned on me that they thought we would be staying tonight and were getting ready for our chicken dinner later.

"No such f***** luck", I said to myself. I went over to the bed, pushed Jim, "We're going!"

Like the market workers we were, we got up and out within five minutes, fresh as daisies and raring to go. The effluxion of time improved vastly at the breakfast farce, mainly due to my insistence. Even though we'd told Kofi not to do it again, there were still many liggers[3] who were given short shrift. I carefully monitored the output

---

[3] ligger – someone who attends social gatherings for free food and drink

35

from the kitchen, restricting the eggs, and acting as restaurant commander-in-chief. The flea bitten place mats were requisitioned for Air Traffic Runway Controller duties, like two table-tennis bats I gesticulated madly, dispatching most of the 'breakfastitioners'. Jim and Will were in fits, but it got the job done.

Kofi excitedly took us outside and pointed across the road, about three hundred yards down, by a small row of shacks and shops, where we saw a silver Mercedes, and our luck was in. It looked good, at least from a distance. We crossed and walked down to a rough workshop area and yard, the vehicle parked up. We were enthused although anywhere else it would have simply been a car. For us it represented hope. We got in, I don't know why, as we had to drive back to the hotel and stop again to check out and load the luggage, but I wanted to stick to the car like glue. Mercedes. Air Conditioning. I'm getting in and not getting out again, I thought. Kofi sat in the driver's seat. We hadn't seen him drive, but presumed he could get us back over the road to the hotel, at the very least. He held the ignition key up to us for approval, smiling his vast grin.

"Mercedes Nina, Jim! Mercedes!"

I'm pretty sure sunlight glinted off the key, like a halo, and a bell rung somewhere in the distance, 'ting', like a toothpaste advert, the key held the answer, the dream, the prospect of a pristine future. He held it there for an unbearably long time, all of us looking, keyhole theatre.

"Let's go." said Jim.

Kofi placed the key in the ignition. I held my breath. He turned it. Nothing. Not even a click. He tried again, half a dozen times, but nothing, completely dead. No cranking, no turning over, not a birdy. Jim got out first. I wasn't moving. Once out, he lifted the bonnet, briefly looked in, and then lowered it. Jim chuckled, suppressing trauma.

"There's no engine."

Will sat looking ahead, waited for a minute, then announced:

"Jim, I'll sort it mate!"

Kofi was silent. I sat dumbfounded in the back, but Jim pulled me out, taking me back to the lodgings as some sort of stifled violence played out behind us.

Kofi had bought or 'obtained' a car without an engine. Will threatened and Kofi shouted at the mechanics. An engine was ordered. They hadn't realised he'd wanted an engine as well. Within twenty-four hours, unbelievably, it was fitted. Because of the high number of road accidents in Africa it was common to part engines from their bodies and fit them elsewhere. We reluctantly spent time taking a cab to Makola market, with Kofi dragging us around Accra in the heat and grime. One more night at Beauty, then we were on our way to Takoradi. The sisters prim had been right.

Eddy drove because Kofi was sulking again. He wanted to stay in Accra and presumed we'd feel the same, hence not taking us to Takoradi on the first night. Accra is where his family was and it was likely that he regretted the arrangement he'd made with us. Every half an hour they stopped the car at a roadside food stall to eat and chat. This was grinding us down. Will said we shouldn't eat at the stalls but the day wore on and there had been no-where else to stop and buy food. We were starving, and the sight of Eddy and Kofi stuffing their faces became too much. We succumbed.

※

As Thomas ate lobster and oysters, washed down by brandy and iced water, he stared intently at the poster on the wall in the restaurant. He had never seen anything quite like it. Actresses with white faces and bunched hair, dainty locks falling around their thin stature gossamer necks, looking fey and alluring. The letters jumping out from the bill 'Rosendale Music Hall, £-2/6-. 3, 7, 10 o'clock showings'. Thomas paid for his meal, asked directions and went straight to the theatre. The building couldn't be missed, a throng milling outside. More gas lamps than he'd ever seen and marble pillars. On entering, red velvet lined walls, and a vast central elegant iron staircase winding into the mezzanine bar from the ground floor. Thomas bought a ticket for the front row and entered in anticipation.

Gentry in top hats, ladies with faces that had been puffed with powder, delightfully rouged cheeks and the smell of pomade and scent wafting throughout the room surrounded him. It was a din, the noise of chatter and laughter. The band struck up, a real battering drum set, a trap full of glittering percussion. Looking down into the pit Thomas saw gleaming trombones, a huge bass drum, the drummer taking a sweeping roll, a crescendo across the side drum, and glimmering cymbals, the conductor keeping a fast tempo with his baton. From each side of the stage came kicking showgirls, the whole audience erupting into clapping and whooping, making the dancers kick their stockinged legs even higher, revealing a row of frilly knickers and lace garters. Dazzling.

From the middle emerged the most beautiful thing Thomas could ever have imagined, singing like a bird. The whole room went silent, dancers disappearing off to the sides. The numerous brass tortoiseshells disguising the stage lighting, set across the length of the front of the stage suddenly lit up as she drew close to the edge, facing the front row. It made her skin incandescent and Thomas fell in love at that moment.

"A little of what you fancy..." the theatre joining in for the choruses.

The violins chirped in and she was gone, as if she'd glided away on ice. He had to see her again, and he did, she was back for two more numbers, a comedy routine and finale. He couldn't take his eyes off her and she noticed him. The only Negro in the audience and in the front row Thomas couldn't be missed. She was referred to as 'Ettie' and she was the Star turn. As soon as encores were done and the roaring had subsided he politely pushed his way backstage.

"You can't go there guvna," and the stage hand was suddenly the lucky owner of a half crown piece from the suave dark-skinned gentleman. "Upstairs on the right."

The rear of the hall was cramped, awash with hyperactive giggling chorus girls, but Thomas found the door. It said 'Ettie Cinders' with a small star underneath. He straightened his cravat, leaning down he shined his patent loafers with his handkerchief taken from his pocket. He could see his hair in the shine of the shoes and tousled it into position, then knocked.

"Come-in-if-ya-comin'," so he entered. "Oh," she swung round from her dressing table.

38

Ettie Cantor (stage name Ettie Cinders) early 1900s

Thomas, lost for words, stood for a second in what felt to him like a few hours, and the hush became filled with her London brogue.

"I saw you's out there, I saw ya in the front row, that's an unusual sight down 'ere."

She stood up knowingly, intentionally letting the dressing gown fall partially open. He glimpsed her thin waist in a red bodice, which had been half undone, her stockings showing, and frilly panty hose. Thomas found his voice but it was a pitch or two above his normal resonating baritone.

'I mumbled, introducing myself, mentioning my business and Africa, whatever was whirling in my head wasn't connecting with my mouth, I know I said 'enchanting', complimenting her performance, and stammering similarly about supper'.

"Delightful Thomas, I can't make suppa, I have a prior engagement, but I'm free for lunch, twelve o'clock, below the clock at Charing Cross tommorra."

He stood in awe because as she said this, she pulled off her wig, blonde cascades falling from under the brunette hairpiece. She shook her head and Thomas was taken aback, for Ettie was even prettier with blonde ringlets framing her soft milky skin. Some of her stage make-up remained.

"'Ang 'round, I need to take the rest of this off, would'ya like a drop o' bubbly."

The drinking episode on the boat flashed in his mind, and having already had brandy that evening, he replied:

"I'm very grateful. I must decline, but dearly look forward to your company tomorrow."

"Please yerself, see ya tommorra."

Ettie gave a mischievous wave and smile and drawing closer, held her hand out to be kissed. He took it, arching modestly forward, but she grabbed and pulled him in, kissing him full on the lips. He nearly

40

fainted, overcome with sexual impulse, holding her tight waist close. She pulled back, taking the base of the long-stemmed glass on the dressing table between her forefingers, and floating it around in the air between them, with delight.

"Ooooh, that's a first, I've never kissed a black man before." Thomas smiled his wide charismatic smile and backed out of the room, trying to keep composed as he stuttered:

"I look forward to it," or something like that.

Thomas was unaware that Music Hall starlets had a scurrilous reputation in the 1900s, that *actress* was unfortunately almost a byword for a lady of ill repute. But he was biased and would not have cared one iota. He stood panting, his back against her door, noise of the performers in their changing rooms resonating round the stairwells. He got his breath and exited into the night air, her perfume still filling his nostrils.

It was dark now. Having not eaten for hours the splodge on the end of the stick looked like a kebab from a deli on the Old Kent Road and had never done *us* any harm before. We dug in. The locals were delighted we were eating their food; we were the main attraction. This was something we would become used to, where there had been no foreign visitors before. Will had a burger-looking affair and Jim and I opted for the kebab-style dish. It tasted delicious despite not being able to see it that well, although when I finished I could see two small paws. Now I felt ill. We got in the car and left.

"No more stops!" Jim told Eddy.

We soldiered on to what seemed around midnight, but it was only seven in the evening, when Eddy admitted to being lost. It came as no surprise. We could hardly see a thing, no signs, no illumination. The road would precariously split at various points with no hope of knowing where any of the turn-offs took you. The map we had indicated one solitary road from Accra to Takoradi and no landmarks. NASA had Apollo rockets that were more economical on fuel and, as the indicator sank down to empty for the third time that day, we

41

started to get tense.

"We just need to find somewhere to stay," pleaded Will.

No one answered. We'd been cooped up in a dusty oven since first thing, with malfunctioning air conditioning and jostled along hole-ridden trails. I suppose we'd been buoyed with an engine, forgetting other essentials. Even with the paw-based delicacy earlier, I was hungry and the unprecedented salt and flavouring required to make a rat tasty, had rendered the water ration officially 'dwindle' level.

A spaceship was following us. Dehydration and food poisoning were catching up as I peered behind through the gap in the headrest. Kofi was first to see faint lights in the distance ahead, but as soon as he mentioned them Eddy suddenly exclaimed:

"Everyone down, we're being followed!"

"It could be kidnappers." Kofi piped up.

"Or robbers." Eddie added.

The hurtling alien war-machine illuminated the cloud of dust the car churned up in its wake.

"Duck down." said Jim, pushing my head into my lap, exacerbating the heady sensation of nausea and hallucinations.

Everyone ducked down, including Eddy.

"Not you!" shrieked Jim, but it was too late, we careered into the ruts at the side of the track, the potholes banging the suspension and turning our stomachs to jelly. The aliens shouted as they went by, kindly slowing so we could hear.

"Stop, Stop!!"

We all looked up together and saw it halt in front of us. A man was yelling and pointing out of a car window.

"The road is up... see the signals? It's dangerous. There's big holes up ahead!"

He got out, a tall coffee-skinned smooth looking man, cool in cotton robes, compared with our sweaty, traumatised condition. I leapt out. I was so relieved, shaking the man's hand vigorously with both of mine, but unable to talk. Jim and Will followed.

"We're lost, we're looking for the Takoradi road, and a hotel," said Jim.

"I followed you for thirty minutes. Didn't you see me flashing my headlamps? You're way off the main road. I knew you were lost. No-one comes out this way."

He was shocked to see white people here and we struck up some conversation. He was Faysal Barakeh a Lebanese timber merchant. We told him what we were doing and he offered to lead us back to the main road and a hotel. He had water in his car and offered food at his house on the way.

"Oh Lord, pray to God for your sins, the Lord is omnipotent!" came the loud exaltations from the preacher standing on the wooden fruit box. There was a tussle, the London 'Bobby' roughly pulling the preacher off the box and cuffing him.

"Disturbin' the peace! Down the cells. This is a respectarble combudity. Can't 'ave your type round 'ere."

The second Bobby, in blue tails and tall top hat pealed his whistle for back up, swinging his wooden truncheon.

"Everyone move on, you all move on there!"

Thomas had visited the Zion Tabernacle the morning after seeing Ettie at the Music Hall, and sent a note of regret, an apology, to the theatre, delaying his engagement with her at Charing Cross. Religion and raw desire churned. The emotional conflict compelled him to visit the makeshift chapel in Hackney instead. He rose early having rested badly in his new bed. He took a tram via Mansion House interchange, with a note from his landlady showing the numbers of the carriages and where to change. Thomas was not himself. He had toned down his dress, wearing a simple dark suit and a grey round collared shirt buttoned to the top.

'31st October - weighed myself at Mansion House Station - 10 stone, 2 pounds'. Seen Revd Campel and he laid his hands upon me in the names of the Lord. Signed card'.

43

Ettie Cantor (stage name Ettie Cinders) early 1900s

Thomas had been inaugurated into the Zion movement and went out the following Sunday preaching the order.

'I am Recd now in Zion Church - sat on the Lord's upper. Went in 3's to Berkeley Square. I joined the Saloon Seventies and distributed Zion Literature. Quite a crowd had gathered on the corner of Berkeley Square, and there was some pandemonium'.

His first experience of spreading the word amongst London city dwellers left him vexed. He snuck away, retreating from trouble, and walked down through Piccadilly and Green Park, ending up outside Buckingham Palace, marvelling at the scene for a little while before making the decision to see Ettie again. This was a confusing start to his religious exploration in England with the Zion order. Thomas took a taxi back to his rooms and arranged for a telegram to the theatre. He asked her to meet him again, with sincere apologies for the missed date 'due to business'.

The following lunchtime at twelve o'clock, he waited under the vast timepiece outside Charing Cross, the trams hurtling up the Strand, street traders, horses, carriages, newspaper sellers, noise everywhere. His heart pounded and he was not expecting to see her again. Then there she was, in front of him. Passers-by strained their necks at the sight of the luscious Ettie, with the tall, raffish Ghanaian. A more unusual sight in Charing Cross you could not have seen.

"You're a cheeky devil, cancelling me out, aren't ya?" she said, placing a peck on his face and slipping her arm behind his, when Thomas had been intending to follow a more formal protocol.

Thomas made his apologies, keeping his voice in check this time, and she swept him across Charing Cross Road, avoiding the carriages and buses. The huge stone lions of Trafalgar Square to their left and the monolith of Nelson's column rising above, the top piercing the mist that hung in the London air. The Lyons Tea House on the corner was packed with lunchtime office girls who literally swooned at the

45

sight of the two of them entering. They found a table.

Ettie Cantor (stage name Ettie Cinders) early 1900s

Maps were spread on the dining table, enticed out by Faysal's interest in my 'Legend of Thomas Brem-Wilson' tale. I'd pulled them from the battered leather Box and was pointing enthusiastically whilst Jim and Will looked on despondently. I hadn't taken much persuading, explaining to Faysal about the 'lands', describing the diaries and the gold I was going to find. My sickness lifted as soon as cold beer and a decent meal passed my lips. Faysal and his wife Lulu were fantastically hospitable, a dinner of locally grown food erased the last days events from my mind, and I was now talking in overdrive, describing our mission and what I thought was the family 'legacy'. Eddy and Kofi had gone to fiddle with the car, promising some air conditioning, after Jim and Will berated them once again for the unholy mess. Faysal examined the maps, keenly recognising the area and the names of villages.

"I know where this is," he pointed, "I can send you in the right direction."

It felt like things were at last going our way. I liked Faysal and this was the luckiest coincidence so far away from home. We made tracks at ten, Faysal in his car up ahead with Jim, and following in the Mercedes Will, the Africans and me. Faysal mentioned to Jim:

"Watch the two Africans. They are trying to double cross you. I overheard them outside discussing the lands and the gold."

"Don't worry, we don't even know ourselves if there's anything - you can't steal what's not there," said Jim, although he did agree they were both dubious characters and more than likely scheming.

The hotel was on the outskirts of Takoradi. After twenty minutes and the loan of a can of petrol from Faysal, suddenly there were lights and some civilization. We were thankful and gratefully checked in. The hotel was lush and expensive but we didn't care about the price. We paid for a room for Eddy and Kofi sharing. Faysal, who was familiar with it because of his timber business, gave Jim a hand drawn map to get to the 'lands' and briefed Eddy.

We were up early, breakfasting among businessmen, our shorts and t-shirts giving us away. Kofi and Eddy had been sent out to fill the car up and check the oil, water, and air conditioning fluid and to see if they could get it working. It was going to be an endurance test on bad roads. They'd apparently done a good job, as surprisingly they also came back with it washed and valeted. Jim was in front with the instructions and a couple of maps Faysal had lent us. I felt a little more confident. We headed out of Takoradi into the country, then the bush, the heat increasing, the air conditioning not working. I stayed as close to the window as humanly possible whilst trying not to breath in too much dust. We did have water and provisions. The hotel made sandwiches and we stopped at a small supermarket on the way out of town. We were looking for the village called Tuasi.

◇

Thomas gazed into the lagoons of crystal clear blue, with hints of green and brown.

"Maybe your eyes are hazel, one of my favourite colours," he said.

Throwing as many compliments at her as was humanly possible, he was unaware of the gogglers ogling through the full floor-to-ceiling windows at them like shop manikins on show. Ettie was used to a bit of attention being tall, stunningly pretty and outrageous. Her skirts were always a little bit too high above the ankle, calf-length lace up boots teasingly visible, a mink stole nonchalantly thrown over her shoulder, barely disguising the heaving cleavage it was intended to cover. Ettie showed as much bosom as she could without being arrested. Her waist was thin, pulled in, and she was completely dressed in jet silk, her skirt finished with lace edging. No wonder chaps would walk into things as they passed her in the street. A small sable bolero topped it off with thin velvet lapels and gold buttons, and cerise ruffled shirt cuffs covering her delicate palms.

Ettie had many admirers but never a black man. She was equally as taken with Thomas. Cake, tea, chat, disguised the torrent of passion bubbling under their skin. It was as civilized as they could make it with the fireworks going off. Ettie flirted insatiably and he reciprocated. It was all they could do to restrain themselves from making love there and then on the tearoom table. The window gawpers would have liked that. They had ballooned, the snowball effect, and with some commotion, so Ettie and Thomas went. She lived above her father's shop on Shaftesbury Avenue and Thomas offered to walk her back. He did not have a game plan as this was uncharted territory, but he did know that she had been very forward when they first met. Whether or not this was the affectation of an actress he could not be sure, so he intended to be as gentlemanly as possible and see what happened.

Their arms entwined. Thomas liked this and she reached across with her other hand gently squeezing his. Hers were peach in comparison - thin, and never tainted by any type of manual work. The tension of the onlookers was left behind as they cut through the graveyard at Saint Martin-in-the-Fields Church, through Trafalgar Square and up Haymarket towards Shaftesbury Avenue. The sun graciously pierced through the November wintery London mists and the whole town twinkled with brilliance and movement. They spent some time window-shopping in and out of stores. The pavements were busy and they were able to melt into the afternoon's jam-packed city. Thomas was in his element, his failed religious exercise now miles away. He bought Ettie several little trinkets, a single rose from a street seller and costume jewellery. Up through Piccadilly Circus and into Shaftesbury Avenue. Ettie stopped at each theatre, recognising the actors on the posters, saying what she knew about them, describing and laughing out loud at the gossip and scandals, making Thomas laugh as she was so animated. Past Shaftesbury Theatre and into a shop on the corner of Oxford Street, above the vast curved glass and wooden doors at the entrance, was the sign General Merchant Store. For the first time Thomas saw electric light bulbs and lighting and was so absorbed he missed the introduction.

"This is my father, Joseph."

"Can't you hear me, I'm telling you it's down there!" I yelled in Jim's ear.

I thought I knew the map better than him, and with Eddy and Kofi putting their penneth[4] in it was a racket, stressful and confusing. A far cry from Faysal's cool, calm directions, but we *were* going *somewhere*.

"This is it," Will chipped in and Eddy veered off stopping the car.

We were at a village and what looked like a small school in the centre, under a thicket of trees gently blowing in the breeze. It was so inviting we ventured out strolling towards the school and very soon we

---

[4] penneth – as two-penneth - Old English saying - when someone gives you his thoughts and views or opinion on what you should do

were surrounded, the children coming out of their classroom and villagers coming up to see the 'visitors'. They were polite but started gesturing in our direction, laughing. I knew we were different but I suddenly felt like the butt of a joke. Will was getting annoyed.

"What's goin' on, I'm not 'avin' this?" turning around to walk off.

Then we saw. The back of him was red from head to toe. We'd been dyed. Necks, arms, back, legs, completely red. Two-tone white people, no wonder they were pointing.

"It's the soddin' seats - the idiots." said Jim.

The red velvet car interior wasn't colourfast. In the humidity we hadn't noticed they were still fairly damp, splodging stain everywhere.

"Bleedin' 'ell," said Will. "That'll never come out."

A disgruntled looking gentleman of thirtyish, in a cool short-sleeved blue shirt and smartly ironed khaki trousers appeared. He had an almost military appearance, looking stern through half-lenses. We were the centre of a scrum but his flock quietened when he spoke in very polite English with a deep well educated voice.

"Good afternoon. Welcome. Can I help you?"

I took the map attached to the Indenture from my Grandfather's Land.

"Is this Tuasi? I'm looking for this land - it belonged to my Grandfather Thomas Brem-Wilson?"

He came close, marginally taller than me, and glanced down at the detail. He grabbed at one side, which I straightaway resented. I didn't say anything. He pushed his spectacles tight onto his nose with his free hand. Some sweat dripped from my brow onto the map but I knew I didn't smell of sweat, and *he* did. The smell was familiar to me now, stale BO. Even with his smart appearance he was a bit whiffy. It flashed in my mind that everyone is not what they seem. He glanced at it almost too briefly. He turned to Will, ignoring me.

"This *is* Tuasi, but I don't recognise this land you are looking for. You are in the wrong place."

The 'free-for-all' huddled to stare at the map. I sensed I was being corralled, so I hastily folded it and snapped it in the Box. It was a long way to come to hear 'no', and it felt like a clout. This emotion held no logic, as we'd just arrived, and had hardly made any proper investigations. Armed with old maps and bumf[5] held little credibility. We had Faysal's information, but that was a fluke, so nothing concrete. I still felt let down.

"Thank you." I mumbled, turned and went to the car, some of the children following.

⬡

Joseph nearly fainted. This was the first African he had ever had in the shop and, regardless of his daughter's bohemian associations he was still knocked off kilter. He did not know whether to shake Thomas's hand or throw him out of the store. There were a number of customers browsing, so to avoid a scene, the staid half-bespectacled Jewish merchant shook. Joseph Cantor was a respectable orthodox Jew living in Earlsfield, Thames Ditton, who had built up his business over many years to a prime position in London's West End. He did not approve of his daughters' colourful lives. Ettie (Esther) was one of three siblings - Rachael or 'Ray', was also a performer, younger, and jealous of her sister's success, and the youngest Carrie, twenty-two. Carrie was attending the Italia Conti Stage School studying dance. Being on the stage in Victorian times was not an upstanding profession, one of the reasons why the girls were still single. This was a great disappointment to Joseph and by Victorian standards they were already past their 'shelf life' for potential suitors.

Thomas was distracted, enthralled by the goods in the store. This is what he needed for his business in Africa. Making off into the recesses of the shop, (no thought of formal introductions) with Ettie and Joseph following behind, his cane tapped on the wooden floorboards as he dictated an order.

"I'll take a thousand of those in sizes a quarter inch to one inch thickness and varying lengths," pointing at the boxes of precisely-laid-out nuts and bolts. "Twenty boxes of those, ten bicycles cartoned and ready for shipping, thirty wheel-barrows with five spare wheels, thirty

---

[5] bumf - reading materials (documents, written information) that you must read and deal with but that you think are extremely boring

five pulleys, rope, fifty lengths of one hundred feet."

Joseph produced his notebook hurriedly writing down the order, Ettie in tow, quite amazed at the sudden change in Thomas. He was in business mode, his voice monotonic. He was instructive and fastidious over the detail. It was clear that Thomas was used to having his own way, his word followed to the letter. After perusing the store corner to corner he turned to Joseph.

"And I'll expect a family discount of fifteen per-cent," slapping him on the back and laughing out loud at his own audacity.

"Well, I'd never have guessed Esther." Joseph laughed nervously almost lost for words. He took a pencil; one of several consecutively lined up in his apron pocket and flicked it as if trying to attract a waiter's attention.

"Junior! Junior!"

His son, who had been practically invisible until now stacking boxes behind a counter, hurried over, a thin pasty looking lad, the epitome of his Dad. Ettie ignored him.

"Have these written up straight away Junior and an invoice prepared with a family reduction for Mr... Mr?"

"Thomas Brem-Wilson," Ettie said smoothly. He ripped off the notes and handed them to his son who poked them in his brown jacket, edgily affirming with a shake of his head at Ettie and his father, avoiding eye contact with Thomas, withdrawing to the till to mark them in the ledger. Any prejudice Joseph may have felt toward a Negro was conveniently expunged as Thomas counted out gold sovereigns. Joseph fussed, inviting Thomas for dinner the following evening at Thames Ditton. The wile merchant saw an opportunity. He was fighting a repossession order on the shop lease. On three floors, with a flat above, it was in what had become a sought after area of central London. Even though Joseph had a good business, the building was not his and was being called in by the landlord for development.

I sat in the car away from the village. I could still see them from the corner of my eye, Jim and Will in conversation with the schoolteacher, their red backs giving the appearance of bronzed statues. They were in the cooler shade of a small copse by the school, the pale green leaves rustling in the afternoon heat. I was sitting in the heat box, with my Box, trying to work out what the hell I was waiting for when I heard something.

"Ssshhhh..." it came again, "Ssshhhh..."

It sounded like air rushing from a puncture.

"Don't say anything," said a voice. I looked down out of the window and there was a small old man crouching beside the car with his finger held up to his mouth.

"Ssshhhh... your land is there." He was pointing, his hand now gripping the windowsill, as he could no longer balance. "For ten dollars I show you where. Through the back of the village, follow the path, it begins at the Mango tree, don't let them see," he croaked, "in ten minutes."

"OK." I said.

We had lunch and water, Eddy moving the car into a cooler spot. Jim and Will liked my 'old man' story. The general consensus was that we had come this far, ten dollars wasn't going to break us. We drove on once the schoolchildren had been called back into class, parking a little bit out of sight at the opposite end of the village. We got out of the car. I took my Box. Jim and the others took some water, hats, and provisions, and we went towards where he'd said.

It was more like thirty minutes but he came, waving. He had a Gandhi look, skinny and sprightly, a bit spooky. Jim approached first.

"What's the story then?"

The brittle little voice crackled.

"The schoolteacher is Chief of Tuasi and thinks he owns the land around the village. He takes money for timber and rents. That is why he will not tell you anything. Follow me... where's the money?"

Jim pulled ten dollars from his pocket and stuffed it into the man's bony old hands. There was a rambling concrete house, run down. We entered past a yard full of chickens and ducks, and a couple of pigs hoovering the ground for food. Followed in by half a dozen children who'd been playing outside, beaming smiles. They tried to touch our fair skin, brushing our hands and wrists. I thought they should have

53

been in school.

"Queen Mama! Queen Mama!" rasped the old man, the children mimicking it in an amusingly similar style.

The Queen Mama, contradictory to the grand title, was cooking in the kitchen, a squeaky confirmation in dialect emanated, validating his presence. A musty odour pervaded the whole house, the old man showing us to a 'past it' settee, where we sat, to be polite, even though it was the source of one of the rotten stenches. She bumbled in, portly, and little. The old man introduced and translated, raising his voice when addressing the Queen. He explained what we were doing (I presumed so, as this went on indefinitely). He asked for the files. I pulled them out of my Box and he took them. She glared as he trailed across the worn out bare wood boards. She scrutinised the information for several minutes asking the man to retrieve a magnifying glass from on top of a pouf in front of us. I felt like we weren't getting anywhere and the smell was becoming a bit much for me. She'd left the kitchen door ajar; the aroma of seemingly a hundred cabbages being boiled was wafting in. I was about to get up and make our excuses, her focusing the magnifier was interminable, combined with the dainty stink. Ten dollars wasn't making it worth staying but she suddenly became animated.

"Ek is jou tanti."

"She's saying she's your Aunt!" the old man said.

My heart literally skipped a beat. She beckoned him to go to a weathered cabinet in the corner. He accessed the top drawer, rustled around, and pulled something out - we couldn't see. He passed it to her and again, she beckoned. He paced the floor.

"She wants the case."

I gave it to him. He handed it over. It was like a game of pass-the-parcel. She held the case up to the sunlight (what there was of it coming in through the mucky windows) and placed a sizeable gem in its socket on the case. It was one of the missing jewels. I went over to see.

"Thomas, Thomas," she smiled and said to the old man.

"This is it," I said to Jim, "we've found the place."

Queen Mum of Tuasi (daughter of Thomas Brem-Wilson's brother Joshua) and Nina

Centre: Queen Mum/Nina's Aunt Rose (African name Nan Gyanama) with two schoolteachers (left: Nana Akula)

It was amber, semi-precious, she had taken it from the case at some point or it had fallen off, the eye of a carved elephant, an exact fit, deep in the leather. As I leant over the Box she pulled me in and gave me a tight hug. I could feel her huge rolls of fat under her pinafore and the smell of overcooked vegetables.

After more lengthy toing and froing translations, and a bit of delving, it turns out she was the daughter of Thomas Brem-Wilson's brother, Joshua. My Aunt Rose! The old man said that the Chief treated her badly and didn't offer her the respect that a Queen deserved. She started talking about the land, saying that a tribal man will give you nothing, but a white man will always give you something, and then we knew what she wanted. Out came the dollar bills, and Jim donated something for the children who seemed to be living there, even though she was too old to be their mother. I was excited at my first real African relative and the prospect of discovering our 'Lands'. She sent out one of the boys and after a little while he came back with two strong looking teenagers.

"They will take you into the bush to survey the land as it's too far for me," the old man said. Rose indicated on the maps, took a scrap of paper out of her bib pocket, drew a diagram for the two boys and spoke to them, as did the old man. She told us to return to her at the house when we'd been round the land. The giant Mango tree marked the corner of a boundary, at the edge of the village.

Thomas met Ettie at seven in the evening, at Oxford Circus, and they made their way by tram and cab to Thames Ditton. Thomas had had Ettie on his mind. Today it had also distracted him from his business of arranging export for his newly found goods. He had been to see Mr Renner, his African lawyer in the UK.

'Friday eighth of November 1901… Renner in London. Removed to Vernon Chambers, Recd from Coates £10.0.0'.

He had a lot of money going out in the UK on rent, and now on goods and shipping.

'Two weeks on - need to get tithe and rent money in from Africa. In my absence the money is unpaid... Will put pressure on through Renner so royalties come in. Taking too long to come through. I can't forsake my exploits in London, not now I've met Ettie'.

Ettie was vivacious and alluring, and the goodbye peck outside the shop left him upbeat, feeling desirous toward her. Thomas was particularly refined tonight in expectation of some sort of dalliance with Ettie. He was infatuated and religion was not on his mind as he stepped out in his trademark patent shoes, shined immaculately, brown suit, green silk check shirt and satin cream cravat. He certainly did not look like a man who had spent the afternoon at his solicitor's office trying to find money to pay the rent on his lodgings.

Joseph Junior met them at the door, again a little mute, well mannered but almost inaudible.

"Mr Brem-Wilson, Ettie."

The house was typical of the area, comfortable, middle-class, an imposing terraced Victorian residence; twin pillars at the front porch, a brass gas lamp shining above their heads and a marble doorstep. Thomas felt like he had arrived at the heart of conservative Victorian respectability. Curtains twitched down the street. Word had got around. Blanche, Joseph's wife, had not been able to keep quiet about the visitor, and the whole neighbourhood knew by now.

Inside was surprisingly uncluttered and bright. A feminine majority influenced the décor. The reception was airy and warm, exposed oak floorboards punctuated with smart Persian rugs. There was a king-size circular elaborate bamboo table in the centre, a glass top resplendent with orchids in a vase. Drinks and hors d'oeuvres lay prepared on trays. Joseph Jnr passed them around.

"Sherry, Mr Brem-Wilson?"

"Please call me Thomas, young man."

Thomas was probably about the same age as Junior, but Junior was outwardly younger and nervously introduced everyone. Blanche was gracious and inviting, yet could not hide her incredulity at a black man being in her home. She had only seen them in books or on film and usually portrayed as natives dancing round pots of boiling missionaries with bones through their noses. Negros were perceived as slaves or servants. Blanche looked down to see if colour had come off in her hand when Thomas shook hers, she could not help herself even though she had been fully briefed for the event.

"Dinner," the maid came in to announce.

They retired to the dining room. She served the courses from a hatch, the cook sending them up in the dumbwaiter from the kitchens below. It was standard English fare, although well prepared. Joseph was agitated, trying to draw the conversation towards his business and the huge resources required to keep the landlord from the door at Oxford Street. Thomas showed some interest in his plight but preferred the light-heartedness of the girls, who were hotheaded pubescents in his company, trivialising over the theatre, music halls, and the acting fraternity. Ettie, Ray and Carrie, who were made-up perfectly and showing a generous amount of cleavage, as was the fashion, were fawning, offering Thomas wine, taking every opportunity to lean into the table to upstage Joseph's discourse. Junior kept his head down, only murmuring during the meal, beaten back over the years by the girls' relentless banter. Blanche observed as if a tornado was eddying through their dining room.

As pudding was served Blanche suggested Ray show Thomas the gardens and house, if only so that she and Joseph could be temporarily unburdened by the hurricane. Ettie was seething but Blanche plainly had her reasons for asking Ray, possibly to split them up and quell the girls' over-exuberance. It was a chilly November night but Thomas was glad of the air and pulled his Crombie collar up around his neck as Ray took his arm, dropping down from the terrace into the gardens, which were illuminated by the glow from the house. A few gas lamps were set out in a row alongside the borders of the trim lawn, the corners of the hedges and trees lit.

The path was overgrown and the tunnel vision was turning my mind to jelly. We'd been following them for approximately twenty-five minutes and it felt like twenty-five days, the heat turned up to full, I was 'alight'. The water had been insufficient and the two strapping Africans seemed to jog rather than walk. Eddy and Kofi hadn't come. I'd heard them talking to 'Gandhi' in some sort of vernacular, as we'd descended the rickety old veranda from the house. Scenarios churned in my head, as I could only focus on their scheming, oblivious to the landmarks that the guides pointed out at intervals. We could have been anywhere, my cognitive faculties were in reverse, but I moved forward.

"I need food and water, I can't go on any further." said Will.

"Hold up! We need to drink," Jim called out.

The lads took out their knives, which actually were more like machetes. I hadn't noticed them before and now I thought that's it, we're for the chop! But off they scuttled.

"Wait here," they said.

We did, as we had no energy to go anywhere. After ten minutes we were overjoyed to see them return with coconuts and pineapples they'd chopped down, and they sliced off the tops. I'd never had coconuts fresh like this. It was nectar. A fruit salad was made using the coconut shell as a do-it-yourself dish. Feeling rejuvenated we were able to get to our feet.

Will was complaining about blisters. It all looked alike and we'd been out over an hour. Maybe the 'old man Queen thing' was a ruse. I had Faysal's words spinning in my microwaved head, putrefying with the teacher's statement, and the 'pidgin' of the Queen Mama, a whopping gemstone blinding my brain, in a boiling pot of confusion about Kofi and Eddy's intentions. Suddenly Jim proclaimed:

"There's the Mango tree!"

We stopped. We were back.

"Where was our land then?" said Will to the two young guides.

They looked quizzical.

"You just walked round the land Sir."

I felt like I should have been concentrating better, like a naughty

59

child on a geography field trip. Beneath the Mango tree, they placed the piece of paper between us as reference. One drew with a stick in the dirt the diagram from the paper, the other drawing in the groves, trees, ditches and forest they'd pointed out. I got the map from my Box, covered in sweat where I'd carried it. I laid it out on the dry ground. Jim and Will got on their hands and knees carefully comparing the two.

"They're right, that's it," said Will.

It looked like Wales, both maps with the same outline, same relief, the Mango tree at one end in the Queen Mama's scrawl. We were quite sure we'd found Thomas Brem-Wilson's first piece of property. What to do with it now? And how to officially confirm it? I felt elated, mixed with exhaustion (probably dehydration) and maybe yellow fever, which culminated in me falling asleep as soon as I got in the car, in spite of a pair of chickens pecking at my head.

We'd gone back via my Auntie Rose's house, Eddy and Kofi still skulking there. Unexpectedly she had a few words of English.

"They are lands sold by Chief Amuku to Brem-Wilson. The lands of Tuasi. Thomas, Thomas." she recited, like some mantra.

She managed to pawn a couple of scraggy chickens off on me. We didn't want them, but we couldn't abandon them there in the village, they might be recognised. Now the clucking and pecking kept disturbing me from my slumbers. As if the car wasn't chock-full enough. It didn't escape my attention that she didn't offer up the gemstone. It would have been natural to replace the stone in the Box now it was back here, but it was not to be. They do say 'when you leave something behind, you are destined to return'. We'd left a fair amount of cash, Jim doing a round of tipping - the teenagers, the kids, Auntie, and Gandhi again.

The rumbling noise was the thing that woke me as well as the sick feeling in the pit of my stomach. I pulled the Box close, a chicken flew at me, not having fastened her safety belt, and we ground to a halt. We all got out, except the chickens. I felt like deserting them here, as we stood inspecting the flat tyre. It must have been three in the afternoon. Darkness would be upon us in three hours. Jim and Will got the spare. It was flat. Will gave the tyre to Eddy and Kofi, telling them to go find a garage and get it fixed. They sluggishly pushed the tyre off into the distance up the track, and we waited. We gathered robes and blankets from the boot to sit in the shade of the surrounding scrub by the track. Crickets clicked, the bush crackled, animals, trees, undergrowth, heat.

Rachael's long blue velvet dress was ruffling up against the winter leaves on the ground. She seemed contemplative in comparison to Ettie, with soft brown hair worn flowing, down her back, something completely novel and enticing to Thomas as it swayed gently against him in the chilly air. She wore a short fur coat pleated at the waist showing off her dancer's figure. Whenever Thomas replied to her questioning, he had to look down and the sight of her breasts was unavoidable. She was well spoken and softer than Ettie. He did not understand why they would have different accents. It dawned on him that Ettie's cockney brawl might be an affectation, her 'Ettie Cinders' character. Ray named the trees commenting on the planting, asking what gardens Thomas had at home in Africa. He described his houses and his tenure at the Wesleyan college, their laid out grounds, the ornamental trees and palms. She listened enthusiastically, enraptured by the image of exotic lands.

"What did you teach dear Sir?"

"Religious Studies, English." he answered.

"I wish too, to be taught by you," turning and kissing him.

He succumbed. Ray was blossoming, girlish, luscious and assertive, pushing Thomas against one of the oak trees, forcing her thigh up against his, and passionately placing her hand in his trousers. She looked up at him, her ravishing aquamarine eyes alight with shock and desire, a gas lamp flame reflection dancing across her pupils like a devil's tail. She placed Thomas's hand on her breasts, pulling her blouse and dress down to her waist, her nipples reacting to the cold and his fondling. Thomas breathed heavily, her hand moving more rapidly and, as she did so, she let out little gasps, her thigh pressing more intensely against his leg. Thomas stifled her screams of delight, a hand over her mouth, as he caught sight of backlit shadows at the house. Her stroking became charged, she reached down between her legs, pulling her skirts up, uncovering high-buttoned leather boots, stockings and suspenders.

"Press, press, press harder on my mouth," licking between his fingers, wanting him to increase his dusky grip on her lily skin and red lips.

Ray had now unbuttoned Thomas's trouser and was delighting him in the open, moaning at the sight. Her eyes rolled back, her lids half shut. The vision of her toned legs and her explicit fondling between them brought Thomas to a climax. Ray reaped the harvest pleasuring herself in unison.

"Ray, Ray. Where have you taken him?!" came Ettie's voice from the veranda. Ray French-kissed Thomas.

Thomas spent much of the next few weeks glum, not himself, defaulting to the religious order at the Tabernacle. He took to visiting the Zion meetings regularly, taking solace in their readings. He also occasionally undertook some preaching when invited. Thomas had done so in Africa and was an adept orator with his booming voice. He became increasingly involved with the movement, also socially. Ettie had gone away the following day after the dinner at Earlsfield, on tour, promising to write. The garden incident left him anxious, as he had hoped to woo Ettie that night and make a more serious liaison.

'I loved Ettie the moment I saw her, her sister is dark and strange, exciting my curiosity, the lips incident repulsed me, a frisson unfamiliar to me... I want to see her again, is she a... masochist?'

In Africa Thomas had many relationships and dabbled in the tribalism of the villages. He had a predilection for the ritualistic element, the unruliness a direct contrast to his ordered life but it gave him unadorned pleasure. The rebound was deep guilt.

'English ladies have a veneer of sophistication... beneath the elegance is a base, animalistic instinct, a hidden meaning I've yet to find. What perplexes me is the permissiveness of these women – on the ship and in the garden. Am I totally to blame for my sins?'

Ettie sent him letters regularly, from Brighton, Worthing, and Bexhill-on-Sea. Thomas continued to write back, but also saw Ray for coffee out, then onto to his lodgings where they made love. Thomas capitulated to Ray's sexual preferences, he the master and she the willing victim, and he became embroiled in an emotional struggle of his own making.

Thomas was wedded to England after a few months, his funds depleted, having to borrow money from his lawyer as advances against rents coming in. He kept afloat by attending auctions, buying up dress diamonds and jewellery, selling onto shops and dealers, often visiting the pawnbrokers, Smiths in Hatton Garden, EC2, making minor amounts from his endeavours. It was not ideal. His rent was always late now, it was not the lifestyle he was used to, but something kept him in England - he had no desire to go back to the Gold Coast. He shipped the goods bought from Joseph to Africa, but without being there, they remained in storage and Thomas lost money on them. Bit-by-bit he was losing his connection with the Gold Coast and his family, having no thought for them. He would occasionally send a telex or letter home, but it was a case of 'out-of-sight-out-of-mind'. Having left his brother and a wife Efuru in charge of matters there, inevitably, the income from Africa slowed up. Thomas was distracted, drawn toward a different life. Through these stormy weeks he had thoughts of self-doubt that manifested themselves in bad dreams and nightmares. He judiciously wrote these up in his diary as he regarded them as an omen, a portent of ill health or even death, which only fed his sombre mood.

After a final demand for rent at his lodgings, Thomas decided to harass his lawyer in Africa, Mr Casely-Heyford. A warning was issued to those looking after his palm oil and timber operations. A substantial sum of money came through. This buoyed him up for the moment, but the situation could not go on. Thomas was not carrying out his duties, as he should have been making commercial deals, selling gold concessions and timber contracts in London. Thomas *had* been doing a lot, but it was mainly socialising with Ray, and mixing with a club of fellow countrymen he had met through the church in London. He had friends both African and European now and was intangibly linked with life in London.

The City oozed thrills for Thomas, the rain, the cold, gas lamps, fog, the electric bulbs, and something spontaneous emanated from every street corner and pavement of the capital. Also, Thomas could not get Ettie off his mind. He was intrigued with her theatricality. As part of the publicity for the show she was in, Ettie became Miss Daily Mail. It was a national beauty pageant promoted by the newspaper, a prestigious award. Thomas cut out the clipping and had it framed for his bedside table, which he hid before Ray's visits. Ettie's absence had made their letters and communications more fervent and suggestive. She'd be writing everyday.

'It is true! Absence does make the heart grow fonder... often when I read Ettie's letters I have a hot sweat!! But her winter tour is almost over, and spring on the way. Cannot wait for her to be back in London... trying my utmost to lessen the number of encounters with Ray, she is an endearing and a vivacious companion, I feel I am being drawn toward something I shouldn't have started'.

The daffodil and snowdrop bulbs started to show through, the days warming and Thomas felt rejuvenated. Casely-Heyford set him up to meet solicitors Emanuel & Simmonds in London who had customers for timber felling; the hardwoods on the lands were valuable and sought after in the UK. Casely-Heyford was on commission and telexed Thomas to organise interviews with the London contact. Thomas did the deal and got the advance. The whole affair was dogged with bad luck for the client, since, as soon as the workers reached Africa, they contracted smallpox and malaria and many died. The agreement ran out before any timber was cut. Nevertheless, Emmanuel & Simmonds earned a good sum from the arrangement, as well as Thomas, and it was to be an enduring relationship.

Thomas and Ray had taken to cycling out, visiting the nearby parks and woods, Kew and Richmond. They ate out and met mutual friends. Inter-religious mixing was frowned upon by the Jewish contingent. Joseph concealed his true feelings less they cloud potential business dealings, so he presented no barrier between his daughters and Thomas.

Ettie arrived at Waterloo station. She had returned. Thomas was shaking, feeling like a cheat, which was quashed as soon as they met. She radiated a presence and he was immediately entranced once again. With four stage boxes dispatched to her flat at Oxford Street, she and Thomas walked arm-in-arm over Waterloo Bridge, turning heads, like the original date at Charing Cross. They were the King and Queen of London *that* morning. They took brunch in a small restaurant off Parliament Square, then a cab to Thomas's flat at Hyde Park. Ettie took her clothes off, leaving on her stockings. She did not notice the lack of grandeur of the rooms, the poorly sprung single bed with its quaint metal frame and the ageing wall covering. She only had eyes for Thomas. With a chiffon scarf between her and Thomas's body, her firm breasts pressed up against his chest, they had sex. Thomas then used the scarf to tie her wrists to the barred headboard and placed the hard feather pillow under her buttocks, an act subconsciously appropriated from Ray. This gave Ettie multiple orgasms, enabling Thomas to penetrate deeper and harder, jerking her fulsome hips toward him again and again, her wrists chaffed. They spent the remainder of the day looking out through the skylight in the roof at the passing clouds over the rooftops, kissing, cuddling and making love. Thomas felt there was some connection, like he belonged. It was the only occasion he had fully unrobed with a woman, it was a turning point in his life.

Ettie Cantor (stage name Ettie Cinders), Miss Daily Mail winner
early 1900s

We'd been waiting for an hour. The option was to walk. We knew we were near the town of Acquidah, which we'd skimmed on the way to Tuasi, and thought we could get there by dark to find some temporary accommodation. We hitched a lift as soon as it approached. I'd never ridden on a tractor at home, being a townie. We may as well have been the British Royal Family the amount of attention we were getting moving at five miles per hour over the sandy road.

We passed through small settlements, gathering an ardent following of children. Skipping and tagging alongside, they were going faster. But at least we weren't walking. We *were* baking though, cooking alive. Getting up onto the old tractor nearly burnt the skin off our hands, the metal bonnet red hot. It was difficult to know what was worse, relentless walking in the overhead sun, or the inferno of this huge antiquity. Will changed his position; he couldn't stand it any more. He got down and stood on the back bumper hanging on to the bonnet catches. He was right about one thing he wasn't getting burnt. He was being thrown around like a rag doll, juddering with the vibrations. The sight of three whities being shaken around and barbecued on the ancient contraption was like the fair coming to town, and tickled onlookers lining the roadside. I made the best of it, waving like the Queen.

Then Jimmy bellowed above the noise.

"Car!"

The silver Mercedes was approaching in the distance. We thanked the tractor driver, who dropped us by a small church and waived down the car. As we waited little girls, neat in their ship-shape school-wear ran up, trying to touch Jim's face. They'd never seen a straight nose before. Jim obliged, bending down for them, one-by-one, the girls giggling. Kofi and Eddy facilitated the tyre repair, got it back to the car and fitted it, a small miracle. The return to Takoradi was mercifully uneventful and I looked forward to the luxury of air conditioning, a shower, and a decent bar. I wanted to get as far away from Eddy and Kofi as possible. I told Jimmy to get rid of them. Our car pulled up at the hotel. We went one way and Jim told them to go the opposite, giving them both fifty dollars. I had no regrets. Eddy waived cheerfully; he was coming to England and would contact us. Why? Our trip had been successful, as I'd found my Granddad's lands, but they were a liability. On collecting our key at reception we had a message, an invite from Faysal to spend the evening. We got a cab, arrived at eight, and had a fantastic time with our new friend and his family. We ate chicken and suddenly I remembered we'd left the chickens in the car. My gift to Eddy and Kofi. It was the last we ever saw of them.

Thomas had continued to see Ray contrary to his better judgement, unable to resist the attention of the sophisticate whenever she called on him. He was in love with Ettie but could not refuse the dark furtive sister, keeping their dates secret. Ettie had taken advantage of the leap year, utilising the lady's prerogative to propose to the man, requesting marriage. Thomas did not reciprocate immediately and the two relationships staggered on.

The proposal caused more problems, apart from juggling the various liaisons he now had to keep a potential father-in-law at bay, who wanted Thomas to use his contacts, influence, and money to help with the onerous legal wrangling. Joseph had heard about Thomas's recent business success, the timber agreements negotiated, and was constantly hinting at a cash injection to replenish the drained coffers.

A marriage between an orthodox Jew and a Pentecostal immigrant was completely unheard of. The insular Jewish society in London was outraged, but Joseph ignored the controversy.

Ettie exited the Lyceum Theatre on the Strand, where she had been for an audition for the next season's pantomime. She turned left up Bow Street heading towards Drury Lane, where she was lunching with a friend. She glanced inside a restaurant opposite the Royal Opera House as she walked up the street. They were there, fraternising - Ray and Thomas. Ettie saw red, clenched her parasol, and marched in screaming at the top of her voice in a distinctly different tone to the cockney drawl.

"It's her or me. Make up your mind!" The parasol came hammering

68

down in the middle of the table, sending the first course of soup flying. "You have a week to decide, or it's over."

With that, she about turned, the bustle on her voluminous dress turning over a sweet cart. Ray gathered herself up in shock. She pursued Ettie who was striding apace. Twenty or thirty yards, she nearly caught up, calling out.

"Et, Et!" Ettie skidded round and pushed Ray over, who landed face down in the gutter amongst the bad fruit and vegetables discarded from the market opposite.

"Hussie!" Ettie screamed, bending over Ray, Ray not looking up. A policeman's hand came down on Ettie's shoulder. Constabulary whistles pealed through the lunchtime workers. Traders from Covent Garden market sidled over to see the attraction.

"That's it missie. You're under arrest. Breach of the peace," and Ettie was unceremoniously dragged off.

Ray was weeping and Thomas, who was shaken and drenched in soup, looked on inanimately, not knowing which way to turn, distraught because of the onlookers pushing to view the scene. The police broke up the sideshow. He got Ray into a taxi, sent her to Thames Ditton and went back to the restaurant, as the owner had tailed him into the street ensuring that someone was going to pay for the damage. Thomas settled the bill and went to the police station at Hyde Park. He enquired after Ettie, paid her fine, and she was released into his arms. He apologised in his own way, by accepting her proposal. Usually, Thomas was in control, especially in Africa, but now his defences were down. He shed a private tear as Ettie hugged him, and they strode off, crossing Hyde Park to her flat where they resided on-and-off until they got married. It had been a costly afternoon for Thomas, financially and emotionally, and it had set a precedent in his life - say an epiphany.

The incident had disturbed him and he was determined to alter his philandering ways. He had, by the nature of his stature and charm, always been the recipient of female attention. His father, also Thomas, was the son of the veteran missionary Thomas Birch Freeman, and his family had been Wesleyan Methodists, attendance at the Dixcove church compulsory to his upbringing. In fact Thomas had known

69

nothing else but the Pentecostal church. He strayed as soon as he could, perhaps as a rebellion against his strict youth, becoming involved in indigenous tribal rituals, which had an overt sexual element. He had dalliances with young female students taking advantage of his senior position at the Wesleyan college, and fought emotionally with himself over his conduct. It did not align with his beliefs, he knew *that*, and with *this* marriage he resolved to take a fresh step. Nevertheless, he kept his African marriages secret from Ettie, possibly because they had no legal status in the United Kingdom, and visa-versa. Although a colonial nation, the marriage ceremony in West Africa bore no resemblance to the agreement made in England.

The entrance to the flat in Falconberg Mews was separate to the shop below, but Thomas could not completely avoid Joseph. Thomas was as personable as ever and kept smiling through the pestering, as was his character. As soon as the marriage had been announced, Joseph expected that Thomas would be obliged to inject cash or the assistance of one of his powerful lawyer friends into his tenancy battle.

As part of Thomas's quest to mend his ways and to be a good husband he became more connected to the Zion movement. He took Ettie to a couple of rallies and she was surprised at the outlandish nature of the services after the conservatism of the Jewish worship. He also involved himself to a greater degree, with the colonials, having regular assemblies with members of the newly formed United African Association. Thomas knuckled down and took his business more seriously, working on selling concessions for his gold mine at Sarnie and Kobala Kasa. This is something he should have done when he first came to London and Emmanuel & Simmonds were more than happy to oblige, putting potential clients forward, also finding per diems for Thomas for travel and expenses, in advance of deals being expiated. Ettie liked this and Thomas liked the regular money coming in.

The rift between Ettie and Ray continued. Ray could not accept the proposed marriage. She had fallen in love with Thomas. She tried to commit suicide.

'Sunday 26th June... Ray took poison chlorodyne owing

70

to a quarrel between Ettie and her about me. There was a mob. Blanche banned me from the house at Earlswood, and Joseph keeps making further entreaties to me about his problems.

Top from left; Ruth Cantor, Joseph Cantor (junior), Joseph Cantor (senior), unknown (friend of Thomas Brem-Wilson from United African Association), Carrie Cantor; middle - Maud Cantor, family friend, Blanche Cantor, bottom - John McCann, Ettie Cantor, Thomas Brem-Wilson, Rachael Cantor, 1906

Thomas had not bargained for the sister rivalry. It was beyond jealousy, as what had been teenage style tantrums turned nasty. Joseph wanted nothing to do with it, Joseph Junior would not get involved, Blanche observed, powerless.

On 11th July 1906, Thomas and Ettie were married at Fulham

registry office. Ray had threatened to throw herself under a tram and could not bring herself to attend. Straight after the ceremony they travelled to Westcliff-on-Sea for the honeymoon. Although Westcliff was agreeable and Ettie had friends there (as she'd performed regularly at the Palace Theatre), after a couple of days Thomas longed for London.

The metropolis pulsed, it's diversity and grandeur infused him with pride and zest. He liked to stride up Tottenham Court Road, looking at his reflection in the long windows of Heal's department store, the huge concave glass entrance hall, the perfect place to observe the ladies, window browsing. He observed the host of street vendors, listened to the calling out of newspapers, and the fruit and veg. Electric bulbs were nearly everywhere now in London and stores were already stocking electric powered gadgets. Thomas was fascinated by innovation and commerce; every day felt a new lease of life. In the Gold Coast the pace had been slow, sometimes like time was in reverse. He loved the bristle, the pubs turning out and the hordes, girls made up, every type coming from theatres, variety halls, and dancehalls that lined the streets. In the day, he would cut through Warren Street, crisscrossing Marylebone Road, meander into Regents Park, through the Zoo, and up to Camden Town to see the vibrant markets. Then take a tram down Camden High Street or train back to Ettie's flat.

In Westcliff, he felt constrained, disliking the palaver of bathing and beach-huts. Ettie's contrivance of being born within earshot of the Bow Bells was dropped in private, and she spoke in the same way as Ray, quite posh and a little finished. He had been so entranced by the 'Ettie Cinders' character he had almost forgotten that Ettie Cantor was the real person. Some of the shine had been rubbed off when the pretence went. Thomas returned to London a week earlier than Ettie, into a three-week break, pretending he had important business and left her to her theatrical pals.

I was glaring at the clock, I'm sure it was going backwards. Probably a delusion brought on by the conditions. Jim had fallen asleep. It was just as well, as the heat was very uncomfortable. I picked up my hand and it made a sucking sound, popping off the leather Box that I'd placed on the seat next to me, my sweat had been holding it on. The noise woke Jim up.

"What time is it?!" he said.

Even though the clock was only six feet away from him this was his affirmation that we had been here too long. Time wasn't at a premium when dealing with African officials. The twelve-thirty slot we'd arranged on the phone with Mr Hutchful at the Land Registry office, at Faysal's suggestion, had turned into one-thirty. Plus, we'd been twenty minutes early, because we're like that - courteous. Will had the right idea staying by the pool for the day. I had the feeling he lacked the backbone for this type of thing, and the 'Eddy and Kofi' show had left him bruised over further endeavours. He bottled out saying he had a stomach upset. I had an upset stomach now, from hunger.

"Go and see her again," I said to Jim for the seventh time.

Albeit disgruntled, he rose and went out into the hall, and into the next office. I heard raised voices, unusual for Jim. He came back, sat down saying nothing, also out of character. Fifteen minutes elapsed with me tapping my fingers on the Box, fingering the empty elephant's eye, Jim nearly nodding off again, my mind playing tricks, taking me back to Deptford market, gazing at the stall selling handbags opposite me for hours on end, waiting for customers, waiting, waiting.

We were asked through, the secretary smiling sweetly (the same way she did on our arrival, as when we asked for the umpteenth time) showed us in. The offices were cooler, with old-fashioned cast iron fans pumping the air overhead. The old Colonial building was well kept, whitewashed ceilings, magnolia walls, red tiled windowsills, and old style metal frames with the windows open. The place had a look of efficiency, neat desks piled with maps, ribboned bundles and correspondence. The junior workers were at their desks, heads down in their notes. No one looked up. Now *we* wanted something, nobody was interested. Mr Hutchful was orderly, his watery eyes behind what looked like ivory frames, bookish, fortyish and had the look of someone, who quietly, in their own way, had been punishing us for the past two hours, for having the audacity to ask for an appointment with him. A sense of his own worth, but I bit my lip. Jim, ever enthusiastic, went ahead.

"Nina has come to confirm her ownership of the lands at Tuasi, as the granddaughter of Thomas Brem-Wilson."

Mr Hutchful watched as I put the Box on his desk, taking out the death certificate, my birth certificate, and the maps and bits. He called to one of the youngsters, wrote some notes on a pad, and sent him off. About ten minutes later the young man was back with the maps for Tuasi laid out on the draughtsman's table next to Hutchful's desk. In the meantime one of the lads was instructed to transcribe details from my identification items. Mr Hutchful spent some time looking at my Indenture with the attached map, cross-referencing it with the oversized Ordinance map. He didn't say anything. After a period of listening to the fans turn and the lad scribble, he spoke.

"Make an appointment for three months time with the secretary on your way out and we'll have the formal ownership registered. I'll need your lawyer's details for correspondence, and I'll need to see your original Power of Attorney from your father or grandfather."

This sent me reeling a little as I'd expected to do everything there-and-then. Yes, some form filling, a fee to pay, but not this complicated. Surely the land was mine, I had the proof, and no one was contesting ownership?

"B... bu... but," I stuttered.

He cut me dead.

"Three months."

Placing his head down in some files, our signal to exit. What we didn't realise, and something that Faysal alluded to later that evening, was that, people were used to 'back-handers', and we hadn't cottoned on. He told us to go back.

"Go straight through to the office and give him some money."

We tried this the next day. When the girl went to lunch Jimmy went into the office with an envelope with so many cedes jammed in it, it felt like we were giving him everything we had, but it was about fifty quids worth. Jim told Mr Hutchful we'd forgotten to submit some dockets, handed it over, and the job was done. We called Mr Hutchful later, got through, and he said 'three weeks'. Now I was on a mission.

We added an extra week to our stay, visiting the airline office in Accra, paying the administration fee to alter our tickets, and started rounding up everything we needed to make the transition from hopeful vacationers to successful speculators.

"Goldfinger, he's the man, the man with a spark in his eyes," I was singing in the shower.

The experience was so out of our normal routine, something so different, I was able to make light of the initial disasters. Kofi did get us here - I hadn't forgotten that he got us out of the airport in one piece - but everything he'd told us in England had been a lie. I liked Africa, the pace of life, the characters, and was getting to like the heat.

Faysal was a guiding light. We had now become a firm fixture at his family home in Takoradi. We liked his house; it was a little out of town, but not too far; a three-storey building with a flat roof. This was typical in Africa, and Faysal told us it was so an additional storey could be built easily at any time. Opposite was a school, where there was always a game of football being played. The youths were skilled and enthusiastic, playing on uneven scrubby ground with no shoes and a hand-made ball. We liked to sit outside, watching them past the baked track, with a cool drink in our hands. Some days we spent on the beach at Busua, about twenty miles from Takoradi, and although the seas were a bit choppy, they were cool. It was deserted apart from a few gofers who would manage to produce delicious pineapples and coconuts for pennies at the drop of a hat. This really was my sort of place; we'd now acclimatised. The Gold Coast touched me. We'd slowed down to the style of life, were appreciative of every smile we came upon and the friends we were making. Was I being pulled back to my roots? I was mystified as to why my Grandfather never came back to the Gold Coast.

We hadn't seen much of Will, we spent more time with Faysal, and Will was off doing his own thing. We'd split up. The events of the first couple of weeks had perhaps put him off. Jim and me took it in our stride, ready for the next challenge. It had to be better than getting up at five in the morning every day to set up a stall in the street, battling the British weather and the British public.

Faysal had recommended a budget hotel near Labardi beach, close to Accra, called the Liberty Court, which was good for us, clean, with air conditioning, and we liked to people-watch in the bar by the pool. C.P owned the hotel, a young, rotund larger than life African. He had a great sense of humour, his whole body wobbled every time he laughed. We became buddies and visited his family for dinner a couple of times. There were all-sorts coming and going in Accra, a lot of European and American businessmen frequenting the bar with tales of cashing in on the booming gold market. This was music to my ears and made me more determined that my family lands were properly accounted for. I wanted to get on the lands right now and find my gold! Government buildings were in Accra. It was where we needed to be to navigate the African bureaucracy.

In the evenings we met up with Will in the bar, filling him in on what we were up to, but he didn't seem that interested and steered away from any serious business, happy to keep it light hearted, sharing tittle-tattle and poking fun at the American prospectors hanging about. Wearing thick denim jeans and cowboy boots in thirty-degree heat. I guess they were used to it being from Texas. One pair, Eric and Ernie, resembled the Clampetts from the American television show The Beverley Hillbillies. The preceding year they'd formed an African company with a Ghanaian citizen as a board member. This was a requirement of the Minerals department before any licences could be granted. This African partner, entrusted with the money to take samples and pay for workers to start surveying, had done a runner with their cash.

They had to start from scratch, compiling records again so that their application didn't expire. I picked their brains. They liked to talk. Eric and Ernie needed to get their project off the ground and the clock was ticking. They managed to hire a German geologist, a van, and some labour for their first 'recce'. We saw them off along with the rest of the hotel labour force, who appeared conveniently to have some jobs to do at the entrance. They wore cowboy hats, plaid shirts, sweating profusely from every orifice, and more.

"Looks like they're ready for some chilly nights on the prairies," I murmured to Jim.

The van was loaded with surveying paraphernalia, tools and camping equipment tied down on the roof. Eric and Ernie squeezed in alongside the German and three African labourers in the front.

"It's a twelve hour journey," Jim told me.

They pulled away, waving goodbye, their arm movements restricted. I quivered, not with anticipation, all of us stifling our collective jocularity until they were out of sight. Eric and Ernie were back in two days, worn out and despondent. The hire van had broken down relentlessly, and they'd realised it was impossible to sleep outside in Ghana, the mosquitoes making mincemeat of them. By the end of the week, a member of the Minerals Commission visited them at the hotel. Their concession was defunct. They were ordered to vacate the country. The third week into our trip, I'd just witnessed what I hoped to avoid myself. We couldn't afford this type of pitfall.

I called my Dad in England and persuaded him to give me Power of Attorney, having to explain what I was doing. He was a bit vexed by it but I organised a visit for him to a local solicitor. I called my brother Jason to take him, with more explanations. He happily agreed, for a cut, so I had to fax him a guarantee from the hotel, a small percentage share of anything found. Jason in return faxed me Dad's committal. C.P managed to get us a date to see Mr Kessi, the Minerals Minister, who advised and recommended a lawyer to help form a mining company with a Ghanaian board member. Since my Granddad was dead and my father was a British citizen, this was the only option to commence prospecting. I wanted to see the piece of land mentioned in my Grandfather's Box, called Assor Brompon, where there was meant to be gold. This time, Faysal suggested we go direct to the Chief.

"The Chief still holds a great amount of influence. If you can make him believe that you are here to make good use of the lands, then it would grease the wheels."

This meant we would have to swell the Chief's coffers. We kept missing Will who'd been out to the beach, coming back late, and spending the evenings in the music club, where they had local jazz bands every night. C.P set up the car hire. Jim and I drove out fully prepared, with air conditioning, water, spare fuel, spare tyre, shovel, tools, rope, compass, and maps. The onset of the rainy season in the bush was our first obstacle. We hadn't driven in Africa, but Jim was a 'Hell's Driver', a trucker from the 1960s, the first ever of a team of transporters from the United Kingdom to drive a convoy of deliveries to Russia, so he was up to any challenge I could throw at him. He'd once said he would follow me to the ends of the earth.

On arriving back, Thomas headed straight for the Tabernacle in East London, taking the bus across town. He wanted to see the Head Pastor, Reverend Cantel and share his dilemma. Thomas had doubts about his sanctity in marriage already, and his ability to stay on the straight and narrow. He had taken an unhealthy interest observing the girls who paraded up and down the promenade on sunny afternoons in Westcliff. The Pastor was tidying up after the afternoon prayers in the small Tabernacle hall. He invited him into his office, a tiny closet off the vestibule. Thomas confided, and the Pastor prayed for steadfastness, falling to his knees and taking Thomas's hand, their heads bowed, absorbed. This intensity lasted ten or fifteen minutes, then the Pastor sat back in his leather armchair. He regained his composure which took a while, with Thomas still submersed. The trams trundled outside, the Pastor was thinking concertedly. Finally he spoke.

"I'd like you to conduct a 'laying-on-of-hands' service this Saturday. For a young lady whose lost her way."

Thomas thought, his head rising, a hint of a smile lifting the look of despondency from his face.

"I'd be honoured sir."

"Knowing you've undertaken the ceremony in Africa I feel it would be a good choice. Give you a chance to reflect on your own path."

"I'd be more than grateful," Thomas replied. "My wife comes back Monday, and it's an opportunity to confirm my vows prior to her return, say, to cleanse my soul."

"Then Saturday, ten thirty Mr Thomas," they shook hands.

The hallway had been shadowy when Thomas entered earlier as the doorway was closed. The front door hinges and Victorian oak suffered from lack of maintenance and moved with difficulty. He had done the usual for out-of-hours visitors, prizing them a small degree to push through a gap. Two attendants would wedge both open during services so singing could be heard down the street, in order to attract likely members. When alone the Pastor shut them. Regulars had come through to the church to prepare for the evening, jamming them open, light flooding in. Thomas was blinded a little by the late afternoon sun shocked upon the limed wall opposite, and when his eyes adjusted the bolt of light illuminated the otherwise obscured sign.

DR. DOWIE. EUSTON ROAD TABERNACLE
THE ONE AND ONLY VISIT TO GREAT BRITAIN OF
THE ORIGINAL FOUNDER AND SPOKESMAN OF THE
ZION ORDER.
INVITED GUESTS, TUESDAY 13th AUGUST 1906, 7 O'CLOCK
THE TABERNACLE HALLS, EUSTON ROAD
OPPOSITE CAMDEN TOWN HALL

Thomas, astonished, turned on his heels, tapped twice, stepping back inside the Reverend's office. He had his back to Thomas, preoccupied, counting out bibles into boxes.

"What of Dr. Dowie, Reverend Cantel?!" Thomas blurted.

Cantel turned.

"Of course, of course, apologies, naturally, you are invited, it slipped my mind with your confidences."

"Ah, ah..." Thomas mustered, and reiterated, "Saturday, ten thirty."

With that Thomas left, feeling stirred both about his holy task and the Dowie visit. Dapper, Thomas had a spring in his step down Shoreditch High Street, heading for Liverpool Street Station, turning his cane as he walked (and turning a few heads). Reflecting, he felt he had done the right thing coming to England and with his marriage. Everything was looking good for him. Back at the apartment in Shaftesbury Avenue (where he was finally ensconced with Ettie, having given up his own meagre lodgings), Thomas answered mail and spent the rest of the afternoon composing a telegram to her. He felt better, invigorated.

At six in the evening the bell rang. Thomas went to the door and peeked through the spy-hole. He knew Joseph Cantor was downstairs in the shop, but there was no direct entrance from there and they had never been disturbed by him before. He saw it was Ray, looking desirous and refined, returned to her former glowing beauty. Thomas let her in flashing his special smile and she was unashamedly pleased to see him. He was in his silk dressing gown and slippers, relaxed, and Ray, with a mischievous beam, gave a soft brush on his cheek. She had found out he was back in London on his own, but had not come to take advantage of the situation.

"A party, John and Ruth McCann, they're the rage!" gushed Ray.

She had an invite to the banquet in Greenwich with the London socialites the following night, Friday, from her mutual friend Minnie M, and it was difficult for Thomas to say no, such was her enthusiasm.

"He's a business bigwig, you have to make the acquaintance of, you'll regret it if you don't come, Mr T," her old nickname for Thomas. Minnie was a student from a well off Spanish family, spending time in London hobnobbing, under the pretext of education. It seemed hopeful that things were resolved between Ray and Thomas, with her acceptance of the marriage, so he said nothing of the previous incidents, receiving the invitation with grace. She left after taking tea and biscuits, Thomas loved the Garibaldi, and Rachael had brought a packet, knowing his sweet tooth, with one more peck on the cheek and a time for tomorrow's rendezvous at Greenwich station.

After a day with solicitors, Thomas was ready for an evening dabbling with the London cognoscenti. It was a fantastic summer, late August weather of 1906, glorious, and Thomas looked chic in lightweight cream trousers, cricket-style blue striped blazer, an Ascot shirt worn with a narrow pastel grey patterned silk cravat, and a lounge coat slung over his arm in case of a shower. He left at six thirty, taking the London Underground that trundled below Oxford Street. He could sometimes hear the first carriages at five in the morning rumbling below when he was in bed, before it was drowned by the street cacophony of trams, callers, and shoppers. He had not taken the underground before. Ray had recommended he take the tube to London Bridge and then a bus. He did not know about this subterranean world.

The first thing that hit him was the noise of the trains, then the beggars that lined the many tunnel walkways, veterans with limbs missing. Africans were poor, but he had not seen vagrants before. Ladies of the night, bright rouge visages and skimpy bodices pushing toward him, everyone was rushing past in both directions, the vast thundering of trains into the tunnels. This was as far away from Africa as could be. Thomas liked it but was hesitant until he had purchased a six penny ticket and found the Northern line to London Bridge. The wood panelled carriage was roomy with air blowing through from the window louvres and door apertures at either end. Gents sat reading the evening papers, with couples on their way out to the many taverns that populated the streets around London Bridge, Borough, Bermondsey, and the busy Elephant & Castle railway interchange. Thomas was so engrossed he did not see the looks he invited, or he chose to ignore them. Either way, he was imposing and distinctive and could not help being noticed. He sat thumbing the tiny bible in his inside pocket, looking at his reflection in the window opposite until someone sat there.

Ray was waiting, although Thomas was easily on time, having got there in only thirty-five minutes. It had not occurred to him that it might be a little out-of-the-ordinary spending the evening with his wife's sister (with whom he'd had an affair), without his wife's approval. In Africa Thomas could do what he wanted, the master, he pleased himself. He did not know it was odd, but Ray did. She looked modern in the latest fashion, slim, graceful and elegant. Her figure-hugging dress fell to ankle length, revealing leather boots, lacy cuffs and hemline, a waist belt accentuated her figure, and a smart green cotton bolero to keep cool. Even when he saw her he did not go up immediately, watching from a small distance. The image change transformed her. Looking nonchalantly into the sky and at passers-by, her head was in the air, not concentrating on anything in particular, carefree, hands behind her back, turning around slowly, serenely. One heel was at an angle and she rocked gently forward as if practicing one of her dance moves.

'I felt sick and nervous. I thought I had made a huge mistake. That Rachael must be the one for me. I felt I loved her, as I stood out-of-sight, observing, illicitly. She would have liked that, unknowing of my vantage point. She was an apparition, an angel floating on a summer's night, her new chic - I had almost not recognised her and I had to take control of myself'.

A cursory hug and they walked off arm-in-arm, Ray directing. Beside the busy Greenwich High Road, turning towards the Royal Park, Thomas stopped to admire the grandiose Maritime Buildings. Up the steep slope he strode with Ray hanging on, stepping nimbly in her heels to keep up. The lustrous sap of freshly cut grass in the parks swamped the atmosphere, twilight falling and leaves twitching in a fresh summer breeze as if in anticipation; past the Observatory and to Maze Hill. Before them a vast vista of three storey Georgian mansions, a row of silver birch adorned the park border, which they overlooked, their mottled hoary bark diffracting gas light from the dozens of carriages arriving. Traps and hansom cabs lined both sides of the track, drivers patiently waiting to ferry guests away when it was over. The large pillar-box red double doors were already agape with so many invitees arriving at once. Thomas was rattled as they came up the steps, confronted by a fellow identical to him. He knew straight away that it was not a servant greeting everyone in such formal attire, as smart as Thomas, but more subdued. They were in a queue, which also rattled him. He did not like to queue and squeezed Ray's arm gently, whispering.

"We can go if you want?"

"Don't be mad Mr. T, we've only just got here."

Ray looking directly at him, smiling reassuringly, knowing his discomfort, in a way that Ettie could never have sympathised. The greeter ushered Ray forward in front of those fumbling with coats and cloaks, having caught her eye. John McCann had a broad smile.

"Ray, darling! And this must be Thomas! You're a lucky chap, marrying one of the prettiest girls in London and already out on the town with another beautiful woman!"

Laughing a huge laugh, he shook Thomas's hand robustly inviting them over the threshold.

"It's a pleasure meeting..." Thomas could only utter, as Ray funnelled him to the first drinks tables, where she was acquainted with the majority of partakers.

Cupid's Bows had Thomas spellbound, lustrous red lips, painted in. A lady risking the latest haute couture similar to Ray, held court, a willing contingent hanging on her repartee. Ray pushed through, drinks in hand taking Thomas with her.

"Ruth, Ruth."

"Darling, darling," the 'Cupid's' replied and the group dispersed, quickly distracted by the music and mingling.

"This is John McCann's wife Ruth, Thomas, call her Ruthie."

Thomas took Ruth's hand, bending forward, and kissed it.

"Delighted, Ruthie."

He was close as he straightened up; her hair was glorious, wavy, swept over her head, with ringlets and curls falling alluringly around her pink highlighted foundation. Thomas had never seen lips like these. She smiled.

"The best suitors have gone in London. Fancy you marrying Ettie. I hear you're from the Gold Coast, my husband's also from Africa, the Ivory Coast. There are many opportunities to be had from links with Africa, you and John should talk business."

"No business tonight Ruthie," said Ray, her eyes flitting about the room, "excuse me, take care of Thomas Ruthie, I've seen M."

Ray skitted off, meeting more of her friends on the way. They talked. Thomas was surprised that he had not bumped into John in his circles, with the small number of black people in London at that time. He mentioned his interest in the Tabernacle, Ruth affirming her approbation of men with moral values, by tapping Thomas on his chest as she spoke. An odd gesture and over familiar, Thomas thought.

Ray returned with Minnie M.

"I didn't know you had so many friends?" Thomas breathed in

83

Ray's ear.

"If you'd married me you would have been privy to best kept secrets," Ray replied, winking improperly at Thomas.

A heartfelt expression crossed his face, taking another slurp of champagne and procuring one of the treats that were circulating on trays, something elusive in pastry. Ray introduced Thomas to Minnie and John finally joined them, only to take Ray off dancing, capitalising on her agility. She flicked her bobbed hair at Thomas as she went, leaving him with Minnie and Ruth.

Generally speaking, they were an appreciation society for exotic gentlemen, as Minnie and Ruth would not let Thomas go. Minnie was wearing more formal evening apparel, her dress, off the shoulder, shiny long red hair was pulled back and tied, a ponytail falling down a low-cut back, and her silky brown cleavage was partly exposed. Thomas discovered that the 'M' was for an unpronounceable Spanish surname, so it became her nickname. When she laughed at Thomas's little jokes, her breasts gently moved, and he found it hard to keep his eyes focused in the right direction. Minnie was a little younger than Ruth, in her twenties. Her glistening gown clung to her slender figure, the subtle lace detail highlighting her Latin skin. She reminded Thomas of the young village girls he had known at home.

I was feeling a bit down in the dumps as we tried to dig the car out of the monsoon battered terrain. The rains had come as we'd left, falling on land that had been baked so dry, it had no place to go except down the road where we were headed, like a deluged river bursting its banks. No drainage gutter here, the surface immediately turning to slushy red mud. Potholes became lakes and we got stuck, going nowhere fast. Jim suggested sitting it out, before having a go at digging, maybe the deluge would ease up in a while. We should have brought Will and I felt a wrench of guilt. Right now, it was more of a mud rush than a gold rush. I couldn't see that we would ever get to any mining. The whole idea was becoming more ludicrous. But Jim was right, it soon eased up and the sun came out. For a bunch of gratefully received cedes, four boys, who had been watching by the roadside, were employed rocking us back and forth. With a bit of digging we got going again.

They told us to watch out for the bridge up ahead which was always out of use in the rainy season. I was mystified. Shouldn't a bridge be used to cross a river - not the river crossing the bridge? We'd headed west from Accra, back towards Takoradi following the bustling Cape Coast route, avoiding lorries that wanted to take up both sides of the road. We'd turned off into the bush towards Tarkwa forty odd miles north of Takoradi. With the Land Registry maps we knew where Assor Brompon was, at least in theory. We were close, but without any signs or landmarks to go by, we were going to have to pull over and start asking. Soon enough we were stopped, stopped at the bridge, cut off by a torrent of water from the swollen stream. It was a small tributary, but the little bridge was now impassable. There were various bikes, herdsmen with cows, and a couple of old vehicles queued up, so we got out.

Jim took the map and started talking with the locals (his favourite past-time) and they were eager to help. He quickly accumulated a fan club. I enjoyed stretching my legs, as it had been a two-hour lumpy ride. A lot of 'arm-waving' off into the bush and 'finger-prodding' at the maps was now under way. All and sundry had become involved. The gist was, that it would be quicker to go off, onto the track that ran beside the stream, and traverse further up where it would be easier, as it narrowed to a shallow spring. That's where Assor Brompon was anyway, two miles on apparently. The track looked similar to the one we were on, which was confirmed by homegrown knowledge. Part of my brain was saying, 'this makes sense', but a small voice said, 'don't drive into the bush'! I ignored the latter and so did Jimmy.

After five minutes, the result of our endeavours struck home, when overhanging trees bounced off the window screen, and the waters engorged the track. Jim slowed up, engaged the four wheel-drive, and we slugged it out, the alternative being to reverse back, where we would be sure to get grounded. There was no turning place, simply a muddy, bumpy, overgrown track with thick bush closing in. We slid around. Jim was positive.

"Don't worry darlin', I've had much worse than this through Mont Blanc in the snow and ice on the way down to Italy."

I didn't believe him and clutched my Box. Sweat dripped from Jim's forehead and we crawled on in silence for ten minutes, the car clock ticking. I didn't want to get marooned out here, and I swore under my breath 'Thomas Brem-f****** Wilson'.

"That's it!"

Jim had spotted the clearing visible up ahead, and beyond that, on the opposite side of the now lesser bubbling rivulet, a small village. A picturesque African scene; typical mud dwellings in the midst of shrubs and bushes, a few skinny cows and chicken pens, and a school hall in the centre. Women were out and children playing.

Jim carefully edged into the brook, only a foot deep, something the Toyota could easily handle. It ground to a halt. He tried reversing and managed to superglue it.

"That never happened in Mont Blanc, but I did have me snow chains on."

Jim was laughing but I wasn't amused. We both got out. The water was clear and cool between my toes, slithering through my sandals. By now we had an audience. Every child from the village was over in the water and the ladies were coming as well. The children were screaming excitedly and touching us. I said 'hello' about a hundred times. The truck wedged in the stream must have given the impression of something from another planet. Soon we had everyone shaking our hands, smiling, talking to us, and they all mucked in. It worked. The car shifted. Jim started it up, and it moved out.

"That's a first, wish I'd had my camera," he declared.

The truck careered up the bank, I scrambled in, waving, and we drove to the village centre toward a gang of fellas milling around the hall. They were typical village types but I could make out sticks and machetes. It flashed through my head that none of them had come to help in the brook. It made me a little nervous as we drew nearer.

"Park round the back." I asked Jim.

"OK Luv."

We avoided them, pulling up a little distance from the building, getting out and approaching on foot.

"Ask them, is this Assor Brompon?" I said.

"Is this Assor Brompon, is this Assor Brompon village?" Jim called out, and the answer came in the form of Will's voice.

"Yes, and what do *you* want?!" Will's voice. We both froze on the spot. "Beat you to it."

Then we saw him. Will was surrounded by the entourage, who looked like a bunch of tribal sentries. He pushed through to the front of the gang.

"It wasn't a race." Jim blurted.

"I got here first, the gold's mine, don't expect to hog it." Will said.

"But.. But.. Will," I said, "we're sharing everything, you weren't interested…"

Before I could finish, he really started up.

"You always were an arrogant cow, hogging the Box, cocky, acting like you own everything."

"How did you get here?" said Jim, veering off the subject.

"I worked it out before you, that's how it works mate," said Will.

"Don't call me mate." Jim said angrily, and swung for him, narrowly missing his jaw, but succeeding in pushing him into the wall behind.

"Don't Jim, let it go!" I was screaming, as there was a melee brewing.

Two blokes roughed Jim, but he pushed them both off.

"All right all right, that's it, insult Nina again an' you've 'ad it," Jim clenching his fist. "We had a deal, everything down the middle, and we're the ones who've been doing the bollocking work, who do you think you are?!"

"This isn't 'Dallas', we've only just got here." I added.

"Too late. Deal's done, I found it first, and the Chief's with me."

Will turned his back and skirted off to the main road at the other end of the village, the crew encircling him like a raggedy band of skanky football thugs on an afternoon's rampage at Millwall. He disappeared. We were left cold. Will had always been the quiet sensible one.

"What shall we do?" Jim said.

"For Christ's sake, there's only dirt, no gold yet, what in f****** God's name…?"

I snapped but couldn't finish, my words stifled with anger and frustration. Presumably Will had his own ideas, something had niggled him. Maybe he was in collusion with Kofi and Eddy; that would be a fine thing. I realised that I didn't know Will in the least. The women had come over and took us into the public hall, where we had some water, sat down and cooled off. My head was spinning.

"Blimey, that's a day by anyone's standards, unbelievable," Jim grunted, "f****** git."

I didn't know there was more to come. The Chief had been summoned and the hall was now filling up. The disturbance had drawn everyone in. No one had bothered about Assor Brompon since my Granddad had been here. It *was* going to cause a stir I suppose.

Thomas headed for the washrooms. He felt like the hobbyhorse and needed a break. They'd insisted on dancing, and took turns. There were elements of déjà vu. He escaped temporarily, avoiding the guest toilets and taking the stairs, inconspicuous in the maelstrom. Elegant hosts but intense, and he did not want to overcomplicate the self-doubt he had already experienced so near to his betrothal. He ascended the huge oak stairway, which straddled the hall, a showcase chandelier illuminating every part of the reception area clad in walnut and marble floors, a grand English residence. Taking a breather and inhaling deeply, looking out over the lavish surroundings, he felt at the centre of the universe. Even with his status in Africa, this type of lifestyle had eluded him. Thomas immediately knew he could be more successful in his business making a mark in London, following the example of John McCann. He was young enough with a beautiful new wife everything was possible.

The jumble sale stained drinking tumblers were passed around. 'Libation' was tradition and who were we to question it. The Chief was fishing for money. He had some from Will, and we had to up the stakes in order to mine Assor Brompon. I didn't know why it made any difference, because surely the Mining Commission would have the ultimate say, but the peculiar alcohol and airless sweaty hall, stacked full of elders and villagers, clouded my judgement, and now I wanted to outdo my cousin. Jim and I needed a drink after the incident our anxiety was eased by the petrol liqueur. We had become involved in some sort of initiation ritual with the Chief, that didn't require much more than being noisy and drinking the dirty looking fluid.

"Can't do too much harm." I said to Jim.

But it had undeniably already got the better of him (he was mainly a beer man). He suddenly jumped up and declared.

"Let's see the gold then!"

The Chief had a faintly ridiculous massive ostrich feather headdress on, with traditional African clothing and bare feet. He was maybe in his fifties, a little overweight, cheery, lined face beaten by the sun and happy to be drinking and asserting his rule over the flock.

"Big cheese, small pond." I whispered to Jim.

"Let's see the gold then?!" Jim repeated.

You couldn't argue with that. The Chief came to life.

"Gold it is!" he said, taking us by surprise. "Take them! Take them!"

He pointed to three young men at the doorway, beckoning us to follow them, which we duly did. Out of the hut and into the afternoon sun. They led us into the bush speaking in broken English.

"You come. This way. Gold."

I had a flashback, as I was hungry, thirsty, and I believe, hallucinating to a degree.

***

The glowing linen-covered tables literally heaved under the weight of food. Everyone was eating and drinking from the banquet that the McCann's had organised. Not so much a band, but an orchestra played, on an especially built stage, curtained round by flags from the colonies. The raised sprung dance floor was crammed, traditional routines alternating with modern hit tunes from America. There were servants, Negro and Chinese, serving from silver platters: small roasted chickens, hams, fresh vegetables, fresh sweets, cake, cream, champagne, anything you could want. Thomas looked down in awe at the scene. His eyes glazed a little at the bobbing heads, colourful regalia. He thought he saw Royal colours, reds, golds, and epaulettes. Thomas continued, found a washroom and it was a masterpiece; huge porcelain sink, the latest plumbing with silver swan neck taps, lined in marble from floor to ceiling. He washed up, combed his hair, and went on a little reconnoitre. Along the corridor away from the party, music and laughter echoed throughout. Walls were hung with artworks, mainly hunting and English country scenes, and at the end of the hall, he took the stairs up to the next floor. More corridors, wood panelled, recently buffed, they shone with the reflection of the electric lamps. Thomas was besotted by the opulence: objets d'art, mahogany and oak furniture, paintings and statues. He peeked in a couple of rooms where the doors were open: well furnished, warm, comfortable, and one with an enormous four-poster Edwardian mahogany inlaid bed.

He mooched around, thinking about Ettie and Ray, his head gently buzzing from the 'bubbly' he had drunk. Ettie's theatrical drawl gone in favour of elocution English, and Ray, so relaxed, natural, part of a decadent set, eloquent, he felt cheated. Thomas found a full-length mirror in one of the bedrooms to adjust his look and check on the spotlessness of his get up. When done, ensuring strands of hair were in place, he patted his bible and headed back down to the party, descending to the first floor, his patent pointed shoes clicked against the oak floors, until the roar of the party drowned it out. He heard ladies' raised voices from one of the rooms in the corridor, and poked his head round the door.

"Oh, do excuse me ladies. I was having a look around." he apologised.

They laughed. It was Ruth and Minnie powdering their faces, although Minnie's complexion seemed natural downstairs.

"No, come in, please come in," said Ruth, reposed in a sumptuous red leather armchair, the wood surround carved as a huge fan, Minnie reclining on the matching settee next to her. Both ladies giggled.

"Have some champagne with us," said Ruth.

"I'd be delighted, thank you," Thomas accepted courteously. He entered unhurriedly, the door remaining fractionally ajar, "I have been admiring your beautiful home. I hope you don't mind?"

"Of-course darling, join us," Ruth replied.

She leaned toward the drinks table to pour from the magnum. Thomas approached. She politely sat up a little to hand it to him.

"We're merely relaxing having a tête-à-tête."

As he bent down, instead of handing him the champagne she moved up, grabbing his lapel, kissing him full on the lips. It was lingering and lush, the Cupid's bow smudging across his face.

"You naughty girl Ruthie," said Minnie.

She sank into the sofa, teasingly smoothing her hands up and down her long legs. She rucked up her dress, showing off her backside and thighs whilst she witnessed the indiscretion. Thomas was eyeing up Minnie as he French-kissed Ruth.

"Ettie's a very lucky girl, but she can't have you to herself can she?" Ruth gasped.

Taking Thomas with both hands, parting her legs, exposing her oyster silk stockings and calf length boots, and pulling him in toward her. He had no control. His virility overcame him. He knelt and kissed Ruth's long sexy neck, squeezing her trim petite hips. She groaned, baring her breasts by slipping them out over her corset. The tight herringbone pushed her nipples up which Thomas sucked as he squeezed them, her groans becoming deep heavy moans.

Minnie got up from the sofa, taking off her gown and was removing Thomas's jacket and shirt, caressing his mahogany skin with zeal. Ruth managed to gesture to her to shut the door, but Minnie was preoccupied with masturbating, her hand gliding up her smooth brown legs to her mound, as she felt Thomas's body. She breathed deeply as she was stimulated to a sexual frenzy watching Thomas's full lips on Ruth's pearly bosoms, and she came.

She slinked over to the door and locked it, removing the rest of her clothes on the way back to the sofa. Minnie was nude; silky olive skin, taught youthful breasts, a pert smooth bottom, and her ankle boots, which she had tried unsuccessfully to unlace. Before Minnie could return, Ruth had taken out Thomas's penis and moved him over to the sofa, kneeling, and clutching the high back with her painted fingernails,

91

guiding him into position. By now Thomas was having coitus with Ruth from behind. She was crying out with lust, rocking back and forth with his thrusting.

"Minnie darling, have some."

Taking Minnie's hips and pushing her underneath her, Minnie moved into position and sucked Thomas's testicles and girth, whilst Ruth licked Minnie's vagina. Thomas withdrew his penis before he climaxed, Minnie appreciating the cream on her face, licking voraciously. Thomas sat back on the sofa, the sweat dripping from his brow onto his glistening chest, his arms splayed out behind him, trying to catch his breath. Minnie pulled away from Ruth taking Thomas's penis in her hand, salivating.

"Now me, now me."

Thomas was quickly erect again with her gentle persuasion, Ruth continuing to pleasure herself, and caress Minnie's breasts. Minnie mounted him, and jerked on the pole, her eyes widening each time she let the penis pull out, startled at it's magnificence, before she thrust down on him again. Thomas did not need to do anything as Minnie was moving up and down the whole length, her nipples now hard, being squeezed and slapped by Ruth. Minnie's nails clenched the settee, her shoulders arced backwards so that she could rub her clitoris on Thomas's pelvis and push her breasts out. Her deep brown eyes were huge with desire, she gasped, and climaxed repeatedly. Thomas sat back and enjoyed the two ladies swooning over him and taking the treat that he offered, spurting on Minnie, his semen dripping down her breasts, with Ruth tasting it greedily. Thomas had no feeling of contrition, or thought of his wife, or Ray. He was completely caught up in carnal lust. The ladies became absorbed with the juice, kissing, and rubbing their breasts and slim tummies together.

"Darling, you're quite a specimen, don't tell John, he'll want to join in next time," Ruth gushed.

Thomas wanted to get back downstairs. It had been enough for any man. He sidelined the locked duo, pulled his trousers up over his swarthy legs, noticing that he had not taken his socks off. As he pulled on his shoes, Minnie leant over grabbing his leg.

"Don't go Tom."

He had never been addressed by a moniker before, and he did not really like it, even though it was with affection and an endearing Spanish accent.

"I have to go. Ray. The party."

The first words he had spoken since the orgy's inception. He had difficulty with an uncooperative key in the lock, an unyielding Victorian mechanism impeding his exit. Looking back, he saw Ruth get up onto Minnie's face, spread her legs fully, the heels of her boots denting the leather of the chaise longue. He shut the door behind him.

Thomas walked down the hall smoothing his hair, and was struck down by contrition. He had to steady himself against some oak drawers, a valuable gilt vase sitting there rocked precariously from his shaking, and he tried to stop it. An ashen mist clouded in on him. He fell to his knees, hyperventilating, mopping his brow, and putting his head in his hands. Minutes passed, he could feel his heart thumping against his eardrums and a ringing, like a continuous high church bell tone, the dull party noise turning to a reverberating cacophony. Grasping the tabletop, his other hand fumbled around inside his jacket. He seized the pocket bible. Somewhere in the recesses of the disorientation he knew the familiarity of the frayed leather binding could atone. His fingers tensed almost so they were bent back, but his hand pulsed where he gripped and a burning sensation seared his palm, forcing him to thrust the book away onto the wooden floor. Was it a nervous spasm or trapped nerve? He was too panicked to know. Thomas was glued to the spot, breathing heavily, eyes flitting rapidly between the book and his hand as he tried to focus. He turned his hand over and over blinking at the protruding veins. Managing to extricate his hand from the cold marble tabletop, he placed it on his forehead and chilled his face; sweat dripping through the gaps between his fingers. Staring at the open bible on the floor he clasped both arms together in a type of desperate rite, a pain went up his arm, pins-and-needles, he prayed, furiously, between desperate breaths.

"Dear Lord, I have sinned, strike me down, I deserve no less. Oh Lord, take me now, take me now."

Thomas heard voices getting closer. He used every ounce of energy, pulling himself up, using the table as a crutch. Arching down, he clasped the bible and staggered off, heady and unsure, making his way back. He acknowledged the revellers, keeping his head down as they passed in the passageway. He reached the stairs, hanging on to the banisters tightly, descending intently. He felt dishevelled and kept trying to tuck his shirt in, his hand going round his waist. He straightened his tie, and pulled the lapels on his jacket forward obsessively, going back over his hair, attempting to calm the natural Afro into its slicked coiffured condition. He pushed through the party, directly to the buffet tables and gulped down water, calming himself as he ate what was in front of him, not aware of what it was. Ray spotted him and caught up.

"Thomas, you're flushed, you must be enjoying yourself?"

It was hard to see that he ever reddened up, but this *was* the case, and embarrassment swamped him; spitting out some words.

"I have to go, I'm feeling unwell Ray. Apologies."

Ray found John. They said their thank you's.

"You must stay and see Ruthie before you go - she'll be terribly disappointed," John proclaimed.

Thomas lacking his usual social prowess stumbled over his words, Ray filling in. Nevertheless, they promised to meet up in London City at their solicitor's office to see what business alliances they could make, and Ray and Thomas were off into the clear temperate night air. Thomas breathed it in like nectar. After the food and drink he felt somewhat revitalised, and upped his step. The park was now closed, so they made their way up Maze Hill, past the expectant cabs, and stood on Blackheath, Ray hanging on to his arm. A sweet tasting summer mist blowing gently across the ghostly splendour of the heath, and they hailed a cab for Shaftesbury Avenue.

⬦

It resembled Tuasi; perhaps it was an omen that gold could be here. The difference was that the trees stretched up in to the sky, with roots above ground that divided out like tentacles. The forest was older and denser. Maybe it was because we were close to the brook that spurred me on, the thought that I could get to water at any time, even though you daren't drink it. We were probably walking for about twenty minutes, but it felt a lot longer after the libation ceremony, my legs dragging.

"Wait, wait." I proclaimed, and sat down on one of the many overgrown roots that crossed the path. I took a glucose tablet out of my pocket, I can't remember why I'd put it there, but I chewed it.

"OK Nina?" Jim said, "We won't go far... check out the lay of the land."

I looked down my mind froze on a trail of ants, traversing the track and down to the brook.

"Ants can't swim, can they Jim?" I called after him.

"Are you ok Nina?" checked Jim, and I got up and trudged on.

Like before we trusted the locals, and followed. The trees became fewer, and I could sense we were coming into a much different spot. I could hear the clanking of tools, activity, male voices.

"I think we're here Nina," came Jim.

As we walked into the area the scene was indescribable - so enormous. The whole place was a mess of scrappy earthworks dug out at different times - there were piles of soil and rock in a sprawling landscape surrounded by brush and low bush. Beyond this was the Africa I had been searching for, a green vast valley, then a plain, with animals grazing and, far off in the distance, uplands. Looking closer there were trenches in the ground, with rocks and dirt piled up beside them, a lot filled with water from the downpour earlier and about half the labourers working, but not fast. They were more interested in us and, as we navigated our way to the centre of the site, they gravitated toward us, forsaking their various excavations to come and see.

"This is knock-out, I never expected this," said Jim.

From here it looked gigantic with hillocks of red soil, ditches, basic tools lying around and a few bits of string marking out sections. It seemed cooler, a kind breeze, but I could see swarms of mosquitoes building up around the many puddles and mini-ponds that had formed in the craters and I started flicking, even though none had come after us yet. The panhandlers looked bedraggled, muddy hands, arms and knees with the red mud ground into their fingernails and skin. Each wanted to shake our hands, smiling and curious. We got messy but I didn't mind. I followed Jim's eyes downwards. They were wearing scooped out car-tyres on their feet, that had been cut to shape, and fashioned into makeshift Wellingtons, tied on with scraps of string and nylon. If there was gold, there couldn't be that much - either that or they were very lazy. I realised they were waiting for us to say something.

"We've come to see the gold," I said.

Then they piped up in dialect, which sounded a little Dutch to me, a few words jumped out, like 'Kwesi Bruni' and 'Toyota'. The main man, looked like a foreman, mainly because he was older than the rest and a bit less grimy, spoke in broken English.

"Here, come here, yellow, yellow, we show you, here, here."

He took some of the rocks that had been recently dug out placing them in a bucket, and went over to the brook. He crushed the rocks in his hands and they started to crumble. Jim and I gawked, transfixed, disbelieving that anything of any value could come out of this dirt. He kept crushing them, and they eventually turned to particles in the bucket. He placed the muck in a section of rounded cutout tyre, and squatted by the brook, swishing it back and forth. Washing out the bigger particles, he kept sifting with his fingers, gently refreshing the water so as not to wash the whole mixture away. Everyone watched in the heat, mosquitoes buzzing around my ears and the gentle wind rustling the scrub that grew by the brook. After fifteen minutes I could only think about the ants that I'd seen, trekking across the path, maybe the effect of the 'imbibement'. I started reflecting on where they might be going, why, and what was the point, then I thought, 'what is the point? What is the point to this?' I said it in my mind so many times in the silence that in the end it came out loud.

"What's the point?"

"Eh? OK Luv?" Jim said, in his jocular manner.

I was feeling dizzy - a bit sick - the glucose and libation amalgamating with the afternoon sun. The rubberized pan was swaying in the water and I was swaying on the spot. I was seeing kaleidoscopes. The last time I'd felt like this was at a party in Lewisham when I was sixteen and had drunk too much Babysham. The hues flitted across my eyes, a rainbow in the rubber pan; the sun glistened on the rainbow. It was gold. I fainted. As I went down I heard the foreman call out. "Yellow, Yellow!"

***

Ray was on the floor, determined to get Thomas back, and knew his weaknesses. Thomas could not resist as she unbuttoned his fly where she knelt. He had made love with Ray before, but never like this, and in a public place, at the entrance hall to Ettie's apartment.

They had passed St Paul's in the taxi, having driven down the Old Kent Road, the profusion of taverns and pubs turning out, stacks of revellers, brawls, bobbies, girls in make up and their best finery, out for a Friday night. They had traversed Tower Bridge, carts being wheeled out for the morning markets at Borough and East Street, passing up Fleet Street, the early morning lads broadcasting the first editions of the Standard and Times. Thomas was excited by the nighttime commotion and bustle, looking out the window. The unfolding scene was a revelation, the parochialism of the Gold Coast far away, and it revived his spirit. Ray took advantage of his buoyant mood, sidling up to him in the carriage gently stroking his leg, and Thomas was aroused.

In the front hall to Ettie's apartment, Thomas was enjoying fellatio, Ray eliciting his full attention. He took it as a sign of his manliness and status and succumbed with no protestation. Ray had asked for water and let the cab go minutes before. It was her deliberate intention to use womanly powers to win him back. Ray used her lace hanky to wipe away what she had missed from her lips and fragile neck. Thomas was breathless, quickly hiding his modesty. He pulled Ray up and she fell against him pressing her breasts, which were now on display, brushing across his open-shirted chest. Gazing up into his eyes, kissing, she guided his hand, brushing her erect nipples. Thomas tasted salt and could not restrain himself. He took Ray, ripping off her dress in the bedroom. At the summit of his virility Thomas had sex with Ray, sullying the marital sheets in a wanton fervour, indulging their now joint proclivity for erotic deviance.

The alarm went at ten in the morning. Thomas rose. He had a headache. Ray stirred and turned over in Ettie's silk covers. Thomas

97

gazed for a second at her smooth desirous dancer's legs, shapely ankles, and wondered what he had done. Thomas hurried, had some tea without milk and what was left of the Garibaldi packet, shaved, washed and, as he departed for the Tabernacle, shook Ray on the shoulder declaring loudly.

Ettie Cantor (stage name Ettie Cinders) early 1900s

"Ray... Rachael! You have to go, Ettie is due back," and he left.

After the tea and once seated on the tram, Thomas's headache passed but he was still tired and the jerky ride quickly made him queasy. Inevitably the night's bacchanalia left him depressed and remorseful. He was confused about his inability to divorce from the old Thomas. He found women irresistible and any opportunity to indulge his male prowess was overpowering. Ray was a conundrum and he knew it. He was worried now. Maybe the chapel, and the 'laying on of hands' would make a difference, a clean start and the reconfirmation of his faith. Thomas jumped off before his stop and was sick in the gutter by the Kingsland Road - Saturday market, browsers and shoppers deriding him.

"Drunkard!"

"Sot!" And racist comments he had not heard before.

He wiped his face over with his silk hanky as he strode away toward Dalston, ignoring the scoffing stallholders. As the hankie was returned to the pocket he patted the holy book, saying something derogatory about the market workers under his breath, in words he had never uttered previously. He shook his head to himself as if ashamed and made away hastily. He had drawn a lot of attention and rushed off before the police were summoned. The pace and fresh air helped.

◇

I was back on my feet. I was made of tougher stuff than that. They'd put me in the shade with a bottle of water.

"You went down darlin'," said Jim, "probably a bit much." I took slurps and revived. "You missed the best bit luv, he added a bit of mercury to it from a small bottle in his pocket and it congealed into a tiny gold nugget." Jim held it out and I took it.

"Where's my Box?" I said suddenly.

"You left it in the car." Jim replied.

"Let's go, and, give them some money," I got to my feet and wiped the sweat. Jim huffed.

"OK, I already gave them about a fiver each, that'll do, the foreman had ten."

There was no way I was going to be usurped by my cousin. They'd most likely brought him out here, flattered him with the nugget trick and hey presto, the Chief became the recipient of what I liked to call a 'bung'[6]. I had to get my concession in first. Will was now a loose cannon, and I felt a sense of panic. The mines were an unknown quantity.

"It could be a cottage industry, a few extra pennies for the Chief and the clan." I said.

"Yeah, but what a fantastic thing." Jim said, peering at the mini-titbit.

As we traipsed back I remonstrated with him, "I got the power of attorney," the formalities swilling about in my imagination.

Jim didn't answer as he was trying to communicate with the three lads who followed up behind. He managed to drag it out of them that the gold was sold to the Chief. In return they were given the school, money and libation. I listened intently. This is what Jim was good at. It slotted into place. The Chief was on to a good thing. He was a stick in the spokes but he was absolutely open to a bribe. The ants were gone.

When we got back to the village it was deserted. It was now very late afternoon and families were at home, some cooking going on, slivers of vapour trails emanating gently from the huts and shacks. It was an Eden, if you could scrape a living. The Chief couldn't be found. We were too exhausted, so we decided to go.

We drove the car ostensively the logical way through the village, which led to the Takoradi road. At the small bridge the waters had subsided, minor traffic crossing again. We headed to Faysal's place near Takoradi keen to discuss the events. Jim and I debated scenarios in the car. How Will could possibly have arrived at his point of view was inconceivable. 'You couldn't make it up' was Jim's riposte after each declaration of incredulity from me.

We found Faysal's easily, Jim, having been there a few times, could remember the exact spot. The Toyota's lamps carved a route, a million bugs splattered on the screen. We tooted, and he came out to the drive, waving both arms. The house lights illuminating the surroundings, the

---

[6] bung - (slang) bribery, a form of corruption, an act implying money or gift given that alters the behaviour of the recipient

school opposite shut up, and some other settlements blinking in the vicinity. Faysal couldn't wait to hear our news. We discussed the Chief and the gold and Will!

"Even if you had a mining concession, the Chief and his settlement have rights, and he could always cause problems for you. Better you have him on your side, he'll smooth the way with the workers, help out the geologists, or anyone that needs to survey the area," he remarked.

Faysal was always full of good advice, and he gave us the name of his lawyer where we could form our mining company. It was the priority, in order to be taken seriously by the minerals department. He said he had tried lots of lawyers in Ghana, and this one was the best of a bad bunch. This appeared similar to the UK. The Chief could be 'sucked up'[7] to anytime, but I really had to get some 'red tape'[8] completed before Will. We stayed with Faysal, and left early before breakfast for Accra, determined to catch up with Will, and put him on the spot to find out exactly what he wanted. We could still split everything. Will had gone. Taken his ticket out. We had our extended week, forgetting that he was due to fly back home. C.P let us use the phone and we made an appointment with Mr Solo Kwame Teteh, the lawyer, for that afternoon.

We waited in Mr Teteh's office, in the heart of Accra's business district, one of the neat two-storey buildings. The reception was cool and westernised. There *was* the prospect he was going to get paid, an incentive to see us quicker, so low-and-behold, we were soon shown in. We replayed our experiences eagerly and he confirmed with occasional 'hhhmmms'. He was tall and calm, taking everything in. Mr Teteh was even mannered, bordering on quiet. He had obviously seen prospectors come and go, he knew the 'ins and outs'. He suggested we form a mining company, with him as a non-voting, advisory director, so that he wouldn't have direct influence over company decisions, but could carry out instructions in our absence. We did this, and Brem-Wilson Mining was formed. Granddad would have loved this, I

---

[7] suck up - (slang) - to behave in a very friendly, flattering, or kind manner to someone higher than you in order to get a benefit
[8] red tape - excessive bureaucracy or adherence to rules and formalities

thought to myself.

The company partnership was drawn up, signed, and paid for. We gave him extra money to formalise the mining concessions in our absence - three hundred pounds odd. He explained the process. We would need proper geologist samples from each of the sites (taken from various areas, so that they could be sent off for tests to see how much, if any, gold was there, to help us get commercial companies interested in mining), and up-to-date large-scale maps with borders indicated and proper contouring (one for each government department). We'd already seen several in-depth drawings at the Land Registry, so this was curious. Someone may have been lining their pockets, but if Mr Teteh was saying it had to be done, it had to be done. We knew we didn't have the money or equipment to go into full scale mining ourselves. It sounded ridiculous - like castles in the air.

Inside a day of hitting British soil again, as the rain was pouring down (like it did most days of the week when I was setting up my market stall), I knew why I was doing it. Jim and I were cleared out of money what with the solicitors, hotels, car hire, and the rest. We arrived home to the reality of wintertime England, cold starts, dead van batteries, freezing fog, sleet, and jingle bells. Wishing we were back in the African sun, with our recently made friends.

"Baskets, baskets, lovely basket-ware, two for a fiver." bellowed Jim.

Thomas brought the leather Box up toward him onto the bed. Inspecting it, he saw a jewel missing from an elephant's eye. He had not noticed before, never examining the fine detail since he'd brought it from Africa.

'The lost jewel is an evil sign, an emblem of my vice'.

He felt like he was on his deathbed. He had been here before, in this place, a dour repentance battering his fibre, he must be a devilish man. Smoothing his finger in the eyehole, feeling the leather, and taking some small solace from its soft velvety lustre. The case had always been by his side, like an old friend. He pulled the diary out, placing it beside the bible.

'1. I had gonorrhea this morning. 2. Bought syringe tube & sulphate of zinc 5 shillings'.

The laying-on-of-hands at the Tabernacle Hall had turned into a frenzied session. The singing was fervent, many participants 'speaking in tongues'[9], as if possessed, and Thomas was enticed by the turmoil. The Rev. Cantel had led him into the room, a white ceremonial Zion cape slung over his shoulders. A slender girl, who was the daughter of a member of the congregation, was lying nervously on a table covered in green and orange cloth at the temporary pulpit. It was understood that she had strayed, having unions with male friends not approved by her family, and was here to find salvation by casting out the wickedness from her body. Ladies, relatives, guardians, their hands already in the air flanked her on either side, shaking and clapping to the thumping piano music.

The girl had calmed as soon as Thomas had taken her hand between his. He smiled at her. Madeline was an innocent young beauty. Thomas praised the Lord, speaking of her deliverance, 'liberating her from evil'. He started to run his hands gently over her body. The Reverend Cantel stood between him and the excitable believers (about a hundred) raising his hands, encouraging everyone up and dancing and shaking themselves out in the aisles. As Thomas moved adeptly over her she smiled gratefully, shut her eyes, feeling the beat of the music and the heat of the room. Madeline cried out with pleasure, Thomas responded as if gripped by a spell. He ran his hands more powerfully and her thin dress, already ridden up somewhat, pulled up over her thighs. The

---

[9] speaking in tongues - utterances approximating words and speech that are nonetheless generally unintelligible, usually produced during states of intense religious excitement.

whole congregation came forward, waving, and singing. Thomas was sweating, the girl was writhing, his hands covering her entire body, and up her legs. The zeal from the mass disguised inappropriate behaviour. In the frenzy Thomas raved, calling out to the assembled, drawing the girl up to a sitting position, laying his hand on her brow.

"Out evil… In the name of the Lord."

He cast his hand away as if some great thing was exorcised from her body and she trembled, slumping involuntarily toward Thomas and he drew her close. He lifted Madeline up to her bare feet, as she was unsteady, holding her body with his powerful grip, one hand still on her brow, and took her through the baying congregation, down the aisle, and into the Reverend's office. Once behind the door she threw her arms around him, exclaiming:

"You saved me, Thomas, Thomas, I love you."

As she kissed him impulsively Thomas defiled her, there and then, in the back room, with her, Madeline, the willing recipient, opening her legs to him on Rev. Cantel's desk, their sweat blending, the choruses continuing in the hall.

Thomas had caught venereal disease from whom he did not know, and had certainly passed it on, unless the carrier had been the girl at the Tabernacle, his last conquest. He didn't even recall her name, which now disgusted him. He lay in bed moaning and that's how Ettie found him on the Sunday when she arrived back with her many cases being brought up by the cabbie.

"My poor Thomas. I will get you well," said Ettie, determined.

The newly devoted wife went down to Covent Garden to buy vegetables and make fresh soup. Thomas would never divulge the reason behind his ailing, but Ettie was in too deep, a baby due to arrive in only six months.

We knew we had to go back and we wanted to. The phone lines were terrible, and whilst Mr Teteh was doing his job, we were concerned that things weren't moving very quickly. There was no sign of the completed maps of the two areas, and Teteh admitted that he hadn't been able to find a reliable surveyor as yet to go out to the land and get them drawn up properly. I'd questioned the justification for the maps and Teteh told me the government representations were in fathoms. If we wanted to exploit the lands, they had to be brought up to date at our expense. It was a pain, but I accepted it. Now we had a presence in Africa, but it felt like we couldn't cross the first hurdle.

It was our favourite subject, with Jim and I discussing it most days, going through the processes, what was needed to get a mining license. Once we had the license we would have exclusive rights, but I knew Will would be thinking the same. We tried to get him on the phone but he had a 'bee-in-his-bonnet'[10] and wouldn't take any calls. Maybe Kofi had been a good (or cheap) worker and Will resented the way we had treated him. I'd been speaking to my brother Jason, and he was now interested in coming in fully with Jim and me - we could do with some help. We felt out of our depth. We heard through Jason that Will had hooked up with cousin Ken. They were trying to form their own mining company, getting a Power of Attorney from *their* Dad. One thing I knew was that Ken was slow, and together they'd make a pair of lunging rhinos in a china shop. I couldn't take any chances though. Will ran a business, and would be thinking of how to sideline me. Perhaps he never wanted to split it down the middle from the outset?

I tried to think how I could be one step in front, in case it *was* a race. I began by ringing up large mining companies, to see what interest there would be. Obviously, with no experience, I simply picked up the London Yellow Pages telephone book, and started phoning round. Incredibly, there was a section with mining companies listed. I worked my way through a lot of disgruntled sounding receptionists. As one can imagine, my enquiries fell on deaf ears, their job to dispense with crank callers, who'd thought they'd discovered gold, as quickly as possible. With some beginner's luck we finally made an appointment with a company called B.W.P (British World Prospecting). The gentleman who answered the phone was well spoken, took a genuine interest, and listened patiently, throwing in a few 'oos' and 'aahs'. He was obtaining land in Ghana for mining prospects and would be

---

[10] bee in his/her bonnet - a chronic preoccupation, often fanciful or eccentric

willing to meet us. It was a complete fantasy discovering a real mining company - 'pie in the sky'.

Thomas was well enough to go to the Euston Tabernacle on the Tuesday. He had spent time with Ettie in the morning, although he had not made love with her for fear of passing on his gonorrhea. He had to wait for his homemade medicine to work, as it had in the past. Ettie was frustrated, as she had missed Thomas for the week spent alone in Westcliff, although her pleasure at seeing him subjugated the physical desire. His excuse was pressure of work. Ettie was working with rehearsals for the extensive pantomime season. Thomas had vowed to pursue his business interests with more vigour.

He sauntered up through the warren of streets, which ran north east of High Holborn, taking the air, looking in the shop windows (for some reason a variety of umbrella makers frequented this area) and he was looking more like himself, his shiny suit catching the late summer afternoon sunlight. Thomas had taken his Box with him. The thoughts of the depravity and lust of the weekend were fading. As he turned into the northern end of Southampton Row, he could hear the noise. Police whistles, shouting, what sounded to him like a riot of activity - and it was, a full-scale riot. Thomas could now see the throng on Euston Road, banners, loud cries, and police on horseback. On approaching, he heard bottles shattering and protestations coming from everywhere.

"Down with Dowie! Down with Dowie!"

"Burn the heathen!"

"OUT! OUT! OUT!"

It dawned on him and he was gripped with fear. He had no idea that religion could cause such an outcry. He had heard of protests throughout Britain where Dowie had been, and had read some of the coverage of the unrest, but thought they must be blown out of proportion to sell the newspapers. More likely, it would be a few genteel ladies finding a stout afternoon's pursuit before taking tea. This definitely was not the case, and Thomas snuck round the perimeter of the demonstration, the police holding off the baying pack. He squeezed his way down to the front, closer to the Tabernacle, trying to push through with other attendees who the police were attempting to keep separated from the protestors. Thomas spoke with a policeman.

"I have a ticket. A ticket for Dowie."

The policeman scowled and let him through. An egg hit the back of Thomas's immaculate satin frock coat, and the policeman laid into the thrower with his baton, giving Thomas the opportunity to lunge forward toward the Tabernacle into the relative safety of the building. It was a smaller collection than hoped, but still numbered several hundred. Considering the circumstances Thomas was surprised anyone was there. The Reverend Cantel greeted him, but before he could speak Thomas said he 'had been hit' and, removing his coat, he headed for the washroom to get cleaned up.

You could clearly hear the objectors outside, but it made no difference to Dowie, who ploughed into an inspirational oratory. A steely grip on his words held Thomas rapt, and the doctrines that Thomas had hoped to pursue shone through like a ray, made even more poignant by the opposition rally blare bleeding in. Dowie's sombre regalia of full-length gowns pit against his white face and beard set him apart from the poised brethren. Much of his pulpit energy was devoted to the lambasting of medicine, alcohol, berating Roman Catholics and Protestant denominations, and denouncing race prejudices. It was music to Thomas Brem-Wilson's ears, conveniently unmindful of his recent pursuits. Dowie had various medical instruments beside him and proceeded to destroy them, including a crutch, which he broke in two, denouncing it as a symbol of Satan. At this point he asked:

"Those who are afflicted come unto me… believe!"

Custodians helped participants to the side of the stage forming a queue ready to be received onto the rostrum. They were a sorry sight, the sick and invalided. Music careered in with a pounding revivalist hymn and Dowie, in fervid tones, asked that the Spirit of Christ enter the hall. They were helped up onto the platform one-by-one and led to Dowie. The first, an ill lady limping with a stick, was taken by Dowie, one hand placed on her forehead covering her eyes and the other on her back, between the shoulders. He went into a trance, bending her forward. Dowie spoke what sounded like Congolese to Thomas, a rapid jabbering, finishing.

"Hallelujah!"

The excitement caused by this unnatural phenomenon induced a mass exultation. Shouts and cries of 'Hallelujah' and 'Praise the Lord', went out, the music swelling and Dowie pushed her forward ripping the stick away from her as he did. She stood straight, unaided, arms in the air.

"I'm cured. I'm saved," she cried.

The audience clamoured to get a view. The ushers led her down from the stage, to be quickly replaced by the next patient. This happened ten or fifteen times. Thomas lost count, caught up in the exhilaration of the performance. Dowie with his hands raised up and looking up to the ceiling began to proclaim.

"I am the prophet Elijah the Restorer. Give to the cause. Give generously to the Faith. Restore the Faith."

Then he was gone. The stewards were taking round the collection dishes as the pianist continued to pump out a rousing chorus. Thomas nudged his way to the front, he wanted to meet Dowie, and could not let the opportunity pass. The Reverend Cantel was there at the front marshalling the stewards and he swooshed Thomas through to the vestibule where Dowie sat with a clique of hangers-on surrounding him, dabbing his head with a towel, sweating, shattered from the public display. Thomas approached with the Reverend, who announced.

"Mr Dowie, may I introduce an influential and dedicated member of our brethren, a member of the United African Association, and a wealthy businessman with lands on the Gold Coast, Thomas Brem-Wilson."

Thomas wasn't expecting the lengthy presentation, but he realised Cantel was trying to add credibility to the London arm of Dowie's Christian Catholic Church. Being the well versed businessman and orator, Thomas seized the moment, complimenting Dowie on the sermon, how inspirational it was, confirming that he was a true supporter of the movement. Thomas extracted from the Box a letter tied with ribbon to a sample of quartz, explaining it was a gift, a sample of mineral deposits from one of his land concessions on the Gold

Coast at Kobola Kasa. He gave both to Dowie, who was sympathetic to the curious raconteur. Dowie promised to read the letter and was very grateful for the keepsake.

"It will go on display in my cabinet, at my offices in Zion City, which I'm building on ten square miles of land north of Chicago."

The Reverend left them for his duties in the hall. Thomas remained for twenty minutes or so, talking about the Gold Coast, and his great grandfather. Dowie made reference to his last time in Great Britain, his upbringing in Scotland, his theological studies there, also his trips to Australia where he was ordained. He was charismatic; an earthy endearing Scottish drawl combined with a dash of American drew the listener in. He delivered every nuance and syllable with a pithy meaning. Each sentence was enticing. Quieter and smaller than he had appeared at the address, he had with him Samuel Stevensen, a lace manufacturer from Beeston and his wife, who happened to be Dowie's sister-in-law, and Margaret Cantel, the Reverend's wife, and daughter of a Dowie elder in Zion City. Thomas conversed with the coterie but they were interrupted.

"They need to clear the hall," the Reverend called through. "Please leave through the side entrance to avoid the dissenters in the street."

The small group of Dowie devotees followed after him. A carriage waited in Grafton Place at the side of the building, they could see the angry mob at one end of the lane held back by bobbies,[11] the jeering ricocheting down the alleyway, and they took off into Churchway away from the trouble. Thomas spent an hour with the Dowieites at the Cavendish Hotel, but became weary. He made an excuse about seeing his solicitor first thing, and took a taxi home, wiling its way through the nighttime traffic of Piccadilly Circus and Shaftesbury Avenue, where he had first walked with Ettie. He relayed the events to Ettie and she had her own stories about a taskmaster director who kept them working drawn-out days on one song, which they knew well enough anyway.

"What's the point," she said, "it's only pantomime."

---

[11] bobbies - British police are often referred to as "Bobbies" or "Peelers" after Sir Robert (Bobby) Peel, who introduced the Police Act.

"Get back. Get back. Get back to where you once belonged…"

The Beatles were still played continually on the Radio in the seventies, bearing in mind punk and everything else that was in, and this was my song, for the moment. Singing out loud in the kitchen, Jimmy was making our last breakfast before we left again for Africa. He always liked a hearty breakfast, a throw back to his truck driving days, before 'power steering'. You needed to drive on your wits and muscles, and load everything on and off by hand - 'hand ball' it. Bacon aroma pervaded the house but I had no complaints.

"Nina, darlin'," came Jim's call came up the stairs, something I'd heard a hundred times, but now it had a marked ring to it.

I felt like I was entering a new life or new phase. Excitement was mounting I had jitters in my stomach. I went down and joined in.

"Get back. Get back. Get back to Afriiiicccaaa…"

Jim laughed as we sat and ate at our round pine table, next to the boiler, in our little old fashioned kitchen. We had an afternoon take-off, as Sir Wenbergen and Strack Allens had offered us an open-ended ticket in order to meet their experts out there, to help get the maps and a final mining license organised. We had met them at their London offices a month before.

We'd been up with the lark, no different from one of our usual work days, a five o'clock start, but instead of work we were headed into London, to the Mayfair offices of B.W.P, for our 'nine o'clock', and we were definitely not going to be late. As well as my trusty Box, I now had copies of the application forms and materials required, plus everything that Mr Teteh had faxed - the Power of Attorney and company incorporation that made us legitimate in Ghana.

Sir Mark Wenbergen poured coffee, having made it himself, and set it out on the long conference table. When I found out that he was a 'Sir', and his partner was 'Lord' Strack Allens, I was completely knocked for six. For once my cards stacked up.

It was a tall plush seventies office building on Park Lane. We'd parked in the underground Car Park at Cumberland Gate and walked down. There was a security man at the entrance hall, and we were buzzed straight up to the offices, expecting to be shown to an inner sanctum, with some lackeys who would be quick to dispense with us, ejecting us through the tradesman's entrance at the rear. We entered from the lift, a whole open-plan floor, a few desks, typists working, phones quietly ringing, faxes purring, wall-to-wall windows, a panoramic view of Park Lane towards the Hilton Hotel and Hyde Park Corner. A tall very well spoken gentleman with a South African tinge in his voice, wearing a pin-stripe suit greeted us smiling.

"Nina Brem-Wilson, I loved your story, is this the infamous attaché case, let's have a look?"

He introduced himself as Sir Mark and we were bowled over to be introduced by him to Lord Strack Allens, a smaller man, in a smart double-breasted suit, with an impeccable English accent. Sir Mark was the cheery one, with a broad confident grin, and anecdotes about Africa. Lord Allens was the listening type, mulling, asking several key questions. Sir Mark rung out of the conference room. A young lady came through and he asked her to get copies of everything I had. After we'd told our tale of going to both bits of land and the history of my Grandfather, Sir Mark filled us in on what *they* were doing - acquiring land which they would lease out to their contacts to mine. I was a little deflated when Lord Allens pointed out that we didn't have complete rights yet, and that there wasn't proof enough of any gold to make mining worthwhile at the moment, but Jim piped up.

"Well, with a bit of money and help, that can be sorted out a lot quicker."

I thought he did the right thing, as they were certainly interested in obtaining as much land on the Gold Coast as they could. Sir Mark, probably letting us down gently, said they would look over the particulars with their lawyer that afternoon, to spot the likelihood of getting involved.

"We'll fax you in the morning."

We shook hands, and we were off, drained from the early start, and also pleased to have got this far.

"We've really done *something*, its more than most people can say about their lives!" Jim said as we descended in the lift.

"Tradesman's entrance?" I joked as we left through the front. The security guard glared, he had no sense of humour.

I felt sick when the phone went at nine, more likely to be my Mum calling with tales of the latest offers she'd bought from her favourite mail order perfume company Roche. But I heard the fax tone, pressed the button, and through it came, my head turning up side down, straining to see it, as faxes seemed to always feed through in reverse. I saw the words, 'flights', 'flexible', and 'gratis'.

It was now one month after the fax. We were flying out with Jason, to meet the geologist in Accra, and take him out to the plots of land. We wanted to be there a week before to see Mr Teteh, get the maps in order, and go to see the Chiefs again to 'oil the wheels'. We were geared up for them, the young teacher at Tuasi, and the older head-dressed Chief at Assor Brompon. They'd lost our passports at the African Embassy, an employee having taken them home. Either homework, or planning a drug run using my identity, either way it gave us the run-around, finally driving to her house to collect them. We had a contract from B.W.P and they were willing to put fifty thousand pounds into the project if there was gold there. We had a solicitor look at the contract and, with a bit of tweaking, we gratefully signed.

This was it, breakfast finished, we made tracks at ten for the two hour drive to London Heathrow Airport, the afternoon flight of August 23rd, 1975. We'd pulled off getting back to Africa within a year, and with someone else paying. Jason had been a little late but we ignored that, he parked up on our drive and we made up for time on the up-to-date four-lane M25 London ring road. Tired of carrying the Box, I'd bought a suitable bag to put it in as hand luggage.

THOMAS - Phase 2, The Americas

Thomas had made an alternate life in Britain, married, and established himself, be it in a somewhat unorthodox and disorderly fashion. He had whims of fancy, spending his money lavishly on expensive clothes and aftershave for himself, hairdressing appointments, taking hansom cabs[12] everywhere, whilst Ettie would make do. Thomas preferred going out with his West African friends from the African Union, which he had helped form - an alliance of campaigners for the non-Ordinance of the Gold Coast. This usually involved drinking too much and womanising. Nevertheless, Thomas still forged ahead exploiting his lands in deals for palm oil and rubber extractions at Sarnie and Tuasi, through his solicitors Emanuel & Simmonds. In a way his boat had come in. He was receiving very reasonable amounts with royalties accumulating for both, apart from the occasional month if payments were late, when he would default to his little pawning deals. Thomas was well off by English standards at the time and bought a house. He and Ettie moved in that Autumn 1904 to Hither Green, a middle class section of Lewisham, frequented by bowler-hatted city gents, who used the sprawling rail terminus every morning to get into London. They caused a few quivering net curtains but no protestations. Ettie and Thomas kept themselves to themselves. Within a couple of months Thomas started to allow some of his West African friends to stay when church services went on late. Ettie disliked these 'coming-and-goings', but did not want to cause friction, and Thomas had no idea he was being unreasonable, inviting his associates in however 'rag-tag'.

The flat had gone, Joseph Cantor giving way to the behemoth of the British legal system, having no funds to carry on fighting. He downsized to a smaller shop in Fulham. He saw little of Thomas these days, and nothing was heard of the goods that had been purchased, or

---

[12] hansom cab – of the period a two-wheeled horse-drawn covered carriage with the driver's seat above and behind the passengers

further goods Thomas had intended to buy. The changes also distanced Thomas from Ray, her attempts to catch him alone were less frequent and he would no longer succumb to her flirting. He had disgraced himself over that infamous weekend, had heard from Ettie that Minnie was pregnant and had gone away, and he avoided this 'beau monde'. He did meet up with John McCann as promised but as yet they had not found any common ground to do business in London. John did not need to work he had a dowry.

Thomas was always busy, his days meticulously recorded in his diary (despite their apparent complete disorganisation) mainly comprised of flitting between his solicitors offices, sending telegrams, small notes, visiting church, and the African Union. It was Ettie's money that kept the house, furnished it and bought food, and as Thomas seemed to keep and spend every penny of his, her money also found the rates and ultimately the mortgage payments, which were quite small, since Thomas had made a substantial deposit to start off with. It was not ideal but they still retained the greater aspect of their relationship that had brought them together in the first place and often visited the theatre, took teas in the fashionable department stores in Lewisham, as well as visiting the nearby parks of Greenwich and Horniman Gardens and bandstand, where Thomas liked to listen to the public concerts in the summer.

In fact, the summer of 1906 passed fairly innocuously by Thomas's standards, until a letter came from his solicitor. There was a ticket for him from Dowie, for America, to visit the Zion City, and a fifty-pound order to pay his expenses. Thomas set sail that Friday, September 23rd bound for New York on the Luciana.

Nina - Africa 2nd Expedition

We were fully primed. We'd revised our clothing, attitude, and had pockets bloated with cedes for the bribery that we were expecting at Accra Airport. They scuppered us again. They'd set up a medical desk, checking health certificates. Luckily we had ours, but Jason, although he'd had his inoculation jabs, didn't. We were lucky to have ours on us. Jason was tall, pasty, hot and reddening up in the heat. He liked a drink, but we weren't quite aware how much - and he'd had sufficient on the plane to floor an elephant. This wasn't helping at customs, with him slurring, and looking blankly at the border guards. My brother was sent to a room and told that the punishment for not having the correct permit was fourteen days internment. Having just arrived he was about to be 'banged up'[13]. We waited in the cramped terminal so as to avoid the hurley-burley[14] outside, speculating that he would get a small charge and be let off, but after an hour that prospect was becoming bleak. At last the arrival doors revealed an exhausted Jason. He had worn them down with pleas that he 'hadn't known' and 'was only here to see his Granddad's lands'. They'd tried to impose a forty thousand cedes tax, but Jason told them to send him home, calling their bluff, and they had caved in. We then had the rough 'n' tumble[15] with the 'luggage-lads', so he didn't miss out on the full tourist experience. At the hotel, there was a new resident jazz band, and he stayed up till dawn listening to the music, drinking and mixing with the enthusiasts. We found him snoozing by the pool first thing.

Visiting Mr Teteh that morning, we discovered he'd engaged a reliable surveyor, having spent some time searching. The applications were filed with the relevant government departments, and he'd made copies for us. We were purely waiting on the maps. I found it puzzling that he didn't know a plethora of quality surveyors. Apparently the best ones didn't want to go down to Takoradi. He encouraged us to get out

---

[13] banged up – detained in custody
[14] hurley-burley – noisy confusion, commotion, turmoil, or uproar
[15] rough 'n' tumble – disorderly aggressive

there to meet the Chiefs again. Even with licenses granted they could cause disagreements if they weren't involved with plans, and could make life difficult for the surveyors and miners.

We picked up Jason, he was in the bar, and that afternoon we were on our way to Takoradi. We filled up at a garage on the way out, where Jason started taking photographs. Unbeknownst to us there was a military installation behind some shacks and some trees. Two military police arrested him and confiscated the camera. We had to get the film developed round the corner to prove they were inoffensive tourist pictures of the area. Then we stopped at a market to purchase provisions, and Jason took a picture of the stalls with the colourful stallholders selling piles of lush red tomatoes. A police lady retained Jason, accusing him of photographing derelict buildings nearby. We were dragged to a police station. After considerable argument, they refused to let him go, so I had to call Faysal. Fortuitously he happened to know the district police chief. The police chief put in a call, but in the confusion there was nearly a riot. A squad from another station turned up to release us at the chief's request and the two 'districts' got into a huge disagreement. Apparently they were sensitive about their image and the old buildings, as there'd been a camera crew there recently portraying the area as 'run down'. We got away after a few hours delay, I told Jason:

"Ditch the f*****' camera."

Assor Brompon was the nearest, so it was our first stop. I had an agreement and money for the Chief. We parked the Toyota, and were given a lovely reception from the natives, all the children coming round. We asked after the Chief, and he was called by one of the ladies. He emerged from his hut and we had a conflab[16] in the central hall again. We explained what we wanted to do, and that we were sending a surveyor down to make maps. He was very agreeable, studied the minutiae and the original charts of the land that I had with me. The pact was, that he'd smooth the way with the locals and farmers. They'd have first refusal on any jobs, and those already surface mining would receive compensation.

---

[16] conflab – informal discussion

Once we'd signed on the dotted line, he was paid a thousand pounds odd, in cedes. Libation was offered to celebrate. Lady dancers were called in and the remainder of the elders, but we sipped carefully, avoiding the pitfalls, enjoying the entertainment. Even Jason didn't fancy the murky liquid in the streaked beakers.

We walked out to the piece of land, we knew the way, but were still accompanied by a few of the Chief's assistants. As we got nearer we could hear the whine of activity, not the sound like before of clanking shovels. I told Jim to get close. Jason was unfit, puffing, we'd only gone a little way, but he wasn't the walking type. A few more minutes and we were upon it. The sound was deafening. The area was completely changed, huge diggers everywhere, miners in hard hats, a site office, a monster tower with pulleys, and wheels being erected. Trees had been felled, the whole site looked ten times the size, with a rough looking road coming in, cut through the bush. The redundant earthworks were gone; there were two vast conveyor belts across the centre tract of land. It looked like a coal mine, and I knew my cousin was there. We went to the office, a beaten up portacabin, I entered, they were both there at a desk, and I felt sick.

"What's going on, this is my land as well?"

Shocked to see us, Ken spoke dumbly.

"All right Nin', Jas', how are you?"

Will said one thing only to me.

"Piss off, you always were the 'nigger in the woodpile'[17]."

Will backed up knocking his head against the wall behind him as Jim lunged at him.

"What you f***** doing, get out, you're trespassing on our land?"

Before we knew it half a dozen landsmen, including the three that

---

[17] nigger in the woodpile - English figure of speech formerly commonly used in the United States and elsewhere denoting 'some fact of considerable importance that is not disclosed – something suspicious or wrong'. Use of the phrase in English speaking countries by public officials or people in positions of power since the year 2000 has most often been followed by public shame and apology, due to the severely offensive connotation taken on by the term 'nigger' over the decades

had come with us, were holding Jim back.

"I'll be back, I'll f*****' 'ave you," said Jim.

Jason was dumbstruck.

"Yeh, see ya," Will laughed.

We retreated to the village, found the Chief, his aides flanking.

Nina: "I want the money."

Chief: "Sorry it is gone, distributed to the populace as requested," smiling happily at the result of his day's work, "you have the lands, you can do what you want with them."

Nina: "My cousin's already on it."

Chief: "Yes, you can make a happy family bond together to use the land, it is no problem."

Jimmy was mad, ready to pummel the Chief, and Will.

"We're out of here," I said.

I was worried someone was going to get seriously hurt. There was no point in fighting. I had to get away to make sense of it, clear my head, I couldn't think straight with so much anger.

Mr Teteh found out that Will and Ken had got a temporary license to prospect the land, a variation on full-scale mining. And nobody from the Minerals Commission was checking what they were actually doing. I would have to issue a restraining order to stymie the work, which could take weeks or months to get processed, as well as ensuring I had the data to prove my ownership rights. I'd done everything 'by-the-book'[18] and they'd snuck under the door without the proper concessions. We had to get over to Tuasi. With no surface prospecting there as yet they'd hopefully not ruined it.

It took us two weeks to get the licenses in order. We'd been down to Tuasi, persuading the young Chief the benefits of allowing us to prospect the land. He changed his tune once we mentioned money. I was thrilled to buy the gem from my Aunt and stuck it back in the Box. We oversaw the surveyor mapping the land, marking out the borders from the original drawings. B.W.P's man took soil cross-sections from different segments.

I still wanted the maps and samples from Assor Brompon, so we

---

[18] (go) by the book – follow the rules exactly

had to go up there with torches at night with both surveyor and geologist. The site was empty, and the yapping guard dogs made no difference. Jason soon calmed them down. The villagers were probably flat out from the libation fluid. It was rather eerie in the dark, with unidentified rustlings in the bush, but the surveyor wasn't fazed and we paid him extra. The geologist had instructions from Sir Mark anyway, and thought it hilarious. Jason was good company, but wasn't very well organised. He did give us moral support, but we realised he was drinking from a hip flask, trying to hide it from us in the day, and wasn't in a coherent state. What a family.

Glancing up from the *Leaves of Healing*, Thomas was more interested in the passing ladies on deck than the religious magazine. He was chasing the fairer sex, and they were chasing him. Bodies braced themselves against the North Atlantic drift, but Thomas had found a sheltered spot. A bath-chair on the south facing deck, where he rakishly modelled a dark lounge coat, satin waistcoat, contrasting trousers with a smart ironed pleat down the front, brass buttons, and matching cufflinks poking out the end of his coat sleeves. The latest fashion for women was an S-shape with accentuated breasts and pulled in waist, the invigorating wind didn't discourage the amount of cleavage on show.

Thomas tipped his homburg at the females passing arm-in-arm on their afternoon promenade, saying 'good day to you,' with added banter for those who reciprocated with a smile. He always had a weakness for mature buxom females, and had two lustful encounters during the seven-day trip. Not since the hedonistic weekend in July had Thomas been adulterous, but he threw himself into a deluge of sex as soon as he was away from Ettie. The dreary pious propaganda could not distract Thomas from his hobby, or dull his enthusiasm for the Zion movement.

The letter he had given to Dowie was thoroughly researched and skilfully written, reflecting Thomas's education, and gainful employment as a teacher and Principle. He spoke of the great attention

119

Dowie had elicited at the Chicago World Fair in 1893, how he had followed the movement, and of his pilgrimage from Africa. Thomas hit a chord with Dowie, who pursued any type of patronage. Dowie had often said that 'Christians need not be financially poor', and he was practicing what he preached, bringing in money, establishing factories at Zion City and building links with businesses, in alliances that would benefit the movement. Thomas could not miss the opportunity to go. Ettie would have loved to go to New York but Thomas faked 'strictly business', a now familiar mantra.

An expansive pile in East Sussex: acres, swimming pool, tennis courts, and televisions in every room, private cinema, the works. Once the money had started to come in it grew and grew. Apparently Paul McCartney was a neighbour, but we never saw him. I imagined chatting over the hedgerow, but I had to admit to not knowing exactly what my land bordered.

We'd shut up the market stall two years before, the day we received the first royalty cheque from B.W.P. We worked that day and abandoned everything there, including the stock, driving the van home empty. My pal Markus, who mended kettles and iron's on a pitch opposite, said it was still there the following week, intact, a testament to human nature that it hadn't been rifled, or nobody had wanted the tat we sold. Predictably, I received a bill from the local council for 'removal and disposal', with a rambling letter revoking our license, mentioning breach of a number of sub-clauses. I was happy to pay it. It was the era of Thatcher, power-cuts, strikes, three-day weeks, but that didn't affect us.

Jimmy and I quickly became used to an extravagant lifestyle. The soil samples taken from Tuasi were good for deep mining. I had no idea what that meant, but everyone made a fortune, not from gold, but from manganese - using it in Sinclair and Amstrad computers, something to do with circuit boards. I'd been in Curry's, the retailer who'd taken over every Electric Board shop, and there was always a spotty teenager playing some tennis game on one - a fuzzy grey screen, fingers madly pressing the little pads on a plastic controller.

"No chance of catching on," I told Jim.

Our ten percent from B.W.P. trumpeted 'unfair' at the time - but the lawyer pointed out that one hundred percent of nothing equals nothing and he was right - we made a mint. B.W.P. must have been doing very well on their ninety percent. They bought up further land around Tuasi and had the whole place strip-mined. I didn't resent it. They'd taken the chances, paid for our flights, the geologist, ploughing through the bureaucracy. I was celebrating with parties for our old market pals, cars, and a house for my daughter. The Box was in a cabinet display in the hall and I had the maps and diaries framed. Grandfather Wilson had come up trumps.

The blot was the terrible family feud. Will was making money, but not reaping the rewards he'd hoped for. He was challenging my right to my part of the land, engaging lawyers at vast costs to us both, arguing with officials, sending legal letters to Sir Mark and Lord Strack Allens. It went on and on, becoming increasingly bitter. We started to hate Will because of what he was doing, using every trick in the book[19]. I could never figure why Will went out there with us, all nice, then flimflammed[20] as soon as we found the land. Jim and I had even gone over to Bromley when we knew he was back in England, he still had his shop. We tried to talk and get it resolved but he spat at Jim, with Jim going for him again and me pulling him off. Jim would have killed him after what happened at Assor Brompon. I hadn't bothered to assert my rights there - didn't see the point. But now he was trying to get on Tuasi. Jason got his cut and was happy, as long as he had money for a tipple. He kept a second hand Mercedes going (to do his Heathrow Airport cabbying run). I would still have split everything fifty, fifty - there was enough - but Will and Ken wanted to 'have their cake and eat it too'[21].

---

[19] every trick in the book - all possible means, both honest and dishonest

[20] flimflammed - swindled (someone) with a confidence game or trick

[21] to 'have one's cake and eat it too' - used negatively, to connote the idea of consuming a thing whilst managing to preserve it. Also, to indicate having or wanting more than one can handle or deserve

Battery Park was mobbed with dockworkers and commuters, in addition to those alighting and departing on ships and ferries. Three gentlemen, Negros, tailored suites, one older, and two youths wearing cloth caps of checked cloth, with small peaks, held up a sign at the end of the ramp for Thomas. The older man, unshaven, whom Thomas took a dislike to straight away, introduced himself as Judge Barnes, and the cohorts by their surnames, brother Edwin and Theodore. They shook hands, and waited for the bags to be landed.

The ship was docked near the Staten Island interchange, South Manhattan, where there were men and women as far as the eye could see. The large number of Negroes working, wearing uniformly similar caps, took Thomas aback. He was little noticed, merging in.

Thomas had seen the city loom up as the ship inched in, passing the newly erected Statue of Liberty. It was overwhelming. He found it difficult to comprehend his surroundings, and where he stood in the scheme of things, so he desisted from small talk. He needed to adjust, to understand the sheer size of America. They went uptown in a cab, an automobile, a Ford. There were some mechanised vehicles in London, but mainly horses and traps. Cars were the domain of well-heeled enthusiasts. Commercial cabs were few and far between, and Thomas was awestruck by the whole experience; no horses, wide avenues, streets arranged in grids flanked by modern skyscrapers and red brick blocks. First the business sector, then wholesalers, warehouses and outlets, finally the teeming shopping district, the metropolis was beating, a panoramic vista, and the heart of the USA - unmistakably New York. Thomas was wondering exactly what he could do for Dowie in a country like this, where they already had everything. They disembarked at Grand Central station, a black uniformed luggage man taking the couple of small cases from the boot.

"Train Sir?" he asked.

"Chicago, Lake Shore Line," Barnes answered.

"Yessir," came the reply.

A bronze coin was handed over. The porter doffed his cap. They had lunch in the ornate restaurant down underneath the station,

122

accessed by a sea of marble steps, and milling with afternoon busyness. Brass and glass art-deco electric lamps on large elaborate twisted brass stands emblazoning the underground lounge. Thomas listened attentively to Barnes who extolled the virtues of the Zionistic lifestyle whilst all four ate salami and rye sandwiches, with coffee. They found the train, Thomas saw his cases and the guard, and went to enter, but Barnes called him back.

"This way Mr Brem-Wilson."

Thomas followed to the next carriage, separated by the conductor's car. The sign indicated, 'Colored Only'. He felt a homesick London fog descend over him. He was quiet, falling asleep for a while, sitting amongst compatriots.

I sat in the kitchen going through the morning post. I'd never really got used to capacious living and ended up in the kitchen mostly. I had no concept of how to work the cooker, Jim always took charge of household chores, and he was making breakfast. I threw the letter to him.

"That's it, it's all over."

Another lawyer's letter saying Will had reached the first stage of an injunction of our mining license in Ghana. They'd charmed the Ministry, and were 'threatening to shut down the operation'. Sir Mark soon called. He wasn't his usual jocular self.

"I trust you to sort it out Nina, the family obstacle needs to be surmounted, we can't have this flack flying around."

I didn't really think it was my responsibility, as Sir Mark and Lord Allens had managed to get it all going. I agreed the bickering was damaging, so we knuckled down. That evening we were on a flight for Africa, after a two-year gap, only we weren't flying economy class.

"I've forgotten the bloody Box," I said to Jim as we sat on the plane.

"You don't need that old rubbish; should have binned it all ages ago. Surprised you never got smallpox from it," he joked.

It was bad news for me. I should have remembered it. We had

emergency visas, sorted out by B.W.P. and no hitches at Accra Airport. It was less hostile, with not so many 'luggage lads' outside, and I missed the fisticuffs[22] over cases.

We spent the first day with C.P at his hotel. He had expanded his business dealings and we were delighted to see him. He knew about the two mining operations, we'd kept him up-dated on the phone, and he'd even been to visit us once in England. The next day we nervously went out to Assor Brompon, having picked up a hire car. The place was busy, although Will and Ken were nowhere to be seen. We took the recently constructed mine service route that by-passed the village.

Trucks trundled by, full of dirt, heaving muck into the still air. There were armed watchmen and a barbed wire fence surrounding the whole site, several 'portacabins'[23], and a hive of activity. You could see the mining shafts holed up with timber, mini railway tracks emerging from them. The rocks transported from the shafts were tipped sideways from carts on to belts that went into a grinder emerging on one of the two conveyor belts we'd seen two years before, and up the tower mixing with water being pumped from the brook. Waste sludge was chucked out from the tower into the waiting trucks, we presumed the slurry was at some point sifted to separate the gold out, as material was being siphoned off in pipes. These led to the corrugated tin shacks directly below the apex of the tower from which more conveyor belts emerged, to another infinite pile of detritus, which was in turn being shifted by a mini-digger into yet more lorries.

The waste was unbelievable, and I wondered what the hell we'd set in motion. I was hypnotised squinting through the galvanised fence, my fingers hanging on to the chain-link, the sentries got agitated and told us to go. I left my card, wrote the hotel number on the back, and told them to get Will to call me. As we slinked away I saw the sign that had been obscured by one of the patrolmen, Brem-Wilson Mining Ltd & Stamnex Industries.

"They even took the name, what a couple of parasites, couldn't

---

[22] fisticuffs – boxing or fighting with fists
[23] portacabin – a brand name that is now synonymous of a portable building designed and built to be movable rather than permanently located

124

even think one up," I moaned at Jim. "I remember Stamnex from the phone book, and an uptight telephonist."

"Will obviously had better luck," he said.

We drove to the village, flummoxed as to what to do, knowing they were here in Africa, as Jason had done some delving.

"May as well have a look around," Jim said.

It was about three o'clock, a searing and humid summer afternoon. I didn't want to quit the air conditioning of the car.

"Oh, go on then," I gave in.

We got out, the village was deserted apart from a dog sniffing under a tree and the prerequisite chickens scraping. We walked nonchalantly over to the village hall. It had expanded to about four times the size and brand-new, unless my memory was playing tricks. A colossal cross was above the wooden double doors at the front, with broad wooden steps leading up to the entrance. We could hear the din. Inside, we were immediately greeted by almost the entire village. It was some sort of event. They collectively turned, smiling.

"Hello we're Nina and Jim, we've come back to check out the Brem-Wilson land," Jim chirped.

A smart young man came down from the front grinning with a greeting.

"Welcome, welcome. I know who you are. You were here before with the old Chief."

He smelled of soap, freshly scrubbed, had modern western clothes. The whole place was modern and tidy with replacement wooden benches.

"This is our school and church, given by Stamnex," he said enthusiastically. "We are having an auction. Come and join us. I am Chief Nana Panin."

We sat in the middle, with a couple of complimentary drinks, not in chipped dirty containers as before. It was the Libation drink.

"Watch it, it's the imbibement gunk," I whispered to Jim.

He was laughing as we sat and watched something that was reminiscent of a British television programme, 'The Generation Game', where contestants had to memorise a conveyor belt full of prizes as they passed by, then recount each item to win it. No conveyor belt

125

here and the prizes not nearly so grand: a cassette of an African band, some face cream, a copy of Readers Digest magazine. It went on for what felt like hours but we couldn't bring ourselves to up-sticks, they were so keen. It was very difficult to work out exactly what was happening but it culminated in a prize, everyone went wild with excitement, clapping and going crazy. Heartfelt and genuine, you couldn't help but join in the hullabaloo. Jim had a sip from the 'petrol' and was enjoying himself, food was being passed round (something on a stick) and we both partook. I knew I would regret it but we were here now.

We were treated like dignitaries and got caught in the farewell procession, where we were expected to examine every prize with the proud winners. At last extricating ourselves, the Chief introduced us to what he called his lieutenants, well turned out, some in African clothing, sitting on the six inch podium - a small table holding their Libation accoutrements - and what remained of the prizes. Jim explained our predicament, me filling the gaps. Chief Panin spoke to us.

"I saw the contract from two years ago, with the old Chief. He died. Stamnex came with revised contracts using the entitlement from your relatives, William and his friend. I can try to get things sorted out for you as you still have an agreement, but you have to realise, we have work and money from Stamnex, so we can't afford to lose them."

"That's ok, we've come to see Will and Ken," I replied.

"You can't see them at home in England?" The Chief looked puzzled.

"No," said Jim, "we fell out over money and the lands."

"You can choose your friends, but not your relatives!" The Chief laughed.

We sat talking for a while and the Chief brought up his offer again. He was obviously concerned we had some sort of take over plan to stop the work there.

"Maybe we'll be back," I said.

He pulled out a brick sized moulded plastic object with an aerial and mouthpiece and jiggled it in front of us.

"Call me on my cellphone." he said.

He wrote the number on a card and handed it to Jim. Jim and I were dumfounded, we'd never even seen one of these at home. I mimed a phone call with index finger and thumb to my head and pointed at him, and we made a move. In the car, on the way back to Takoradi, where we were going to stay with Faysal, we discussed the situation.

"They'll want money… you know, the Chief… do a new deal for us to come on the land?" said Jim.

"I don't want the land, I'm happy with what we've got Jim."

"Yes, but what I'm saying is, that we may *have* to do it to stop *them* interfering in our operation… you know… like blackmail or something?"

"I don't want it to come to that Jim, I don't want to be that scheming, it's the sort of scurrilous trick Will would get up to. I'm more p***** off with them stealing the name."

"Oh, give it up with that Nina, who cares about the f*****' name."

We went on in silence for forty minutes, looking out the window at the passing villages, small grocery stores and shacks that dotted the route. We were really pleased to see Faysal. We'd missed the hospitality, his children, and the wonderful Lebanese food. It was a great evening chewing over our experiences from the day. I fell asleep early, the result of the Libation mixed with my anti-malarial tablets.

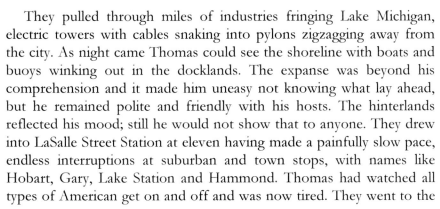

They pulled through miles of industries fringing Lake Michigan, electric towers with cables snaking into pylons zigzagging away from the city. As night came Thomas could see the shoreline with boats and buoys winking out in the docklands. The expanse was beyond his comprehension and it made him uneasy not knowing what lay ahead, but he remained polite and friendly with his hosts. The hinterlands reflected his mood; still he would not show that to anyone. They drew into LaSalle Street Station at eleven having made a painfully slow pace, endless interruptions at suburban and town stops, with names like Hobart, Gary, Lake Station and Hammond. Thomas had watched all types of American get on and off and was now tired. They went to the hotel by cab, the streets more compact than in New York, making the buildings seem much taller, rising up on each side of the road, floodlit everywhere, with human activity even at this late hour. Thomas was frozen by the biting wind when they came out of the station. In New York it had been autumnal, not too cold, but here, the chill air penetrated every part of him. At the 'Christian Endeavour Hotel' they had no rooms for 'coloreds', the last having been taken due to their late arrival. Barnes took Thomas to a more expensive hotel, on the Lake Shore, where they weren't refused entry. He was settled in by the three companions and ate cold meat and potatoes with brandy, alone in the echoing restaurant that resembled an old American dancehall. He deposited laundry with the bellboy to be done overnight and retired, drained.

* * *

We'd tracked down Will and Ken. They had a building project going on in Accra, with an office there. I spoke with Will on the phone, he hadn't said much. We didn't go to our site at Tuasi - I didn't want to see it being closed down - merely deal with the pressing matter, then go. The arrangement was to meet at the Liberty Court Hotel, where we were staying. Neutral territory as Will was familiar with it. It had a nice reception area with a small bar and soft sofas. They were late. We waited half an hour more than the ten o'clock agreed; we were staying here anyway so it didn't make a lot of difference. It was nearer eleven when they arrived.

"On no," said Jim, "they've got three goons with them."

"All right Nina, Jim," came the usual greeting from Ken.

"Hello," Will snorted.

They were both smart, dressed for the weather, shorts - well pressed - and short sleeved open necked shirts. Will had put on a little weight but not much difference in two years.

"Why the heavy mob?" I said.

"Kidnapping." Will said.

"You're 'avin a laugh?" said Jim, and I chuckled.

"You can laugh, things have changed here." Will replied disgruntled.

"No, its real, we've had a couple of threats."

Ken, usually lacking any opinion or point of view, interjected. The goons stood clumsy, embarrassed.

"Oh, for godsake get rid of them Will, that's ridiculous," I said.

"They stay," came his reply.

"Well at least get them a seat," I said, exasperated already.

Jim pulled over a sofa, next to him, slid it across the shiny tiled floor, and Will motioned for them to sit down. All three were Ashanti decked in khaki.

"Oh well, let's get on with it. Drinks?" said Jim.

We ordered some coffee. The minders had water.

"I want what's mine," proffered Will.

"You were due to get half of everything Will, I don't know what happened to you?"

"You're what happened, throwing your weight around, acting like you own the place, mouthy, you always were."

"That's it," said Jim.

Jim rising to his feet, and one of the goons moved forward ready to pounce. Jim pointed at them.

"You better tell these idiots to get lost Will, I'm not having this."

"They're staying, this won't take long, we took Ettie in, you never did nothin', now your gettin' the bloody money," said Will.

"What? You're bringing Ettie into it, that's what this is all about? Ridiculous," I retorted.

Jim sat back down and drained the coffee that had arrived, slumping back into the sofa shaking his head in disbelief, breathing out heavily through pursed lips.

"Why bring that up now? I couldn't take Ettie in, my divorce was going through with me and Melissa's Dad, she turned up out of the blue, we had no-where to put her, the house was being sold, I went to live in a bedsit, doin' the markets!" I said.

"Yeah, that left us to foot the care bill for ten years, no offers from you, then you steal the Box expecting everything for yerself," Will arguing and raising his voice.

"Look," I said, "let's keep this adult and we can all get something. We'll split Assor and Tuasi, like it should have been, and I'll give you

129

the money for the 'care' bill, what is it, ten thousand?"

"More like ten thousand a year... a million," said Will. I fell back, laughing hysterically.

Talk of Ettie confused me and made me emotional, tears were welling up. Jim was fuming, ready to bash Will. It was an underhand trick to bring her up and it broke my confidence. Under pressure my market trader persona would out and quips would flow. I didn't want that.

"We'll talk about it, give us fifteen minutes." I said.

We went up to our room where I washed my face and had some water.

"Let's have done with it Nina, offer them fifty thousand for the 'care', and half of everything, then we can end this."

We returned, I'd changed, even though the hotel was air conditioned, my top had been soaked. We sat back down, they'd been served drinks, a short of some description, with ice, it looked tempting but I wasn't going to drink.

Nina: "Ok, this is it. There's no way Ettie's care cost a million, but we're willing to offer fifty thousand as a sweetener to wrap it up, then half of everything, as soon as the contracts are signed."

Will: "You're joking, you've been creaming off the manganese, do you know how much that mine at Assor costs to run? We're paying to dump every lorry load of slurry from the pit. It's barely breaking even. I want half of everything, half of all the back money from Tuasi, and the fifty thousand."

Jim: "We only get ten percent from B.W.P, we can't afford to pay any back money, we've only just bought the house."

Ken: "Stay out of it Jim, it's family business, you ain't family."

Jim was flushed and I saw his fists clenching on his lap, the 'mugs' keeping watch, checking him, like peas-in-a-pod[24].

Nina: "You took the other site, stole it from under our nose, we didn't know you'd come out here to do that... we found B.W.P. did the bum licking, the graft, you even stole my name."

Will: "You cheeky cow, that's my f*****' name, remember, William

---

[24] peas in a pod – as 'two peas in a pod', two people who are alike

130

Brem-Wilson! I want what's mine, the back money, and the whole lot split."

Nina: "No, I can't do that, you took Assor Brompon. We took the risk on the other site."

Will: "You're a theivin' bitch,"

As he got up Will pointing his finger at me. Jimmy went like a jack-in-the-box. He leapt, the whole table turned over, coffee and milk everywhere. The three goons, who'd been watching him like a hawk, jumped out of their skins, slow off the mark. Jim had Will by the throat and the impetus from the athletic vault had taken them both ten yards, or so, from the table, right into the middle of the reception area. Jim was growling.

"Take it back, apologise you c***!"

The goons were now on Jim and I screamed, grabbing the silver coffee pot off the floor, jumping up. In the ensuing pandemonium the heavies pushed Jim but he held onto Will, and they both went flying through the plate glass reception window, fragments splintering about them. Everything went into slow motion and I didn't really have any idea what was happening. Voices were muffled. The coffee pot had left my hand, I was outside on the ground, and I could see blood and hear sirens.

Thomas felt completely different by morning. He had slept well. The hotel was quiet. He had breakfast in his room, served by an afro-American porter. He was embarrassed, he had no dollars to give him and said he would see him later. Thomas sat writing about his dreams in his diary. For some reason he was predisposed with his nocturnal mind play and often tried to interpret them. He was already brushed, up and out for a walk well before the ten o'clock arranged pick up from Barnes. He walked close to the front, it looked like a sea - he could not see the furthest water's edge. A sliver of haze came in, it was still, the wind from the night before had died down and the sun had appeared. A four-lane highway separated him from the city, but he found somewhere to cross, eliciting honks from the trucks booming past relentlessly. The ferocity of speeding vehicles mesmerised Thomas, a tarmacadam beast flanking the shoreline and framing the giant city. He went walking, through side streets, looking in windows, and eventually made his way back to the hotel, ready at the allotted time. His hosts were punctual. It was Barnes and a different man, introduced as Deacon Barnard, a white man.

They had coffee in the quiet reception area, dark leather sofas, the distant drone of the streets and capital outside. Barnes started to broach the subject of a business liaison.

"Undeniably a good time to get involved with the Zionist movement, whilst it is considering exponential expansion."

Thomas smiled; he knew why he'd been brought here.

"That's fine, I'm looking forward to seeing the Zion City, and being introduced to the members there, but you're aware it's an expensive trip, I'll be needing a little per diem."

"Exactly our thought."

Barnes gesticulated to Barnard who took out a money clip and pealed off thirty dollars handing it to Thomas.

"Sir."

The excursion was rubber-stamped, and Thomas went to his room for the attaché case. He found the bellhop on the way down and gave him a dollar bill for breakfast and a further dollar for portage. Deacon Barnard's automobile was parked outside the hotel entrance. Thomas saw the badge on the front of the vehicle, Holsman of Chicago, and commented.

"It's a Brass," said Barnard.

"The badge is brass?" Thomas questioned.

"No, the type of car, we call it a 'Brass' because they use so much brass in the production," Barnard replied.

The ride was smooth, if a bit noisy, Barnard blaring over the roar of the engine and pointing downwards towards the wheels.

"Leaf springs."

Thomas had no knowledge of cars, but smiled with an approving nod. Roughly thirty miles, it took over an hour, stopping twice for fuel, once at a garage, and once from the can strapped over the boot of the vehicle. They wound their way out of town, Barnard talking of clearing

City Streets of dung and horse traffic, the latest innovations, tram cars powered by electric, and the clean modern technologies Dr Dowie was supporting. Thomas saw the road name sign Stokie Highway Route 41, through many small communities, parklands, tagging along the Lake out to their right, coming in and out of sight as they weaved northwards away from Chicago.

"Madam, Madam, Nina Brem-Wilson, you are under arrest for the murder of William Brem-Wilson on 11th March 1978, you may not say anything..."

These were the first words I heard when I came round. I was surprised because it sounded like Z-Cars, my favourite police television programme - they really said this stuff? I knew I wasn't on TV. I could sense I was still in Africa. I was stiff, and groggy, a drug suffused my veins, and I struggled to wake. There were three figures, but they were fuzzy, two in police uniform and one in a suit. I *could* see the guns in their holsters, exactly level with me, my eye-line following to the end of the bedclothes.

"... And death by a coffee pot," he carried on.

I started giggling, aching, the bruises apparent from the jolting. I couldn't stop. I was delirious. The doctor was called, and gave me a sedative. I slept for two more days apparently. By then Jim was by my side, his face patched, and Melissa who'd been called from the UK, both looking grim and crying. I'd never seen Jim like this, always the cheerful chappy - I knew then that we had problems.

I spent a good day coming to properly, with Jim and Mel quietly getting food and drink, and I made an effort to get up. I wasn't going anywhere far as there was a police guard outside my room. Jim whispered so they couldn't hear.

"Nina, listen carefully love," sitting me at the bedside chair, "Will's dead."

Inside the cavern of my methadoned condition I went hollow. I didn't know what to say. He put his arms round me as I wept. He calmed me, and Mel spoke softly, putting her finger to her lips to stop

133

me speaking.

"There's a Court Case coming up Mum. You've got to attend."
Jim continued in a low voice.

"You lashed out at Will trying to get me away from the musclemen,
and the pot bashed him across the temple. Not hard, but apparently he
had some sort of clot, and they took him to hospital, where he passed
away. But we can't prove natural causes - the police say it was the result
of the blow."

Mel sat on the side of the bed and also put her arm around me
saying.

"We're trying to get self-defence. We have a lawyer coming up from
Johannesburg - someone who knows the law, someone who can get
you off - Sir Mark recommended them."

"I can't remember a thing," I said.

"One of the bodyguards is a witness, the other two have
disappeared, probably worried that they might not get work again. Sir
Mark's been trying to pull some strings, but he's threatened to pull the
plug if there's a conviction, said it can affect their reputation, you
know, bad publicity an' that," said Jim.

I couldn't speak. I cried - tissue after tissue. Bereft over what I'd
done - a 'murderer'. Jim, Melissa and me didn't stop hugging, for two
or three days, I can't remember exactly. I tried to comprehend the
situation - get some words out. I asked about the family, nephews,
Jason, but wished I hadn't - it was so distressing.

In the hospital bed, and the subsequent incarceration in police cells
awaiting trial, I had plenty of time to think, about the miniscule ledger
in my Granddad's diary, irrelevant trivia, 'small-fry', so to speak. 'Two
and six' for this, 'six pennies' for that, 'paid out two guineas for a cab
ride', 'loaned so-and-so twenty pounds'. About the fight - I tried to
rationalise it. And C.P's beloved plate windows smashed. Like a
squirrel on a bird feeder, my Granddad's lists incessantly popped into
my head. What was he saying? He was fascinated by the pecuniary
sprats. Why? He'd followed his heart, a black man from the Gold
Coast, made a life in Britain, and brought to America. He'd tried
things, becoming an orator, an innovator, made an indelible mark. But
why the endless petty balance sheets? He must have known it would be

read, why else does anyone keep a diary? The exact reason I'd never kept one.

Aimless days and impossible questions forced me to look at myself. I'd never been introspective. That was his message, 'I've got money, and I've got time, nah nah'. Can't say I relished reflection, I'd normally blank it, with working, then the prosperity, celebrating with Jim and friends, it all kept it at bay. Jim and Mel were sticking by me, I had to be strong; this wouldn't ruin me. They'd be there, family, Uncle Tom Cobley[25], at the trial. In my murky state, wiling the hours that Jim and Mel were banned from the ward, I remembered Jim's old sleep bedtime ritual. He had a workout method for everything – 'shut your eyes, imagine your toes rested, work your way up to your knees, concentrate on each part of your body in turn, until you reach the top of your head'. A rippling wave lapped over me, cocooning me in a protective layer. Perhaps I'd learnt meditation, but it allowed an inner strength, it might be temporary, but I wasn't going to let an accident take over my life.

On discharge, after about seven days in the cells in Accra, thankfully not in jail, but a type of holding place in a police building, I was able to meet the lawyer and also Jimmy and Melissa were allowed. It reminded me of that first time, before I'd got everyone into this - the fans beating on the ceiling in the Land Registry office, when we were setting out on the exploration of our lives. The lawyer was conscientious and I was neurotic about how much he was costing. My Dad would say, 'the rich-stay-rich cause they look after the pennies,' and I had the willies[26] that mine would ebb away.

I kind of fussed about, like a daughter embarrassed about her downbeat bedsit when the parents come to visit. A bed, two blankets, cup, toilet, and chair, were hardly worth fretting over. Mr Lensah the lawyer sat on the chair, Jim and me on the bed, Mel standing.

---

25 Uncle Tom Cobley – paraphrasing the term 'Uncle Tom Cobley and all' used in British English as a humorous or whimsical way of saying et al., often used to express exasperation at the large number of people.
26 the willies - feelings of uneasiness, nervousness, jitters

Lensah told me to plead, 'not guilty'.

"Whatever happens, do not admit to anything."

His gambit would be to discredit the statement of the bodyguard, claiming there was too much confusion for him to have seen the coffee pot. He said that Will could easily have fallen on it, and that I was not close enough to strike the blow. When the ambulance arrived I was lying about ten yards from the whole thing, having tripped and fainted. He said he would contest with the lesser charge of 'aggravated harm' that Jim was facing separately, and use self-protection, and antagonism from Will and his cohorts as his leading defence.

"What's the worse?" I asked.

"Life for you in Nsawam or the death penalty, and ten years hard labour for Jim in St. James Fort." he replied.

When he said 'death penalty', I thought I was going to soil myself. I looked at the lawyer directly, tightening my fists in the scrunched up blankets between my legs, so Mel and Jim weren't able to see my emotion. We had a police interview, with a lady making notes, and the lawyer present, in another small room, not too hot. I signed a statement, after it had been looked over by the lawyer. I spent another week in police cells, my clothes taken away, and prison garb. They'd paid to keep me out of jail until the trial.

I was up - called to the bar. They led me through the corridors in the police building and then outside. Then I heard the 'maggots'. Flashes went off even though it was thirty degrees and blinding daylight - the mob was trying to get a picture, the police restraining them. Into a bus, not blacked out, chased across town by reporters on small motorbikes, I looked into the minibus so they could not see my face. Fame I would consider, but not ignominy.

Same scenario on arrival at the Court, I had no chance to see the surroundings or get my bearings. There was no further conflab with the lawyer; straight in, more rabble, pulling, some remonstrating, up steps into the room, and the dock. There were screams, insults, I looked forward keeping my composure, it would soon be over. The Judge entered immediately and ordered.

"Quiet in the courtroom."

The superintendents ejected those that refused. I saw the two nephews thrown out, from the corner of my eye, and caught sight of Deidre with her head down, a scarf over her head, sobbing into a hanky. Keep focused, I said in my mind, keep focused.

Zion City, distinguished itself from the scrubby countryside and occasional farmhouse copses, transforming into a pattern of methodically laid out green, tended lawns, industrial areas, houses, shops, parks, cut crossways by broad roads. It was colossal, the impact on Thomas undeniable, he was wide-eyed, as Judge Barnes and Deacon Barnard described the scenes, the investments, the industry. They circuited the site before arriving at the 'tour-de-force'. Octagonal parkland surrounding a monolithic modern church, with leaded windows glinting in the morning sun and stretching the whole length of the building from ground to roof; and the roof, instead of a normal ridge, had steep sloping sides, curved, and made from copper. It was a beacon rather than a church, approached by four different avenues, north, south, east, west.

"We'll attend the midday service at the Shiloh Temple, then go for lunch with Dr Dowie," said Barnes.

Barnard pulled up alongside a number of parked vehicles in the South Avenue. There was gospel singing coming from the open double doors of the church.

"This is quite a place," Thomas said.

"Yes," replied Barnes, "we have plans to build something similar in London. We're hoping to find a responsible overseer who has real estate experience to help," and he gave Thomas a weak smile.

Thomas liked him even less, still unshaven, the smile obsequious. They walked up to the panelled doors, towering at three times their height, almost to the roof.

"Canadian Oak, especially from over the border. We brought it in," said Barnes as they entered.

Twice the size inside than it had looked outside, a Cathedral, cool, with pillars stretching to the vault roof, a tiled floor, and airy. Thomas only knew of small churches and Tabernacles, often dark, or shared spaces. This place was impressive, bright, and a symbol. It was half-full, with seating for a thousand at least. Barnard spoke in Thomas's ear.

"Evensong and weekend is full attendance."

They sat at the back digesting the pontificating of Dowie philosophies. It was quite rowdy, but not as uproarious as some of Thomas's at home. He put it down to daytime preaching. Two songs were sung and it was finished. The hall was large but the acoustics wonderful, Thomas could hear every sound the preacher uttered. He wished he could be heard so clearly, and told Barnard how he often had to raise his voice above the racket when lecturing at home, making a joke of it. Barnard pointed to the apparatus at the pulpit on a stand, wires protruding.

"It's a microphone. 'Western Electric'."

There were metallic boxes either side of the stage.

"Speakers. Amplification of the voice. It's called electromagnetic. We'll send you one if everything works out here."

They left and went to Dowie's for lunch. The house was screened behind woodland at the end of the avenue that headed eastward from the church. It was too far to go on foot so they took the automobile. The churchgoers that were setting-off, walked, had bikes, some with horse and buggy, also a few motorized vehicles. Dowie Drive led into Shiloh Boulevard and they were there.

The first thing Thomas registered as they went through the stately arched wooden gates, unbolted by a servant, was the swimming pools. They were masked from the road by trees and fencing. The only recreational bathing in Africa had been at the beach, and mainly by natives. He had tried it at Westcliff-on-Sea, but hadn't taken to it like Ettie, the changing of clothes, sand and fuss, solely to revel in the freezing English Channel. Dr Dowie came up, a huge smile, he immediately seemed more relaxed than in Britain.

"You like the pools? They're being emptied next week for winter - too chilly! Even *we* can't afford to heat them through winter," he laughed at his own witticism. "C'mon in. You had a good trip? Tomorrow we'll be going to the Lace factory. Three thousand citizens are employed there - a collaboration with Samuel Stephenson. You met him in London - Euston Road."

"Yes, him and Mary!" said Thomas.

Dowie turned to the house. They followed, Dowie continuing to talk with Thomas beside him. It was a colonial style chalet bungalow spread out with wooden verandas hugging every side. Dowie showed it off to Thomas. The chaperones sat on the porch and waited for lunch. Dowie filled Thomas in, how the City was conceived and built - his personal dream - showing him the maps on the walls in his study. Food was served on the porch, an American autumn sun streaming in, meats, bread, cold drinks, and pickled onions laid out by two 'missionites'. Everyone ate.

Jimmy was sat next to Ken. That was the thing about Ken, he wasn't clever enough to pick sides, happily sitting there taking in the scene, probably wondering how he'd ended up here, the only time in his life he'd be following the same thought pattern as me.

The room was medium-sized, similar to how I'd imagined. Like any courthouse in England, wooden panels, timber benches, with lawyers in front of the seated throng at their own tables, and court staff and stenographer between them and the judge. More fans beating above and a wisp of air allowed in from the windows. It was hot but not unbearable.

The lawyer for the prosecution was up first, representing the State. It wasn't a civil case. It was a police matter, they wanting to make an example of me. The Crown Prosecution of Ghana vs. Nina Brem-Wilson. Now that's not the sort of phrase you'd hear very often. Mr Lensah sat on his own at his desk with folders assembled, making notes.

Each lawyer made their introductory speech to the Jury, who were twelve ladies and gentlemen, placed on two tiers of benches opposite to me. The Judge introduced the prosecuting lawyer, Mr Daines. He was a small man with a light beige western suit, and pencil thin bowtie, which I found quite strange. He had the look of a civil rights brother that I'd seen in a cortège with Martin Luther King from black and white television footage, intelligent and indefatigable. He took off his

139

glasses (he'd been reading), and raised himself in his own time, from the chair, as if considering some great tome. His voice was reinforced with steel, despite his lightweight frame - you could've heard him in Deptford. He held his hands in the air before the Jury like he was praying, and began.

"Nina Brem-Wilson. An evil and destructive woman, with the sole intention of doing her family - her cousin - out of his rightful opportunity to share in the wealth of their ancestors' land. Took his money and then when threatened, took his life."

My heart sank, I didn't anticipate the brutality and there was more to come.

"... Deliberately hit, with a coffee pot, heavy solid stainless silver, and brass handles. Poor Mr William Brem-Wilson would have had no chance. And he was scared. Retreating from the violent attack at the time, when Nina Brem-Wilson made a fatal blow, intending to defraud her cousins of their rightful wealth. An evil and despicable woman, whose sole intent has been to come to this country and take land, benefiting only herself. When questioned by her cousin she became aggressive and made no bones about her intentions."

He held up 'Evidence One', the coffee pot, which was at the front on a desk, clearly marked, in a plastic bag. He made a drama of hardly being able to lift it with one arm, and in the end took it in both hands as if it were made of lead. I thought, 'bastard' - it's only a coffee pot. He continued.

"She brought it down with so much gusto, and vile hate, it knocked William Brem-Wilson down dead. Today you will see, with reliable eye witness accounts, that Mr Brem-Wilson would still be here today, but for her malicious intent."

He sat back down, putting back on his glasses, and consulting with the two colleagues who straddled him. They were both in beige suits, and wore ties.

Lensah was already sweating. Don't sweat, I said to myself, look cool, look cool. He wiped his brow with an attention-grabbing hanky pulled from his pocket, and was asked by the Judge to give his foreword. He couldn't top the performance from the prosecution. I was already thinking of escape routes, they wouldn't expect me to leg it now. Only the locked dock door stopped me. Perhaps when I was called up to give evidence I could make a detour out through the in-door before they realised what was going on. Lensah opened using the hanky, waving it as a prop - he'd done this before.

"Nina Brem-Wilson was being leaned upon by the aggressive and persistent nasty tactics of Mr Brem-Wilson - a two year campaign of letters, harassment, and legal wranglings - to try and take her land at Tuasi away. A piece of land legally hers, which her cousin had let go in favour of land that he mines profitably at Assor Brompon. Why, I ask you (and he raised his voice in a controlled manner), would a man already reaping the rewards from his own lands, try and take the rightful ownership away from Nina Brem-Wilson? This poor persecuted woman standing here today accused before you, did the right thing. Gave money to the Chiefs and tribe. Gave work to villagers. Gave generously to projects for churches, charities, and schools. Why, why, why would he want to take her money when he was already reaping the benefits of his own land strips? Because he was a cheat, a thief, and he made a campaign of unbearable pressure on Nina Brem-Wilson to give up her rightful ownership. I will prove today, that, she already had fair legal contracts written up and ready to sign, to give her cousin fifty per cent of future earnings. Yet he wanted more. He intimidated and debased her. She, a woman struggling on her own, against five thugs attacking her, got caught up in a horrid accident, a coffee pot she'd taken to defend herself, to rightfully protect herself from these bullies. I will prove today she never even threw a blow. Witnesses will testify that she was yards from the scene where William Brem-Wilson lay. She fainted from the trauma and anguish caused by the actions of these horrendous tormentors."

I glimpsed Ken. He looked down somewhat shamefully. Lensah sat down. He'd proved his fee. I breathed a sigh of relief. But it wasn't over. Judge Milton, authoritative, elderly, with furrowed lines, wearing a damask mortarboard hat, was intently writing through the introductions, took off his glasses, scanned the court-room his eyes resting on me.

"Prosecution, who do you call?"

Daines stood and called me to the witness box. I heard the key of the dock turning, they let me out, I walked down the few steps and crossed the floor, and 'boos' came from across the room. I thought I was going to faint, each step was being watched and I felt heavy, my mind spinning. Milton asked me to speak clearly, and whether I wanted water. Water was brought. I had loads of questions from Daines - he came so close I could taste his breath. He was a smoker, the smell of cigarettes and mints as he drew near, accusing me.

"You took the coffee pot with the intention of beating Mr Brem-Wilson did you not?"

And with every question came Lensah's retort, standing abruptly each time.

"Objection Your Honour."

I couldn't deny I picked up the pot, and he bent every phrase and sentence, distorting my answers until he made me look like I was Myra Hindley. I fainted and the Court went in to recession. They took me out - I had half an hour, and then we were back, but the prosecution was finished with me. Up next was the security guard. He floundered and stuttered. He had been primed (or bribed) to say I did it.

"Did you not see this lady," Daines pointed to me, "hit Mr Brem-Wilson with the pot and bolt, running away after making a fatal blow?"

"Objection," again from Lensah, but it was too late, the security man answered.

"Yes, that's right Sir."

"I'm done with the witness your honour," concluded Daines.

Judge Milton asked the witness to stand down, and Daines sat, folding his arms, not conferring this time with the advisers either side of him. The Judge called lunch. I was taken and I sat alone, picking, in an anteroom thinking about Jim and Mel.

Thomas sat and wrote up his diary in his hotel room in Chicago. He was at the original hotel they had been to, cheaper, but it was roomy and clean. He was going to travel, then return to Zion to finalise the arrangement. It had been more involved than predicted, taking a month to negotiate with Dowie and his colleagues. Dowie now had time to have the decree drawn up in triplicate. The crux of it being, that Thomas was to input one thousand pounds, in return for a stake in Zion City and a royalty on future earnings; a serious business venture and the equivalent of a small fortune of investment.

Friday 4th: I was invited by Dr Dowie to Ben MacDhui (Dowie's summer house) to lunch with his wife and son and was detained there to supper: then he had a very long interview with me about my properties.

Sun 7: To Ben MacDhui for morning (11.00) service conducted by the G.O (General Overseer). At 3 PM meeting at the Church conducted by Dr Gladstone.

Dowie was struggling financially. Tithes were depleted due to smaller congregations because of his controversial comments, reported in the newspapers. Unhinged with power, exalting his own virtues as a saviour of some kind, there were deep rifts in the Zion hierarchy. Zion City had overstretched itself. The Zionists Thomas met always presented a 'united front', and Zion City was a gleaming example of their money and commitment. Thomas yielded to Dowie's charm; he was being fleeced.

He ventured to St. Louis, staying at Everett House Hotel on Fourth Street. The City was jammed with visitors because of the St. Louis Fair. Thomas rode on a trolley car for the first time. He visited a Tabernacle and Zionist college there, and juke joints in the red-light district, where he heard rag time and blues. Thomas picked up two prostitutes, taking them back to his hotel, and making love with both. One prostitute introduced Thomas to buggery, as she refused to oblige conventionally, due to an infection. Thomas was hooked, and he went back to the clip joints searching for a similar experience, which was accommodated at an extra charge. He went back to Chicago on the Illinois train service answering telexes from Dowie and England. The last month of his three month visit was spent sightseeing, up through Detroit, stopping at Niagara Falls, then returning to Zion City by steamer, the Zion Band greeting him at the jetty. He finalised the agreement in Barnes's office, to receive a third of the Zion income in lieu of his investment.

Mon 19th: the Agreement was entered into between myself and the First Apostle Dr Dowie in the presence of Judge Barnes and others.

Winter was already gripping the cold Liverpool docklands where Luciana made its final drop. Thomas disembarked, taking a cab to Lime Street and the London bound train. He reached Euston and went straight home, Ettie completely overjoyed to see him, the bump on her tummy clearly visible, she wore looser clothing. Thomas shied from childbirth in Africa, had little concept of how to handle this and avoided the subject of the imminent child. Instead, he was full of stories of America, Dowie and the Zion City. He did not mention the thousand pounds, as Ettie would have been astounded at the huge sum involved, and how he could raise this kind of money.

Thomas was tenacious, astutely bringing Samuel Stevenson, the lace maker and entrepreneur, and his partner, a Mr Humphrey, into the equation, already knowing Stevenson's commitment to the Apostles of Dowie. Within a week Thomas had bargained with Stevenson, visiting him at his Northampton offices, extracting half the money. Thomas used his lands as collateral for the outstanding half, which was part of the Dowie agreement. He telexed the assurances to Dowie and made a bank transfer using The Standard Chartered Bank at Cornhill for the transaction, then deposited the bundle in a safe box there. Thomas received two hundred and fifty pounds from Dowie in the first month, the initial royalty, which was the only money ever received.

A year on, and Dowie was in tatters, scuttling off to Jamaica in 1907, after creating bad publicity for himself, having announced he was the forerunner of the second coming of Christ, then denouncing religions voraciously, including Islam, proclaiming Christ would destroy muslims on the judgement day. From the great beginnings of 1903, when Dowie had held capacity evangelist meetings for two weeks at Madison Square Garden, to 1907 - four short years - Dowie had disgraced himself, lost worldwide support, and fallen into alcoholism.

The agreements were never seen again, having been archived when the Standard Charter Bank moved after the war, and then lost. Thomas's gain from the Zionist movement could have been considerable, the legacy from a vast global empire of Zionist supporters, including the proliferation of African Zionist Churches, the result of diligent missionaries sent there by Dowie. Thomas never pursued the contracts again, perhaps thinking better of it. The added complexity of Stevenson's involvement, and Thomas's debt to him, could have turned the deal into a burden. Stevenson had his own concerns after Dowie's failure, and did not chase Thomas.

In June 1910 The New York Times reported - 'Zion City investors vote by 14th July on the disposal of the estate in accordance with Judge Landis's recent order in Federal Court. The three options are: to sell for $700,000 to the bank Cobe McKinnon, sell to Wilbur Glen Voliva the newly voted Overseer of Zion City (having worked as a Dowie Congregationalist), or to hand to a board of Trustees to administer the affairs of the City.'

Voliva took over and supervised Zion City with an iron grip, paying substandard wages to the six thousand strong Zion City enclave producing Scottish Lace, the popular Zion brand fig bar cookie, and White Dove Chocolates. Voliva's route mirrored Dowie's, becoming power mad, adopting an overtly lavish lifestyle. The Great Depression, and Voliva's autocratic rule alienated supporters in droves and Zion Industries was forced into bankruptcy in 1935. Voliva's demise followed shortly, apparently exacerbated by a lifetime's diet of solely buttermilk and Brazil nuts. He admitted on his deathbed the misappropriation of Church funds for his own misdeeds.

The Dowie disgrace did not seem to dent Thomas's own belief. He maintained and increased his involvement with Pentecostalism in Great Britain. In fact, the Church continued to dominate Thomas's life, taking him away from his family.

The afternoon dragged on, Daines calling up a succession of 'supposed' witnesses, none of which I'd seen at the hotel before the incident. Lensah was letting him get on with it, looking on, sucking his pencil and offering little objection to the flagrantly fabricated stories. I was tired, I sat against the hard wooden seat, my bum getting numb, fiddling nervously with my hands, then putting them under my legs, trying to relieve the pins and needles. The Judge, the Jury, the courtroom, were chomping to finish the day off with me being found guilty, so they could go home, I could feel it. The temperature worsened and the grind of tedious witnesses wore everyone down. Daines didn't call Jim and he sat looking down unremittingly, his hands resting on his legs, occasionally turning to Mel, who I couldn't look at in case I started crying.

"I'm done with witnesses," said Daines.

Judge Milton looked up, I was sure he had been asleep, but apparently not, as he instantly glared at Lensah.

"Evidence Sir?"

To my surprise and that of the throng, Lensah exclaimed.

"First witness, Dr Hislett Packerd." Leaping out of his chair with an enthusiasm that broke the collective doldrum.

A very smart young man was brought through, shown in by two ushers at the back, like a bolt from the blue. Lensah hadn't mentioned any doctor or any witnesses besides Jim, Ken, and me. The only other candidate, C.P, hadn't been at the hotel that day and Lensah said he would only call him as a last resort for a character reference if all else failed. The young man spoke clearly stating his name and profession and swearing an oath.

"Dr Packerd, please repeat your profession to the Jury and give more detail about your professional qualification and where you work," said Lensah.

"Objection," came Daines, "misleading the Jury, profession alone is sufficient."

"Objection over-ruled. Please keep control Mr Daines, you were given plenty of opportunity to question your witnesses without interruption."

The Judge was clearly irked at the early interjection, and had a renewed interest in the proceedings with the new witness in the box.

Dr Packerd: "Pathologist. State of Accra Central Morgue. I'm a trained surgeon on a three year internship to the Central Morgue, where I am completing a research project for the University of East Anglia, Great Britain."

The crowd, who'd been murmuring up until now went completely silent, transfixed by every word.

Lensah: "Can I ask you, did you receive the body of Mr Brem-Wilson after death, and did you carry out the post-mortem on the cadaver?"

Daines: "Objection m'Lord, leading the witness…"

Judge: "Sit down Mr Daines, and don't stand up again until I say!" Pointing his pen at Daines.

Daines sat frustrated folding his arms and nodding his head, whispering fervently to his two advisers.

Judge: "Continue."

Lensah: "What was the cause of death Dr Packerd?"

Dr Packerd: "A blood clot to the brain."

Lensah: "When did that happen?"

Dr Packerd: "No more than two hours prior to death."

Lensah: "So a blood clot killed the man and it happened in the hospital?"

Dr Packerd: "Yes Sir."

Lensah: "Did Mr Brem-Wilson have a pre-existing condition that would have lead to the forming of a clot?"

Dr Packerd: "Yes Sir."

Lensah: "Describe that condition please Doctor."

Dr Packerd: "I found that Mr Brem-Wilson had had pre-existing 'micro-bleeds', or very small clots in the brain, probably that were literally swept from his heart over an extensive period of time. He smoked, had mild cirrhosis of the liver from alcohol, probable and proven harmful causes, and ultimately these could have caused a stroke at any time, even brought about by mild exercise, or stress."

Lensah: "I rest my case," leaning against the dividing panel between him and the Jury, addressing the Jury, "I rest my case."

Daines: Jumping up and blurting out. "Objection, objection, irrelevant, objection!"

Judge: "Any questions for the witness Mr Daines?"

Daines wasn't ready, looked clueless momentarily.

Judge: "Stand down Dr. Packerd."

Packerd had only been up there five minutes, but it was five minutes that saved my life. The Jury was called out. Lensah didn't bother quizzing Jim, knowing that if he tripped over his words, or became emotional it could ruin the whole event. We were summoned back after an hour. On their return Judge Milton turned to them, asked for a verdict, a Nana women stood, paused a second, coughed, I didn't breath, then she said:

"Not Guilty."

NEWS OF THE WORLD

'Married To Black Man, Pastor's Quarrel With White Wife' 'Would Bash Their Brains Out'

The headline ran in the 2nd December, 1920 edition of the News Of The World daily newspaper, and this was the account of the sensational court case of Ettie and Thomas's divorce, where Ettie said that, 'Thomas had beaten her and the children severely. He would throw her out and drag her about by the legs whilst she screamed. The child, Philip (Kwesi) was brought to court and gave evidence against his father, saying, that he was tied to a chair and beaten with electric wire or wood, and his legs would bleed. Also he said that they only received paltry rations of food, which were often inedible, his father would give them a penny for bible reading, and then borrow it back to pay for the gas.'

Thomas Brem-Wilson early 1900s

NINA - The Second Coming

Back home in England the news-rags were on the floor in the Hall, Sunday's News of The World headlines:

'Brit Murder Charge Legacy Curse Agony'

A lengthy fax sat immobile, curled up on the floor beneath the machine table, ready to convey bad tidings. I didn't care. I was home. Lensah had forged a bargain with the State Prosecution in Accra in light of their losing the case against me. Jim's charge was relegated allowing his deportation and non-entry into Ghana for twelve years, by way of a sizeable charitable donation made by us (most of which would probably be stolen by the government). Sir Mark's efforts hadn't kept it out of the news, the fax confirming they were upholding a 'discredit conduct' clause in our contract that would see us off the land, with no further payments.

For weeks there were celebrations and crying, we'd never been so glad to be alive, to be together. Back on 'home soil', the BBC, Radio 4, tea and biscuits. Jim had come back to reality ages before me. The bills were piling up and we had no income. He'd got our old van out of the garage, washed it down, charged the battery, checked the oil and tyres, went to one of our old wholesaler friends and filled it with stock, our old 'lines'. He started at 'Addie' or 'Old Addington', a fifteen-foot stall - he had to go back to work 'casual' - we'd lost our prime spots, our regular pitches, but Jim was happier to be doing something. Nothing changed for him; he was the 'rock', preferring the banter of his market pals to the highflying moneyed lifestyle of Sir Mark and Lord Strack Allens. If Jim could have had the Ferrari without the other trappings, it would have been his ideal situation, but that wasn't going to happen.

Mel moved in temporarily, shopping, cooking and cleaning. She found work locally, waitressing. After the initial elation I had become depressed; it was difficult to come to terms with. Jim tried to console, to get me back from down in the dumps, but I couldn't get Will's death out of my mind. Nearly a year passed. I sat, staring at the television, day-in day-out, the relentless daytime trivia and soaps washing over me, entertaining and mindless.

We didn't have the means to fight B.W.P's lawyers, they continued to exploit Assor, and Stamnex stayed on Tuasi, easily diminishing Ken's cut. We were cleaned out from Lensah's fees, the bribes and penalties. My Box sat by my chair amongst the collectables, bits-and-bobs[27], old photos and rubbish that I piled up there, thinking I would look at them at some point. Jim and Mel dared not move it - it amassed dust. There wasn't one moment, no revelations, no sudden undoing of the past, it was a slow unplanned journey, I walked around the house, looking at the framed cuttings in the hall, old pictures and newspaper articles of my Granddad that I'd had framed when we'd bought the house, when the money had been rolling in from Brem-Wilson lands.

Jason sometimes came round, on the way through from a client 'pick-up' or a Gatwick Airport 'drop-off'. He would have a whisky or two (the only reason the spirits cabinet got rummaged) and would chinwag[28] about old times, our Dad, music, Jazz (his passion) and his children. Moving around the house more, and with time, these few small things gradually aided my recovery - Mel's constant cheerful demeanour, Jim's proprietary 'All right Nina?!' every morning and last thing at night. I got myself together, and back to normal fighting spirits.

By degrees I realised what I had achieved, that my Dad and Granddad would have been proud, and it was 'something', however disastrously it turned out. Sooner or later I got out of my dressing-gown, started walking my grounds, which I'd never really got to know, took an interest in the garden, the birds, and went shopping with Mel. A transformation had come about. They say you become stronger from the experiences in your life and I had. I wasn't persecuted by the death - it hadn't been my fault - I'd paid the price. I was accused of being a single-minded bitch, at least that's what the papers had said,

---

[27] bits and bobs - small remnant articles and things, the same as 'odds and ends'

[28] chinwag - have a natter or chat

but at least I tried.

We booked a holiday, this time America - a short road trip. I was taking the Box. I'd been reading in the diaries about Thomas Brem-Wilson's link with the Church, his curious pilgrimage to Zion City, and the transactions with Dr. Dowie. I wanted to see Zion, and visit more of my ancestry. I called it a hobby, Jim was happy to indulge in what he called my 'boxsession', as long as I was laughing and joking again. We'd sold the last of the cars, Jim was gutted to see the Ferrari go, but we put some money in the bank, bought a cheap Daihatsu truck as a 'run around'.

There was a small 'hiccup', a call from our lawyer, who we hadn't heard from since the split from B.W.P. He'd had a letter from Will's son's lawyer. It was the start of civil action for their father's death citing Jim and me, and a claim for half the monies earned from the mines, plus their damages. The solicitor, Mr Morley, said they had little chance, as it had been resolved in Africa already. He would send a legal response - 'It is doubtful your claim will succeed since there has been a final trial in Ghana. Additionally, we would pursue our damages and legal costs vigorously'. His secretary would put his bill of one hundred and fifty pounds plus VAT in the post. He didn't mention B.W.P. Probably thought better of it.

I'd bounced back, we were in better spirits, and so I refused to let it get to me. I left it at that, not giving it much thought, my mind now on my trip. We were headed for Orlando, Disney to start off with, then New Orleans, Chicago and Detroit.

Thomas had tried with the first child, but he wasn't a 'children person'. He soon became frustrated and distracted. Also he had not kept an eye on his business, sidelined by his Church activities and the social sphere that went with it. Not having a regular income, he grew increasingly petty and frugal, with a tight control of the household budget. Nothing was spent on his family but he doggedly invested in his favoured Pentecostal Churches.

Thomas Brem-Wilson early 1900s

He was now preaching regularly, often visiting associated sects around Great Britain, travelling without Ettie, and taking advantage of his kudos in the congregations, dalliances with ladies, exploiting his status in the 'laying on of hands' sessions. By that time there were copious discussions with the United African association and 'Gold Coasters' in London at the Saracen and Head Hotels, and the Reverend Agyer Assam, to comment on plans about the government imposing a taxation on Cape Coast residents. Considering Thomas's lack of contact with the Gold Coast after these years abroad, he was more likely interested in the socialising and the prestige it gave him.

Thomas disconnected from home life, but continued to have children up until 1914. They had six, one of which was a girl who died at birth. Ettie was distraught, but infant mortality was commonplace. Only three boys survived.

Thomas Brem-Wilson the 'Black Pastor of Peckham'

Thomas preached the Pentecostal message 'in the streets', even though he hadn't taken to it in his early days in London, after the incident at Berkeley Square. Signs that he was becoming unhinged showed in his obsession with the Zion message and his erratic behaviour. Bystanders stared in dismay at the outrageous proclamations Thomas was making at his frequent appearances at Speaker's Corner in Hyde Park. Each week there was jeering from the multitudes being provoked by his tirades. He received so much notoriety he became known as the 'Black Pastor of Peckham'.

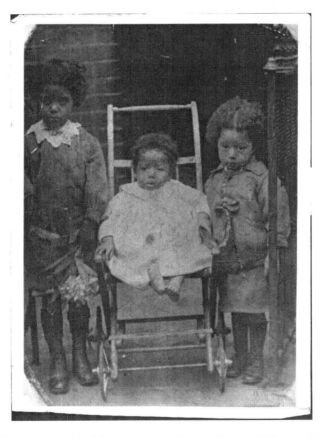

Philip, Raymond and Danny Brem-Wilson (sons of Thomas) 1912

155

Diary entries were more religious gibberish, and never-ending lists of his spending, money in and out of the household. The immaculate dress code remained, but the suits were toned down, the old jackets mended and re-made by Ettie. Grey was showing through his locked down hair do. Whilst preaching in the streets, a hair or two pinged out, and his Afro flared up with the ferocity of his bluster.

The house at Hither Green was sold in 1914, and they moved to a more run down area, Bridge Cottage, Penrose Street, Walworth, which became a popular address for all-comers seeking shelter, since Thomas, conscious of being true to his religious beliefs, was 'practicing what he preached'. The three children often had to give up their bedroom and sleep in the bath, or on the floor, for any waif and stray that Thomas decided to give lodging to. This was not just for the odd night, but weeks at a time. The children took to scrounging for scraps, and became street urchins. They constructed an improvised bed that could be laid over the bath, wood from crates and the straw packing that protected imported fruit acted as a mattress, rubbish discarded from fruit and veg markets at the end of the day, where they also freeloaded food. Charity started in the home for Thomas but to the detriment of his family.

Thomas - The Legacy

A pan cracked across the room, the kitchen only six foot by six foot, had hardly enough room to accommodate a throwing match but it was all too much for Ettie. She had been dragged down from a sought after starlet, to a mother of three with scarcely a penny to buy food or manage a home. She found Thomas's ledger (always having known where it was, but never taken to prying into a man's business). She had had enough and was at the end of her tether. She went to the Box (hardly touched these days, apart from the pecuniary household account Thomas kept there), in the small cupboard bedroom that Thomas and her infrequently shared, under the old metal bed. The miniature script was only just legible. Letters to an African wife and children on the Gold Coast. What was most upsetting, were scores of entries of generosity to Churches and Tabernacles.

'Gave fifteen pounds to Brother Body'

He was only giving her three pounds every six months. Ettie left the diary open on the kitchen table, the only piece of furniture owned in the cottage, and that had come from Hither Green. She wrote under his, in red ink: *'and children starving'*.

Ettie sat in the dark, cold kitchen, the street beams outside illuminating her face, the children put to bed. She wore a stained pinafore over one of her once glamorous gowns, which she had altered and cut up to make work wear. It was a desperate scene but Ettie *was* desperate. She couldn't go back to her family, disgraced, with three half-caste children, and isolated from her friends. Thomas returned late as usual, and on entering he saw something fly towards him, ducking, it missed anyway. A terrible row ensued, Ettie throwing the diary at him.

"Here it is, liar, cheat, religious rubbish, you're a charlatan!"

Thomas hit her in the face and she fell to the floor, crying.

"Take my money, you've bled me for everything, bloody evil

157

woman and children, bleed me dry!"

Thomas stabilised himself on the kitchen table, threw a few coins on the floor.

"Have that, take everything."

Ettie took the small bits of money, sobbing. She scrabbled around kneeling on the thin threadbare lino, some of the coins stuck in the ridges where the lino was thinnest and coming apart. She dug with her fingers. Thomas looked on for a couple of seconds, then turned and went out again.

Ettie persevered, with little choice, a mixed couple was outrageous, they were outcastes in society. Ettie had to stick with the situation. She tried to extricate Thomas from the Church. He had been brought before the Church and given a short suspension, his behaviour with girls not having gone unnoticed. Thomas admitted that he had been 'tempted'. Ettie started attending his sermons, and was thrown out each time for making a scene. She threw a brick through the chapel window. Thomas laid the blame on her, announcing - 'The devil is working his way through her'. Years of lecherous behaviour, combined with his belief in 'divine healing' manifested itself, punishing his body and mind. Self-administered potions for Syphilis had not worked, and his mental capacity and organs were inevitably paying the price. In the reported court case Thomas stated that Ettie was violent, throwing pans and scalding tea over him, that she was the 'devil incarnate' (News of the World), and that he was being misrepresented because he was foreign. It was over in 1920, they were divorced.

Thomas stayed true to his faith, however fanatical and misguided, successfully establishing the first Pentecostal Church in Britain, in Sumner Road, Peckham, which was originally stigmatised as the 'Black Man's Church'. He carried on street preaching until 1922, when he was arrested at the Avenue Royal Exchange, having reeled in over five hundred followers, stopping traffic, ending up in Brixton prison for a four week remand sentence. Ettie visited him, she still loved him but his behaviour was eccentric and demonic. He spoke across the table, the hum of convicts and their guests saturating the austere visitor's lounge. In a low husky voice he leant in as far as he was allowed, the line across the middle of the table a yellow painted no man's land

158

dividing them. His breath, its foulness, made her recoil a little, and an odour, dried sweat on his clothing shocked Ettie.

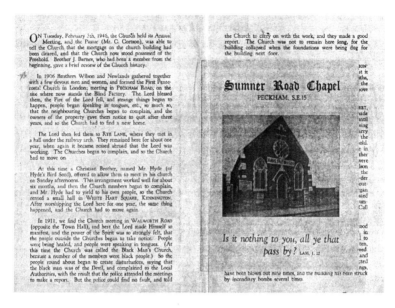

Sumner Road Church, Peckham, church pamphlet 1904

"God has saved me, he's sent me here to repent Ettie, I am cleansed, when I'm set free from here I will be a free man, free of the burden of my sins, I can walk the Earth and spread the Gospel." Then his voice lowered even more, Ettie straining to listen above the noise, "…And I shall be the second coming, everyone will see I am the chosen one, the manifestation of the Lord, I have done the Lord's work, you will see Ettie, everything I've done I've done for you and the children, to save you from your sins, because we will be caste into heaven when the Lord strikes his sword from above."

Ettie leant and kissed him on his curls, tears streaming from her eyes, a stick thwacked down on the yellow, the guard ensuring she did not do it again, reminding her of her brolly slammed on the table between Ray and Thomas. He did not hear her voice as she stood and collected herself.

"I love you Thomas."

He continued to babble under his breath, vacantly searching for her eyes as she walked away for the last time. According to the prison doctor's report, he was 'out of his mind'. His stretch was extended, due to being caught in a licentious act with a young man, for fear of his effect on society. When finally released the rampant public preaching he pursued became nonsensical and frightening, sermons mere rants. The public became afraid of him. He died penniless and alone in 1929, the victim of a ravaged liver and brain, un-treated Syphilis.

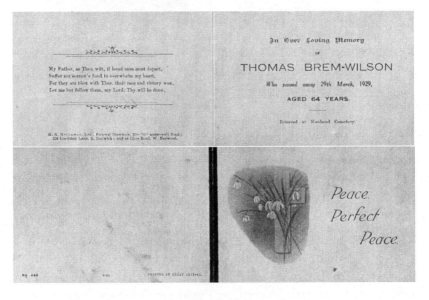

Thomas Brem-Wilson funeral card
29th March 1929

THOMAS - Phase 3, The Children

The ceilings were high, the walls bare brick, red quarry floor tiles continually buffed by the inmates on their knees, two at a time, bars at the wide metal-framed windows. Remand School was hard labour, and cruel. The warders, mostly grey uniformed matriarchs took pleasure in abusing the young offenders. Philip Kwesi Raymond, son of Thomas Brem-Wilson shivered with fear, and cried when he arrived at the borstal, a sinister, dark, bleak corridored Edwardian house with eighty rooms and dormitories, set in its own five acres of grounds in Essex. The gardens and vegetable plots tended by the inmates were enjoyed by the prison authorities and laboured over by the incarcerated. Philip was a prisoner aged eight, on four years minimum detention, handed over to the police by his father. Children were here for a variety of minor offences, from poaching to petty theft. Also, the poor were put here for no other reason than, that they had nowhere else to go.

Philip wasn't helped by his appearance. He had been born a half-caste, in London, at Guy's General Hospital, Southwark, lucky to be brought into the world on 20th September 1908. He was the child of Ettie Cantor, and Thomas Brem-Wilson, brown skinned, tight curly hair like his father, good looking. He was beaten on his first night. His small brown luggage bag was taken away, containing only one change of clothes and a sandwich for his tea, rummaged through by the senior warder, as usual taking any valuable items. For Philip Kwesi Brem-Wilson it was a pair of woollen winter socks, having been knitted by his mother before the divorce.

Ettie was now living on the deprived Downham Estate, an overflow from the slums of East London, which had been built on over five hundred acres of farmland, purchased by the London City Council from The Earl of Northbrook, to address the chronic lack of housing. She hadn't seen the children and had no input, which was the case up until Thomas's death. Ettie was estranged, contact with the children and Thomas too punishing, she tried to re-build her life and shake the shackles of notoriety. She took low quality catering work. Thomas had taken over the household at Penrose Street. With no consideration toward domesticity the children had to virtually raise themselves.

Philip had his own defence mechanism, as he had already suffered at ordinary school, being called 'chocolate', and beaten up by the school thugs. By the time he was sent to Essex he had dispensed with the bullies, thrashing a couple, and nobody picked on him again, but it was too late, as that was the last he would see of regular education, or his home in Walworth.

It had been impossible to please his father; constantly berated and flogged, violence was a daily occurrence. Some excuse from the bible, Thomas had all the 'good words' to take in vain to engender his evil and bitter degradation to his family. He had somehow got it into his mind that they had destroyed his formative carefree and luxuriant lifestyle. The boys were hardly a burden, but their father's resentment festered and was embodied in the unmitigated cruelty that he decided to unleash at any moment. In one attempt to impress his father, Philip broke into his school with a friend and stole books, which were prizes for academic achievement. Replacing the awardees names in the books with his own name, one for literature, one for Maths, so on, he placed them on the kitchen table and waited for his father's return. Immediately Thomas recognised the ruse and took Philip by the neck dragging him to the police.

In the long run remand school became a relief for Philip, as routine was something he had never experienced. They ate well, three main meals a day, tea and bread for breaks, and supper with a biscuit before bed. In spite of the harsh conditions, it was the first moment in his life he had ever had his hunger satisfied. This was to keep them fit for work in the farm, gardens, in-house factory, and the frequent Borough Council inspections. After two years or so, the harshness rescinded as Philip used his looks and charms to flatter the lady warders. As for the deputy and chief wardens - he stayed out of their way most of the time.

───── ◇ ─────

Summer 1985. It was our introduction to America, and we set down in Orlando International Airport - Mel, Jim and I. We got held up in customs longer than the rest, I think the African criminal record was on the file, but we were let in without too much fuss. We'd booked a budget car, a 'compact', although it was capacious by our standards, bigger than our Daihatsu at home. The sun was shining, radio on, Paul McCartney's 'Live And Let Die'. We'd stolen some sleep on the flight and were ready to have our first proper holiday. The six-lane highway swept us away from the Airport, Mel with a map folded out on her lap, directing us to the hotel. Two huge swimming pools, sunshine, and the beach minutes away. Once settled I didn't want to move, but after a couple of days Jim was keen to get around, down to the Everglades to check out the alligators! We did the outings, queuing at Disney Epcot Centre. Coming 'out of school holidays' hadn't quantifiably dented the number of parents with children, but we waited patiently for our death defying rides. An hour's wait for five minutes of heart attack inducing activity wasn't my thing, but we were here anyway, so I gave it a go.

After two weeks in Orlando, constantly dodging the timeshare salesmen who pounced at every opportunity, in the hotel reception, and at the attractions, we went north. I had completely forgotten about our African exploits, it sounds cruel, but I had decided Will had only himself to blame. Jim couldn't be held responsible, he was only trying to protect my interests, and *I* wasn't going to berate myself forever.

We went up through St. Louis, Jim had wanted to go down to New Orleans, but Mel pointed out that it had to be north or west. The distances were much further than they looked on the map. It wasn't like driving in the UK, a lower speed limit at fifty miles per hour here. Jim was amenable, he liked driving, and would have spent all day, every day, truck spotting the gargantuan chrome emblazoned lorries, stopping at diners en-route and re-living his trucking years. It took two days, about a thousand miles. We stayed in a motel near Nashville overnight, but didn't really visit the city.

"Perhaps on the way back." Mel had said.

She changed into the sightseeing guide, always keen to please, even more so now, after what we'd been through. My mind wasn't on anything in particular, the Box stayed in the boot of the car, which Jim was happy about. Mel always liked hearing my stories though, maybe she was being polite, but I took the time on the road to retell my Dad's recollections of his father, and those of my own childhood, with a black father and white Mum, Nellie.

"Philip was the most successful businessman in Lewisham, have I showed you the press clippings?" I shouted over to Mel.

Jim had the radio on, always flipping stations between the AM chat, church preaching, and the FM, which was mostly 'country music'. Perhaps that's what put me off going to Nashville, as I couldn't stand 'country', well except Dolly Parton of course.

"The Rivoli!" I recounted to Mel. "Built it from nothing. I went and worked there, making sandwiches, counting the pennies from the 'slots'. Made a fortune from Bingo nights at the Rivoli ballroom in Brockley. Nellie and him split, she's in a council flat now… council."

They'd both heard it dozens of times.

"I know Mum, I do visit Grandma."

The countryside eventually turned into patchy out of town diners, small plazas, the usual garages and motels lit up with garish neon signs, and then strip malls, Wal-Mart's, J.C. Penney's, and industrial units. We followed the overhead gantry's 'City Center'. The city was up ahead, we could see the magnificent St. Louis Gateway Arch reflecting in the sun - framing an urban sprawl of heavenward towers. Mel had the map out, and we went on a street sortie to find the hotel, managing to pull off the interstate onto the correct freeway, from which we located the 'West End' turn off. We were staying near the Central West End quarter, a resort hotel and we pootled round looking for parking admiring the colonial style architecture en route.

On our first evening we explored what had once been the red-light district, now gentrified, filled with restaurants, bars, and cafes, ragtime blues, and rock 'n' roll blaring from the numerous doorways. It was warm, mid-summer, and we enjoyed the stroll. I imagined my Granddad's visit here; perhaps the sounds and look of the place had been similar. We sat outside one of the many porticoed venues, eating and taking in the atmosphere. The following day we did the Tom Sawyer steamboat trip and visited Forest Park, where they'd had the World's Fair. I knew my Granddad had come here, to the exhibition, and I was suspended in time for a little while. Perhaps emotions got the better of me as I had a little cry, Mel giving me a hug, but we came out laughing again as always. Back to the hotel, a few beers, dinner, and easily ready for bed.

We left at half-nine the next day, 6th June 1985, for Chicago, and Zion City. I sat in the back, with the window ajar, and we found the freeway, Mel with her super directions. I wanted to be in the back, as I was looking through the diaries again.

"Hardly any entries for America, not much of a pilgrimage, so little written down, you would have thought it would have had more impact on him wouldn't you?" I said.

"Well where's your diary?!" Jim came back.

"It's in my noggins." I replied, tapping my temple.

"Yeah, until senility kicks in, next week!" Mel quipped, setting Jim off.

"I'm not talking to you if you're both gonna be naughty."

I snapped the diary shut, but kept flicking through the few photos that were in the Box. A strange one of Dr. Dowie, I hadn't clocked before that he was white, with an amply ridiculous beard, and he wore some weird emblazoned robes.

"Looked important - at least 'thought' he was important." I said.

"Who?" Jim replied, "Dowie?"

"Yeah, they all think they're it, take the funny clothes and hats away and you're left with a lot of perverts," said Mel.

"You're biased because you're the product of a good Convent School!" I said. We headed up Route 55, through Springfield, Bloomington, Pontiac, and at last the city of Chicago, the enormous skyscrapers piercing the clouds. We bypassed the City heading for Zion, keeping the lofty towers to the east we kept on northwards. It took about a day, with a stop for lunch. Jim had the car in cruise, eating up the miles, the lorries pounding by feet from our windows.

The Country Inn & Suite, an acceptably up market motel, was two blocks from Shiloh Park at central Zion City. It had an indoor pool, although not exactly designed for swimming. Mel, nevertheless, put on her cossy and did as many lengths as possible, before the chubby American trippers got a bit disgruntled - a fitness addict sharing their leisure pool. We had a good walk out, the evening falling, and found a

165

small Italian restaurant on a mini mall; Jim's favourite food.

"I can feel something," I said to Mel, as she tucked into the garlic bread, hungry from the freeway and her swim.

"Is it a bone in your chicken?" replied Mel.

"No, I get the feeling I'm close... close to my ancestry."

"Well he only visited, Thomas - it wasn't any big wotsit. It's like your grandchildren visiting somewhere *you* went on holiday," said Jim.

Mel chuckled, accidentally choking on her garlic stick.

"That's presuming I'll have children - which I'm not!"

"They're nutters," said Jim.

"What?" said Mel.

"In the hotel, religious nutters, here on pilgrimages, and that," replied Jim.

"I didn't think there was much interest in the Zion church now?" said Mel.

"Must be a few - the receptionist told me. Apparently they come on packages, you know, coach outings, jollyups."

"I want to find my roots." I said.

"We already found your roots, and look what happened, you nearly got sent down for murder, and me G.B.H.[29] Don't get us into trouble here!" said Jim.

Mel spoke up.

"Let's not go over that, it doesn't matter, we've come to have a good time, and do something different. It's probably rubbish anyway, everything I've read about him makes him out to be mad, apparently they had riots, thousands in tow, hundreds of police, Dowie was deranged."

"Well this is the last bit of the chain for me, I'm pleased I'm here. Ima goin' back to ma 'Roots'." I emphasised the word 'roots' loudly, in my patois African, as per the hit television series.

"Mum, ssshhhh." said Mel squirming. Diners sneaked a peak, and I laughed, amused at my own pun.

We entered the Shiloh House, which was also home to the 'so called' Zion Museum. The house was fresh smelling. It was a mansion

---

[29] G.B.H. – grievous bodily harm

really, apparently extended at various times, twenty-five rooms, 'wrap-around' veranda; I could imagine them sitting outside in the summer 'counting their money'. We'd walked there, after breakfast, three or so blocks. Mildly parched manicured lawns fronted spacious suburban residences; the wide-open tree-lined avenues were not that busy. The Museum, had been quite deserted, a single lady taking the few dollars at the door, postcards, booklets, and interesting pictures from the Zion City manufacturers set out on the desk in front of her. She wanted to sell us a guided tour, but we were happy poking around ourselves. I think she was the guide, so I didn't want to separate her from her money collecting duties. A small team wandered in after us, doing a sort of strange ritual at the entrance, kneeling, then mumbling quiet words.

"Nutters." whispered Jim.

We recognised them from breakfast, they had piled their plates from the buffet, elasticated shorts a prerequisite. Gluttony clearly wasn't a sin in *their* book. Lavishness, also a byword for Dowie by the looks of his house, no expense spared, solid silver ostentatious bathroom fittings, marble, huge oak staircases, one at the back for the servants and a master stairwell, chandeliers, fittings imported from Europe.

The Museum was a teensy bit spartan. It was more like a boot sale full of bric-a-brac - a few pamphlets, old receipts, crockery that had belonged to Dowie's wife, desks and vases. Not exactly Tutankhamen. Mel read from the display.

"Fifty thousand migrants came here looking for work, the lace industry employing five thousand alone at one point. Amazing."

"You'd never think it looking at it now," said Jim, " there's hardly a dicky-bird here."

Jim glared down at the sepia photos of the female factory workers in front of huge lace spinning frames.

"The machines came from Europe, the industry was worth a million dollars in 1906, imagine what that would be worth these days?"

We had guests coming in behind us; cameras strung round their necks, although a sign had said 'no photography' in the reception. Jim stopped fiddling with the leaflets. He looked fairly sure that we weren't meant to manhandle anything, as he frowned at me, shaking his head. I looked closely at the Victorian ladies in the shot, toiling at something, great sheets of material lay at their feet, their hair and clothing identical, floor-length beige skirts, and fresh utility blouses. As I stared at the print I felt a kind of connection with them. I was momentarily transported. The room around me detached, everyone's presence fragmenting. I was right there in the photograph, a nervous emptiness gouged my stomach, a feeling you get on your first day at school, when you're five years old, crying, hanging on to your mother's hand. I fingered the picture in its frame, hypnotised, then abruptly, like a jolt, Jim's voice.

"Says here they worked virtually as slaves, receiving below minimum wage. They flocked here though to find employment, all roads led to Zion eh!" he said.

"I've had enough - that's it now - Let's get a coffee," I replied.

We traipsed out. I was deflated. No welcoming party of Zionists in full garb? What did I expect? My Granddad had been a small cog.

"My Granddad met Dowie," blurting to the receptionist as we were walking out, my mouth had engaged, before connecting with my brain.

When you meet strangers abroad they always say something like 'Do you know John in Leicester?' as if England was preserved in aspic: double-decker buses and red phone boxes, a population of villages where everybody knows everybody else. Now I was guilty of the same nonsense. She was wearing horn-rimmed reading spectacles on the end of her nose, quite middle aged, thinnish, a bookish type. Looking up from her book, she adjusted her glasses and smiled quite patronisingly.

"Yes, I hear that quite often. Hope to see you again soon."

That really annoyed me, which was ridiculous. I wanted to have an argument with the completely harmless lady.

"No, *he did*, he owned a third of Zion in 1906."

She laughed unconvinced.

"I've never heard that one before and I've been the curator here for twenty years."

"Well you have now, and you can take your crappy Museum and stick it, and by the way, we touched everything upstairs. And that lot are taking photos, bye!"

"Mum," said Mel. "I'm sorry," she apologised on my behalf.

The receptionist smiled again.

"That's OK, the memorabilia can sometimes spark strong emotions, why don't you go down to the Christ Community Church, they have some old remnants archived there, you may find information about your Granddad, say Lorna sent you from Shiloh House."

I took a deep breath and apologised.

"Thank you, I'm sorry, just got too involved, suppose I was expecting something else."

We went for coffee. There was a small diner opposite in a mini-mall of shops. We ordered the Starbucks 'grande' style coffee mug brews.

"Can't hurt, we're here now, may as well have a look, I like a nice Church," said Jim.

"No you don't, I've never heard you say you like a Church in your life?" I replied.

"Well I do now," laughed Jim.

"Well that's it," said Mel, "I'm having a cake as well, as it's a few blocks from here, I'll need all the energy I can muster if you're going to carry on being bolshie."

"Yes, sorry about that, don't know what came over me, she was so thin lipped and mealy mouthed."

As usual, I was amused at my own clever remark, but Jim and Mel the 'terrible twins' were blank. The Christ Community Church was easy to find on foot, with Mel navigating, the tourist map page depicting a grid that resembled a British Union Jack flag representing the layout of Zion City centre. The map had colourful little bubbles of handy information next to each location. Mel pointed over to the left up the long Avenue.

"The Church replaced the original Tabernacle which was up there, as it was burnt down by a disgruntled employee in 1937. It says the original church was at the centre of all the city roads and held over eight thousand."

"Why didn't they rebuild it in the same place?" said Jim.

Mel searched through the print on the little sheet.

"It doesn't bloody say," she replied.

We went on the next few hundred yards admiring the lengthy front gardens of the decidedly moneyed houses, ample homes set well back from the boulevard, some hidden partially by trees. Into Dowie Memorial Drive, then the church was up ahead, almost like a Cathedral it was so large, a stretched stained-glass window from ground up, and an arched roof extending into the surrounding woods like a bullet.

"Nice," said Mel.

"Money," I said.

"You always think about money, it's not everything," said Jim.

"I'm thinking of my Granddad's riches and where it went," I replied.

"He wasn't really rich though Mum, he had the lands, but he kept going to the pawnbrokers, that's not the sign of a rich man."

"Hmmm," I pondered, "what about the deal with Dowie, a third of Zion."

"You don't know that for sure Mum, we haven't got any proof, it's probably hearsay," said Mel, "you know how these things get blown up over time."

"Hmmpph," I replied.

I didn't like her contrariness; I thought I knew about my Granddad better than anyone. We entered the Church. A meandering feature granite path had led up to modern stainless steel doors, curved at the top, like the roof of the building. Mel pondered the service notice at the entrance.

"Next service is Saturday, and there's lots of kiddies' activities, playgroups, summer camp, so on."

"Get 'em while their young," I chuckled.

The room was a showpiece, high vaulted ceilings corresponding with the exterior curves, suspended acoustic baffles, spacious rows of wooden seating and prayer kneelers from front to back. About twenty steps extended to an open-plan stage, piano, microphones ready, and a woodland backdrop, put up for a play about the crucifixion, three full-sized crosses erected, and a set made to look like a rocky outcrop.

"I'm gonna be Iron, like a Lion, in Zion." Mel, singing the Bob Marley tune, pulling the camera out of her bag, "I'm going to take a few snaps."

She wandered towards the front of the auditorium aiming it up at

170

the never-ending stained glass window fronted with a cross that dominated the whole room, letting in morning sunshine. From each side of the window there were, what looked like organ windpipes, splayed out down the edges of the building, huge cylindrical timber tubes coursing toward the ceiling.

"Not exactly Winchester Cathedral," said Jim, "but ok."

"Photographs for a small donation," came the commanding American voice from behind us.

We swivelled round and saw a Pastor, in jeans, a clerical collar visible out of the top of his blue jumper.

"Hello," I said, "we were sent by the lady at the Museum."

"Lorna." said Jim.

Mel meandered back towards us. He was a young man, reminding me momentarily of the first Chief we'd met in Africa, the teacher.

"Jon Wizzard, Senior Pastor," he said, holding out his hand.

Jim and I shook.

"How do you do?" said Mel.

He must have been six foot tall, already thinning at the front, a comb-over pre-empting a midlife crisis, and a small grey beard to compensate for the toply loss. Jim started chatting, asking about the décor, and I looked at him. He'd always had thick bushy hair, so much so, that he kept it tidily cropped back to a 'number two' as I liked to call it.

"We wondered if we could look at the archives, if you have any?" I blurted, "I'm looking for information about my Granddad, Thomas Brem-Wilson who came here in 1906 at the invitation of Dr. Dowie."

As I'd interrupted, a moderately embarrassing silence followed. The Pastor coughed into his hand, then pulled out a hankie from his pocket, wiping his hand and then his nose and surveying it. Yuck, I thought to myself, I touched that hand. Oddly, he'd gone a bit pale, although you wouldn't have said he had enough colour to drain.

"Yes, yes, of course, please make an appointment with the secretary."

He flung his arm out, gesticulating animatedly in the direction of the stage and pulpit. We looked over, but could only see the stage.

"I'll take you and she can organise retrieving the files. I have to

171

warn you they're not in a good condition. Many items were damaged in the fire you know," he spluttered harder, and regained his composure, "next month is the earliest we can do it. Very busy at the moment, summer camps, bring-and-buy sales, so on," and he walked down the wide aisle to the front.

We followed to the right of the stage, through a door concealed behind the organ keyboard, into some office spaces, off a short corridor.

"This is where it all happens," he said, "have a seat."

His office was smart and modern, box files stacked upright, and a couple of metal filing cabinets, a multicoloured board up on the wall with dates of events, columns marking out the church's commitments, including names of those involved. A window looked out over the rear lawns and gardens, I could see two groundsmen in overalls tending the plant beds, digging weeds out with a hoe. Wizzard took the pad on his desk, writing down the names and numbers and handing it to me. I could hear talking from a room down the hall. I looked at the note.

"We're only here for a day though Pastor, we've come all this way, places my Grandfather came, you know, following in the footsteps," I laughed a bit nervously.

"No, no, far too busy at the moment. We need some notice. We receive these requests frequently. Have to have a system I'm afraid, Ms Wilson. You'll have to make an appointment. The archives are very important."

"Is that her?" I said, "...the secretary I can hear? Maybe we can pop in and see her, sort it out now."

I jumped up from the seat.

"Oh no, no, it's not a good time," the Pastor intoning.

I could feel all eyes on me as I shot out of the door, no one having the temerity to stop me, not even Mel. Stubborn confidence overwhelmed me. I had to see these mysterious items. I was already out of the room down the hall, tracking the voice. It was a whim, a silly moment, he called out, the words blurry.

She was on the whole a frumpy lady, in that age bracket that said 'no longer young but unlikely to alter much in the next twenty years', greyish hair, a flecked cardigan that could only be described as home knitted, 'Sheri Jessy' written on a plaque at her desk, 'Chief Administrator'. She was on the phone, but immediately put it down when I entered, looking surprised.

"Hello, I'm Nina Brem-Wilson, I'm here to look in the archives to see if there's anything on my Granddad who met Dr. Dowie in 1906. Any chance we can do it now please?"

The three were behind me, Mel, Jim and the Pastor. Before Wizzard could protest, she replied.

"Certainly, I'll get the keys, that'll be a fifty dollar donation to church funds."

"And twenty dollars to take photos of the building," the Pastor managed to interject, "and no copying permitted."

Jim peeled off the seventy dollars, then another bill.

"Take ten for yourself Pastor," he said, teasingly, handing over the money and patting him on the back.

Wizzard smiled sheepishly and took the money.

"Of course it will go to the children's fund," folding it into his jean pocket and with a resigned tone, "Mrs Jessy?"

She got up, ample grey slacks covered quite plump hips and stocky legs, and she fumbled in the metal cabinet behind her, we could hear the chinking of keys. She found them.

"Come with me please Ms Wilson."

"Dead Sea Scrolls here we come," I whispered in Mel's ear.

"Shut up," she spluttered back, poking me in the ribs.

Mrs Jessy parted us to get to the door (as we were squashed round her desk) then out into the hall. I went first, followed closely by the Pastor, so near I could hear him breathing down my neck. Their elephant's feet trundled, herding down the corridor behind me. Jessy stopped so abruptly I fell over her, the Pastor into me, then Mel and Jim onto the slew of casualties. I screamed with laughter, they all joined in, even Wizzard. We were the Keystone Cops. The mood was lightened at least.

I had the impression we'd have a magical mystery tour to a secret underground vault. They could have ejected us with a 'bye bye, see ya' - strangers turning up out of the blue asking to see 'this-and-that'. The only credibility was our English accents, Jim and me South London and a bit cockney, Mel benefiting from elocution lessons, at great expense to her Dad and me, we were hard to ignore.

We straightened up in the thin passageway, staring at Mrs Jessy. I looked down at her patent flat pumps, at least one size too small, which had that look of toes distorting the outer edges. There was a door that said 'Janitor'.

"This is it," she said.

"This is it?!" I proffered, "is it the Tardis?"

She'd definitely never seen the children's programme Dr. Who, where a policeman's telephone box, 'The Tardis', expands into a large spaceship when you enter.

"Yes," she said, "we always have problems with storage. We keep them safe in here. It's dry and cool."

We watched, grouped far too close for comfort, everyone peering over my shoulder at her fiddling with a big bunch of keys. Jessy pushed the door. Sure enough it was a Janitor's closet, buckets, cleaning materials, mop, etc.

"Nice," said Jim, "might do a bit of dusting while I'm here, eh Pastor?"

They both sniggered, like hyperactive boys on a boring school excursion. She pointed down, and we all looked together, at a tiny plastic storage box.

"There you are, the archives, please handle with care." Fifty dollars, what a lark I thought. They had a right little game going on, we'd been stung. Even the Pastor couldn't articulate a sentence. Mrs Jessy was very 'matter-of-fact', like it was an everyday occurrence, not in the least phased by the stunned-silence reaction. The box was so small you could barely have fitted a hardback book in it. She picked it up off the floor, walked to the next-door office, and set it down on the empty desk.

"Please take your time," she said puffing a little, and left.

Jon Wizzard perked up.

"Nothing remained after the fire. A strange metal box was found, half buried below the old lectern - Dowie's lectern. It had impressions in it, carvings of elephants, a jungle scene. It was rumoured that Dowie had seen something like it in Europe on his travels, and ordered one especially. It survived oddly because of the thick leather lining, creating a vacuum keeping it cool. The lining exactly replicated the outer metal skin and had semi-precious stones studded into it. Got sold off. A collector. Went in the bankruptcy auction."

I looked at Jim, and he tipped his shoulders a smidgen, his eyes widening in recognition to me, not saying anything.

"This was all that was left - these remains, everything else destroyed. He'd only kept bills, so on, at his office at Shiloh House," sliding his hand along the plastic.

"It's rather depressing," said Mel.

"Yes, I'm afraid it can be disappointing for those seeking consolation." answered the Pastor, employing a sermonizing, singsong tone. He stayed, took a seat folding his legs, having every intention of checking the scraps with us.

"Time's ticking on, we're very busy Ms Wilson, it's why we make appointments."

"I don't think it's going to take long is it?" I said.

Jim took the blue plastic lid off the box, the musty aroma of burnt paper unmistakable. The smell permeated the room and we went quiet. There was something eerie, a wisp of loss. Mel waded in, everything in plastic wallets, brownish, hand written, some typed. Squinting at the small print, there was nothing relevant. A few copies of a religious magazine, 'Leaves of Healing', article after article on Dowie's doctrines, successes, the work of missionaries, letters, and adverts for the selling of shares in Dowie Lace-making plants. The wallets were passed round... zilch[30].

"C'mon Pastor, lets get the coffees in," said Mel, "we're nearly done here anyway, aren't we Mum?"

She grabbed the Pastor's arm, sensing my disappointment, and he couldn't refuse.

"Put it back Jim, and we'll get a drink," said Mel.

Wizzard cleared his throat, rising out of his chair, not used to being hustled by a young attractive English girl. They went off through the hall, their voices echoing in the church beyond.

---

[30] zilch – zero, amounting to nothing

"That's it Nina, c'mon darlin' we've been an hour in here, time for some lunch doll."

"All right, Jimmy."

He started putting the artefacts back and, a small leaf of paper descended softly, like a hornbeam's spinning seed wing.

"On the floor Jim."

He leaned down; I looked down, the signature read 'Thomas Brem-Wilson' - I went cold.

"Put it in your pocket Jim."

"What?" said Jim.

Me repeating.

"Put it in your pocket."

He picked it up without looking at it, folded it carefully and slid it away. Mel's chuckle rang out, and a clanking tray.

"You devil!" said Mel as they entered the room, releasing his arm, much to his disappointment.

"Complète Ms Wilson? Sorry it wasn't very successful," he said.

"That's all right Pastor, we didn't expect you'd be a real Wizard as well!" I chortled.

He set the tray down on the table.

"We would welcome you back Ms Wilson, and if you have any further enquires we would be grateful if you called."

"No, no, we appreciate it - sorry to have taken up your time."

We were congeniality itself, had the coffee, and were shown out with a handshake, the Pastor lingering with Mel's.

On the lawn I jibed.

"Fifty dollars. What a rip-off."

"God's payroll," said Jim, "You're gonna get us into more trouble Nina, I can't take you anywhere."

"What are you talking about Jim? Mum?" Mel said, her tone rising accusingly.

"Nothing to worry about," I replied, and walked off, the two of them following, Jim recounting the deed to Mel.

"Got to have a rest."

We were approximately forty yards from the Church and I'd come over very worn out. The coffee had kicked in on an empty stomach, it being about two in the afternoon we should have eaten by now. The two morning visits and the whole Pastor thing had been completely draining. I sat down on the grass, reclining against a tree.

"Let's have a break first, then we'll walk to the diner next to Shiloh House and have lunch."

Jim and Mel concurred, sitting in the shade, which was back from the main boulevard. Mel laid out her top and sat on it, Jim plonked straight down like me.

"What does the paper say Mum?"

"Don't know darlin', we'll look at it back at the hotel."

I shut my eyes, dropped off, I could hear the leaves up above shimmying in the breeze, and the odd car glide by, Mel and Jim's voices rumbling like a tumble drier quietly spinning its warm load. At this moment I felt happy, I don't know why. I normally felt a little pressured, scared of life even, the legacy of my Dad, and in turn his Dad, leaving me in a perpetual state of 'dissatisfiedness', always wanting. A better pitch for the market stall. Better lines. Drum up trade. More moneymaking schemes. The insecurity, that nothing would ever quite satisfy, ingrained in me from when I could first understand that taking money on my Dad's market stall was about the profit, adding up the 'x's, working out your 'margins', paying the rents, and keeping your head above water. The predisposition with my Granddad *was* an obsession, Jim was right, a niggling unwillingness to finish with the past, to relinquish the belief that I came from some great moneyed dynasty. Perhaps my Granddad was merely that, what Mel said. A Dandy, not well off, who'd taken chances, done small deals and made his bed.

"Move on ladies and gentlemen."

I focused on the mirrored shades, and an official blue outfit. A car had parked, blue, I could see the name badge 'Ford Taurus', a large seal on the side of the door, a shield in the centre surrounded by the words 'Zion City Sentinel, Peace, Harmony, Security' encircling in gold lettering.

"You can't stay here. Please move."

A two-way radio crackled on his belt, and like a cowboy, he rested a hand on his holster, ready for a shoot-out. Jim, who had fallen fast asleep, raised his head off the green, a bit bleary.

Mel was on the case.

"F*** off. We've been in the Church, leave us alone."

I was a bit perturbed at her abrasiveness.

"I've warned you Madam, don't profane me, this is private property. You'll have to move on," the man insisting.

"All right give us a minute matey," said Jim, sitting up.

"F*** off," Mel swore at him again.

Quite out of character. She had the bit between her teeth. I don't know what had 'got her goat'[31]. Jim and me were on our feet.

"C'mon Mel, it doesn't matter, let's get lunch, it's only ten minutes back to Shiloh." said Jim.

"No f*** them, he can't do anything, he's only some jumped up security plod."

A police car pulled up behind the blue Taurus, and two officers got out, putting on their hats.

"That's it c'mon Mel." I said, and she got up.

"Problem here Greg?" said one of the policemen to the security guard.

"They didn't wanna move, but they're goin' now."

The policeman addressed Jim.

"What's your business here sir, where's your vehicle?"

"Sorry officer, we're holidaymakers visiting the Church, the car's at our hotel," Jim replied.

"Australians Sir?" The policeman said.

"Pommies," said the guard.

"We've got this now thanks Greg, we'll see you later."

The security guard sloped off, sat in his car, filled out a form attached to a clipboard, and pulled away hesitantly, glaring at us over the top of his sunglasses.

"Passports sir?" he said to Jim.

"Back at the hotel, in the safe," Jim said.

"Let's go for a little ride down the station. We'll check you out. Then you'll be on your way."

---

[31] got her goat – to make one angry

I caught Jim's eye, concentrating intently at his trouser pocket containing the piece of paper. The officers corralled us toward the vehicle and Jim shrugged, the 'deed was done'.

It was all out on the desk and my heart was pumping, trying to avert my eyes, away from the items emptied from Jim's trousers spread-out in front of us. I focused on one policeman, his round features, a young chubby face, the product of too many burgers and not enough chasing of criminals. 'Small town cops', I mused, distracting my brain away from the impending arrest and incarceration in Chicago State Penitentiary.

Jim kept-up the chin-wagging, chatting, asking questions, commenting on their office, clothes, police badges, radios, the weather, even managing to get them to show off their guns, pretty well anything that he could think of to distract them. They warmed to us. Jim's continuous banter, and un-relinquishing cheeriness in the back of the police car had got both officers relaxed. It was a classic 'Jim-ism', wearing them down with 'chit-chat'. During the short drive, Jim had been upbeat, pointing out the sights (even though he hadn't seen them before), and the policemen lightened up. Mel stayed quiet. We'd pulled up at the bland concrete building, the sign reading 'Zion City Police Department, 2101 Salem Boulevard'. The security guy was outside, waiting, and he winked to the policemen. I connected Salem to the devil worship, like a horror B-movie, where an unsuspecting stranger stranded in an American backwater ends up a victim of a demonic cult ritual.

I held my breath as the cops sifted though the stuff - wallet, keys, loose change, turning them over half-heartedly. The folded leaf stood out like a sore thumb, it was neither the type of paper you'd write a phone number nor jot notes on, nor a business card, nor anything else remotely contemporary. It had a sepia frayed appearance, and was screaming to be un-folded and examined. They took Jim's driving license and photocopied it, called the hotel to confirm who we were, and completed their write-up. The chubby policeman constantly huffed and sighed, as if it was too much trouble for him. His pal got some machine coffee and a few biscuits, which we scoffed down in seconds, ravenous. After some more 'huffing' he finally spoke.

179

"OK, we don't get your types out here much, so please be careful where you go, no more trespassing."

"What types?" said Mel, the first words she'd said since the swearing.

He went a little embarrassed, choking.

"Those from ethnic origin."

"What?!" said Mel.

"C'mon Mel, let's leave it." said Jim.

"I'll have you know I'm a British Citizen, Founding Fathers, you know!?"

"Sorry Madam, I didn't mean anything by it, it's just, you're a little dark compared to residents out here, makes them a bit nervous, it's more a Chicago thing."

Mel got up.

"How are we meant to get back?"

"Ffffffffphh!" came the sustained sound from the policeman's mouth, puckering his fat lips in an exhalation of air. "One of my colleagues will give you a lift," and at the top of his voice he shouted "Larry!" He came back in, "Take 'em to the Inn Lar."

"Here we go ladies and gentleman."

Jim put the items back in his pocket, intentionally ignoring the paper. The security guy was still outside, Mel made an impertinent curtsey to him, pushing out her backside, and blowing an imaginary raspberry, luckily out of sight from Larry the plod. I cuffed her gently round the head as we got in the car. In only minutes he'd dropped us at the motel. The receptionist said nothing, but we knew *she knew* by the disapproving look on her face. We ordered room service, and examined the loot.

It was a contract, smallish, not quite A4 size, written on one side, a thick vellum, typed out, then signed in ink, a bit faded and charred round the edges, but unmistakably the signatures of Judge Barnes, Thomas Brem-Wilson and John Alexander Dowie.

"He knew we'd find it!" I said.

"We know Mum, we know!" said Mel, who picked it up from the bed and was scanning it. The phone rang. It was odd, since no one knew we were here. I answered. The receptionist's voice spoke.

"Officer Jay?" and he came on the line.

"Officer Jay here, I've been up to the Zion Church, Pastor Wizzard has reported something missing. Says you were the last ones there, I'll have to come down to the Inn, and interview you please Ms. Wilson. Don't go out Madam, I'll be there in fifteen minutes."

"Let's go," I said as the phone went down "the police are coming."

"What? Not again," said Jim.

"Don't argue, we won't get out of this, and I'm not handing over my heirloom… it's mine."

I pulled my bag from the wardrobe and threw everything in.

"Jim, empty the bathroom."

He threw out a huge sigh, getting up from the late lunch he'd been enjoying, and walked to the bathroom.

"Mel," I shouted, "get your stuff!"

"Buggerin' hell," said Mel, stomping off.

We were down in reception in five, and checked out, to the disbelief of the receptionist.

"We're going back to Miami, have to get an earlier flight, something happened at home, an emergency," Jim told her.

"Yes, Sir. Thank you."

She rang up the bill taking the major portion of an eternity, and we walked out, trying not to run. We headed north, in the opposite direction, passing the two officers on the way. Jim had the screen visor down and his sunspecs on, Mel and me, ducked down.

"They're not following, they missed us," Jim said, looking in the rear view mirror.

He sped off, the speedometer rising to fifty, then seventy.

"Jim, it's too fast, it's suspicious," I said.

"Don't worry, the town police are at the hotel," he replied.

I put my head in my hands, to ward off the pounding. We took the 94, tracking Lake Michigan, Mel pointing out that if we carried on north we'd end up in Canada and wouldn't be able to visit Detroit. I didn't fancy Detroit now, but couldn't let her down; she had set her heart on the Motown Museum. So we trailed though little towns, rail crossings, keeping a low profile.

"Anyway they'll be pleased that we were out of town so they can go back to traffic duties," I pointed out, hopefully.

When we reached Milwaukee, we went east on the 94, then at Madison, south on the 39. Once past Chicago, we headed west on the 94 to Detroit, through Kalamazoo, Battle Creek, and Ann Arbour. We were beyond the State line and into Michigan. I wasn't sure it would make any difference, and whether the crime was serious enough for us to be pursued. We didn't discuss it. I think it was silently decided that we'd got away with it. It took seven hours constant driving, stopping infrequently for supplies.

It was night, and Detroit was exactly how you would expect it, but 'twice as much', a city sprawled out, run down, industrial wastelands. We were lost, it was no surprise, interstate's conjoining freeways, untold slip-roads uncoiling into faceless suburbs, the familiar blue highway signs up on the gantries less helpful to Mel, who was not her usual compendium of all things map related. We whittled it down to one area, finding our turn off, bumping down the highway exit ramp, impossible to avoid the potholes.

The hotel looked okay, a Days Inn on Goyeau Street, a generally more up-market district; the typical American hurly-burly of the City, wide avenues, tall business buildings, diners and shops. It had it's own underground car park. We checked in one day early, the reception area still buzzing despite the late hour. They had plenty of rooms available. It had started to rain a little outside, the first bad weather we'd had. The hotel was clean and spacious, not exactly modern, but American from top to bottom, seventies brown carpeting, beige velour walls, quiet and efficient. Mel went for a swim and we went to bed, forgetting about the Zion escape and the perpetual tarmac.

In the morning we found a diner around the corner from the hotel, I remember the name, the Tunnel Bar, because it reminded me of an old club I used to go to at London Bridge, the Tunnel Club, deep in the arches under the railway lines. We had a copy of the Zion agreement on the table, I'd gone to an office shop down the road early and had a dozen photocopies made, the original safely stashed in my Box. Mel started reading, squinting at the small print. I'd had it enlarged, but it was still hard to see.

'An agreement entered into, this day 19 November 1906 between Alexander John Dowie, High Priest of Zion City, Chief Legal Advisor Judge Barnes, and Thomas Brem-Wilson, of Hither Green London and The Gold Coast Africa, under the legal jurisdiction and bound by the Laws of Zion City and of America, Great Britain and The Gold Coast of Africa, and any other relevant Legal Jurisdictions, in perpetuity.'

There was a lot of legal jargon, the 'where-bys, wherefore, and whatnots', as I liked to say, having poured over the B.W.P contracts, I'd seen plenty and been none the wiser. Mel read quietly and methodically the main body of the contract.

'Thomas Brem-Wilson will receive one third of any income from Zion Industries, Zion City incorporated, and Zion City revenues, from whatever source, in lieu of an investment to the value of One Thousand United Kingdom Pounds Sterling payable to Alexander Dowie within one month of the date of this agreement. Royalties from Zion will be paid monthly to Thomas Brem-Wilson, one month from the date of this contract, to be paid via Solicitors, Emmanuel & Simmonds, 10 The Strand, London. As part of this agreement The City of Zion Incorporated will have the right to exploit lands owned, leased and/or favoured by Thomas Brem-Wilson on the Gold Coast of Africa, where deals exist, now or in the future, in a manner that they deem suitable. To include the exploitation of minerals, gold, timber, rubber, fruit production, tobacco, agriculture, land rents, building work, leasing, rental, tithes, tolls, and means not yet determined.'

"Bloody 'ell," said Jim, "that's a lot to take in."

"It means we get a third of Zion," I said.

"Yes Mum, that's if the lands in Africa were handed over, and if Thomas paid the money. Zion has never used the lands, and B.W.P, and Stamnex are on them now, you'd have to get *them* off, and prove that you had the rights. Anyway Zion's worth nothing now, they've got that Church, and you don't know they own that for sure," said Mel, finally pausing for a breath.

"Melissa," I said, "always so negative, it's worth looking into, it's still an agreement. He tried to hide it, you know, 'Pastor-pants'. Actually I'm surprised they'd left it in there, muddled with the insignificant bits 'n' bobs."

"There's a couple of possibilities, maybe he didn't know it was there, it got stuck to some pages in the fire, or he'd been forced to keep it there by the archivists?" Mel replied.

"We'll never know," I said, "it's a bit of luck."

Mel looked down and carried on reading. There was a list of land tracts, including Epirah, Isibu Creek, Assor Brompon, Bentimbaka, Sarko Bonn, Tuasi, Kwedu, Dapasi Tandokwaka, and Asukla. Then accounting clauses, virtually the same as ones I'd done with B.W.P. - 'the right to inspect', 'one month's notice', 'appointment made in writing by your accountant', and so on. I was excited and felt reinvigorated. We got back to the hotel, a message at reception, a small note, awaited us - 'Call Zion City Police Department, 847 746 4088'.

"Bollocks," I said and screwed up the slip. "Where's the nearest DHL office?" I asked the desk clerk.

"Turn right, two blocks down," said the besuited attendant.

We trooped out, past the shops and delis, and found the office services store. It was the same place I'd had my copying done earlier, doubling as a twenty-four hour photo developers, a coffee machine and humming printing presses in the rear. I put the Zion contracts and copies in a padded jiffy bag and sent it to my solicitor; I knew the address by heart, Morley & Co, 65-66 Lincoln's Inn Fields, London, WC2. It was expensive, over seventy dollars, but they'd be there next day, guaranteed. Mel filled out the consignment form, putting 'personal documents' as the description. When I looked at it my heart pounded, I'd stolen from the church, and was smuggling.

Jim called the law department at Zion City from the hotel, having retrieved the discarded note. He was born for this, lying through his teeth, and he swore blind we'd done nothing - we were harmless victims, persecuted by the Pastor who'd taken a dislike to us.

"What bit of paper? He must be mad, why would we want that? What is it anyway? Can't be worth anything, it was a right load of rubbish!" Jim protested.

I could hear the thin tone on the line, asking Jim to return to Zion City to be interviewed, or they'd put out an interstate warrant for us. Jim refused.

184

"You can do what you like, we ain't done nothing, we're innocent, you'll find nothing on us."

By hook or crook they found a compromise, to make a statement at the Detroit City Police Department the following morning, and have it faxed through.

"Sir, take your passport and Driver's License with you," came the response before the phone went down, Jim facing the phone toward me so I could hear the dial tone.

"Look what's happening Nina, is it really worth it?" he said.

"C'mon Mel, you'll stick up for me, you've got to give it a go haven't you?" I made an appeal.

"I don't know Mum, after the African thing?" she replied.

"Don't worry darlin'," I said, "it's over anyway, the contract's gone."

Jim went to the Police Department straight after breakfast the next day, taking a cab to 1300 Beaubien Street. They'd been expecting him so he was back in an hour. We were in the reception area, sitting at a leather sofa, watching the comings and goings, and Jim bowled in smiling his characteristic Jim smile.

"Nothing could be proved," he said, "our word against Wizzard. They took a statement of what had happened in the Church office, I said we'd had coffee and looked at the old records, we paid seventy dollars for the privilege, and that was it. I said the security man had something against us, as we'd rested up on the lawn outside, not knowing it was private, and he'd got ratty. They said that these small town police are hicks. I was warned that the Immigration Authority had been alerted, to search our bags on exit, so we'd better be clean."

"We have some news for you Jim," I perked up, "I called Mr Morley, and he's got the overnight parcel. He said it's very interesting, and that the best plan is, to check out whether Zion has any funds. He has an associate in New York who he'll have a chat with, and I've got to call him at home this afternoon."

Jim sat; we ordered 'elevensies'[32], muffins and coffee, from the small

---

[32] elevensies - tea or coffee taken at mid-morning and often accompanied by a snack

grill in reception, and chundered in[33]. Jim was washed out and starving, and I must admit to having been pretty relieved. Mel separated the top from the stump and picked out the raisins.

We went to the Motown Museum. Mel was more excited about this than anything. The police, contracts, and everything else assuaged. The hire car, with Mel directing, made it a short trip via midtown Detroit, a busy lunchtime business district, workers streaming out of the tower blocks into the diners and coffee shops. Then we were north on John C. Lodge Freeway, via Wayne State University campus, until we came to the wide suburban streets that housed the small two-storey building, on a corner of Berry Gordy Junior Boulevard. The only thing that differentiated it from the neighbouring capacious residential houses was the huge sign out front, 'Hitsville USA'.

"We made it!" said Mel.

We did the full caboodle[34], the recording studio, the office, and the hall that doubled as an echo chamber. Well, that was it, but Mel was excited. She bought bits in the compact gift shop, and we stood having our photograph taken with each other outside, the sun had burnt off the morning drizzle. It was four o'clock we returned to the hotel and separated until dinner. Mel out 'wandering' with her maps, scouting the city.

"Keep in touch," said Jim, as she went off, sunglasses and walking pumps.

We went up to our room for forty winks. I was out like a light, as soon as Jim turned on the afternoon news programmes, more-than-regularly interspersed with countless advertisements for toppings, chocolate biscuits, ice cream, sweets, snacks, fast food. I could feel my voice fade as I moaned to Jim.

"No wonder they're getting fat."

I forgot to call Morley, distracted by Mel's untamed enthusiasm for Motor City, singing her favourite hits in the car, 'Dancing In The Street', 'Superstition', she knew every word.

Pots and pans were spinning, I felt weightless, flying, the wallpaper

---

[33] chundered in - to demolish beyond repair
[34] caboodle - the whole number or quantity of people or things in question

of 1950s decorative kitchen patterns, flitting. I was reaching out teasing the vinyl - I liked to stroke it - feel the redolence of the eggshell surface, trace the patterns, my youthful nerves stimulated by the texture, recognisable, safe, home. Mum was at the back door, going out, I could smell the perfume, Yardley, well known, not cheap, but not expensive, it could be applied in abundance.

"Nell… ready?" came the deep baritone voice.

My Mum and Dad side by side, her whiteness emphasized with a puff from her gold powder compact. It sat at her dressing table upstairs, in their bedroom. The vanity top white painted wood, not plastic, but so shiny it may as well have been. Atop, an oval mirror, tarnished a bit in places on the edges, but always polished and gleaming. The compact had an oyster design. My hand ran over it, following the shape with my palm, daring not to open it. Caressing the red lipstick holder, the eau-de-toilette sprayers, the gold edged hairbrush, and the elaborate glass cigarette lighter with a geisha girl inside. The voices reverberated great gusts of sound.

"Jason, look after your sister, bed at nine o'clock," and the door slammed behind them, my last sight was Mum's cream kitten heeled dancing shoes and a stocking seam disappearing from view.

"Nina, Nina, it's the lawyer, Morley."

I woke with a start, Jim tapping me on the shoulder. He was holding the phone. I came round and put the earpiece to my head, rushing with nerves from being woken.

"Hello" I said, supporting myself on one elbow.

"Nina I've had trouble getting this information for you. I've done some odd things, but this has to be one of the strangest. I've got the whole low-down, and this is going to cost you more than the usual one hundred and fifty plus VAT."

"Ok," I said, "go ahead."

"There are very approximately six million African Zion Christian Church members," he continued, "with leases, Church revenues, and donations, bringing in around ten million dollars per annum. Plus rents on Zion City leases, especially for the Zion Nuclear Plant, that bring in around ten million dollars a year."

"Who gets it?" I said.

"The beneficiaries in the bankruptcy of Zion Industries. The Zion City Christian Church. Relatives of Voliva. Descendants of one Samuel Stevenson, one Judge Barnes, and various further recipients named in the insolvency from 1942, as well as The City of Chicago, who tried to annexe Zion City in 1958, a controversial agreement allowing them certain rights of independence, in return for modernisation amendments to the constitution of Zion. Residential land with a view of Lake Michigan the most expensive real estate in the area, part of seven thousand odd acres still falling under Zion jurisdiction, sold as lots, with Zion having one thousand year leases on them. Residents pay the leaseholder a yearly fee. It amounts to about a hundred thousand dollars per annum. In total, about twenty million dollars coming in per annum as a result of the various endeavours of Dr Dowie and Voliva. How did you come by this contract Nina?"

I was silent.

"If it is by scurrilous means it will invalidate any claim you may have against Zion. By admitting to owning it, you are admitting to theft - if that's what's happened?" he said accusingly, in that way lawyers have.

"I'll call you back," I said, putting the phone down, "get me a drink Jim, our ship's come in."

I made an appointment with Morley for when we arrived home the following week. He didn't mention Will's son's lawsuit, I guess not to trouble us whilst on holiday.

***

Philip went home aged eight in 1916 to his father's. Once out of remand school, the brothers did everything together, sticking with each other, like a gang. Philip had matured quickly in borstal. Thomas had not visited, and Ettie only twice a year, the experience too painful for her. She struggled to afford the train and cab fare out to the towered, round-windowed Edwardian block, which dominated the surrounding Essex marshlands.

It was four years before Ettie moved from Bridge Cottage to Downham, and it would be another nine years before she was re-united with her sons. Philip was grown up, twenty-one, Raymond

Kweku, born January 1910, was nineteen, and the junior Kwami Daniel born in January 1912 was seventeen. Ettie had made a new life, held down a catering job, obtaining her hygiene certificate. She had not expected the boys, but was not going to turn them away. They had endured schizophrenic behaviour from their domineering father, a fractured life, so were appreciative of the mother's influence. They were tearaways but towed the line in the house.

The three looked different, Philip, the eldest, was darker, inheriting Thomas's hair. Raymond, in the middle, was fairer, completely covered in freckles, and topped with curly copper locks. The youngest, Danny, was auburn, again freckly and an Afro-style ginger mop. They were exotic, tall, acquiring their mother and father's good looks, drawing attention wherever they went.

Philip, Danny and Raymond were never in mainstream employment. Their image and lack of education did not deter them from digging up their own opportunities. They became well known for their weekend parties at Downham, playing jazz and bebop[35] and charging a couple of pennies for entry. The neighbours could not complain because most of them were in attendance. They had never come to terms with their Mum walking out, but they were glad of a regular place to live so the subject was never discussed and Ettie took it all for what it was worth.

Ettie knew about the covenant that Thomas had deposited at Standard Charter Bank in London and made an appointment to see them, taking her original marriage certificate and decree nisi. The bank allowed her to view them but she was unable to take them away because the children were the direct heirs since the divorce. She planned to sell whatever she could, and went over Thomas's diaries, pragmatically avoiding entries about his African wives, relatives and indiscretions, making judicious notes about any assets and pacts signed during his lifetime. Ettie sent letters to Africa and America, to the various lawyers and businesses she had found in the logs. She had no

---

[35] bebop – a type of jazz originating in the 1940s and characterized by complex harmony and rhythms

response. This continued for several years, Ettie having bouts of perseverance, but it led nowhere. She had no experience in this area and was directionless in her search.

In 1939 after numerous enquiries, she had a response from African lawyer Archibald Casely-Hayford, who had negotiated a number of Thomas's business transactions. He was establishing offices in London and was keen to meet Ettie. She attended his office in a mainly run down area of Shoreditch, home to small warehouses, firms linked with the docklands. She wore the last of her smart clothes, a tidy grey outfit, a well-fitted trim jacket finishing above her hips, a skirt down to the top of her ankle boots, and a cream blouse with a tall stiff arrow shirt collar. Ettie still retained some of her figure. Work and worry had kept her in shape.

The office was above a leather-tanning workshop, with the smell of chemicals filtering through. Two rooms were nevertheless well appointed, and Hayford had two Girl Fridays. He was statuesque, as handsome as Thomas but a lighter complexion, intense eyes and his hair cropped close, which made him look more English (Thomas's hair fizzed, never completely tamed by the pampering). Quietly spoken, a soft Gold Coast tinge to his voice, his suit was a slim cut, thin blue piping highlighting the pockets and shoulders. He made a fuss of Ettie, ensuring she had coffee and biscuits and asked her to call him Archie. Once seated, he leaned forward each time he addressed her, laying both palms on the desk, as if to emphasise his point. He spoke at length about Thomas. They had been friends, linked through Archie's tenure as Minister of Agriculture and Natural Recourses on the Gold Coast. It was revelatory, as she knew little of Thomas's alter ego, which he had kept close to his chest. He had been a keen recipient of Archie's knowledge, employing him to act as his legal adviser. Thomas had been methodical, businesslike, educated and studious, a family man, an aeon apart from the dogmatism and chaos that came to dominate his life. Archie said he had been as shocked as everyone else that Thomas had never returned to the Gold Coast. And his jail sentence, intimating it may have been some illness in the mind, as it was certainly out-of-character, not the Thomas he had known.

Ettie, having read the diaries, was cynical about Hayford's view but did not voice her opinion. She was aware of Thomas's flaws when she met him, but young love is blind. Mr Hayford couldn't have known Thomas like she did. Casely described the operations he had set up for Thomas, and Ettie gave over her information. He offered to take on the case, regularise the lands, and register them in the name of the three sons, with her and Hayford as the trustees, taking a third for himself. Ettie promised to think about the proposal. After mulling it for a month she wrote to Archibald Hayford that his percentage was too high. She never heard from him again and the offer lapsed. Ettie remained living in relative poverty. She never recovered, the Box remained redundant, a 'thorn in her side'. Her sons occasionally passed it round, as a curio, but had no grasp of its scope. The country was on the cusp of the Second World War and the past held little consequence.

The 'Brem-Wilsons', Phil, Danny and Raymond, knew only 'hand-to-mouth', 'living it up' one minute, 'on the breadline'[36] the next, never certain where their next job would come from. When work was scarce they went without. The travelling Fairs which came to town lured them like a magnet, and they found work there as didicoys[37]. They started off taking fares on the rides then graduated to the Boxing Booths. They slicked down their hair, wore bespoke brown suits with a fine coloured check line, pencil trousers with lengthy turn-ups that revealed the silk lining, showing off their patent boots, shined to a finish. Custom jackets only buttoned at the bottom hole stressed the silk waistcoat, with ample pockets where they hid the pennies that they would take from punters on the dodgems.

They were prototype Edwardian Boys[38]. Living life in the fast lane, picking up girls where they could and hitching food and money from whoever would oblige. They were high-spirited, with the 'gift of the

---

[36] on the breadline - estimated boundary line, separating an income on which it is just possible to survive from the income that is just less than that
[37] didicoys - one of a group of caravan-dwelling roadside people who live like Gypsies but are not true Romanies
[38] Edwardian Boys - UK post-war period 'Teddy' Boys created the 'first truly independent fashions for young people', they were 'the first teenagers'

gab"[39]. Each played a musical instrument by ear, soaked up from the numerous Ministry duties with their father. Being able to pound out the latest tunes on piano stood them in good stead, culminating in their own 'act', the Wilson Trio, booked for good dates in dance halls, and topping the bill at Catford Town Hall. Danny was the pianist, Phil and Ray tap-dancers, a solid 'all song and dance act', which was in great demand and unusual in Great Britain. By the mid-1900s the popularity of black music and images coming through from America allowed the Wilson Trio some notoriety. They even got booked to mime to the latest minstrel style hits imported from the USA - the first lip-syncing.

"Two for one, two for one!" Came the call. "Survive two rounds with these two strapping fighters, one round with each, only one round, and you win the big one, the cash prize, ten guineas, only one bob entry, one bob entry, two rounds, who's the lucky taker?!"

Danny was holding up Philip and Raymond's arms, either side of him. The electric light bulbs around the front of the makeshift stage flickered, glistening on their brown sweating skins, the array they had enticed alternately jeering and laughing.

"I'll bash ya'. Yer black bastards!" taunts flying.

Danny laughed, continuing his well-spun banter.

"Who can do it, who can try it, anyone who can survive two rounds, one with each, who's the brave man?! Two for one! Two for one!" came the loudhailer. "On the hour every hour!"

Phil and Ray danced round the stage, punching imaginary opponents, goading the herd, jogging backwards, and dancing on the spot. Both wore colourful baggy satin shorts, down to their knees, that shook and shimmered in the stage lamps, they punched their gloves together, and threw their arms in the air, steam rising from their lithe athletic torsos.

"Can you beat them, who's man enough?!"

Girls screamed with delight, swooning at the black physiques, pushing their boyfriends forward.

"Come on Sir, come on stage, you look strong. Are you strong

---

[39] gift of the gab - the ability to talk readily, glibly, and convincingly

enough to survive two rounds?!"

Every man (and even some of the women) wanted a go, and as always, several volunteered. Hod carriers, miners, mill workers, dockers, shipbuilders, working classes, labourers with a few pence to spare came to the Fair, for a night of escapism, a night to remember, a night to lift the spirit from toil and drudgery. Strongmen who could throw Philip and Raymond across a pub in a bar brawl and wiry characters who had a dangerous left hook. Any street fighter or psychopath could be a contender. This was the public at their most raw, the unknown.

Phil and Ray took their lives in their hands for the summer months, skirting the country with the Carnival. Men, strong as oxes, pumped up on beer, came to bash up the interlopers, the outsiders the alien invaders. The brothers, as unfamiliar and tropical as one could find in these backwaters of Britain, Scotland, Wales, Yorkshire, to Cornwall, or Essex. Every 'big fish in a small pond' could have their moment to be the 'king of the castle' and it was a license to print money for the Fair. Not enough to survive on year round, but it kept them afloat until autumn. Playing the game to get by, a hollow timber platform, bright electric filaments strung out above them, and a gaudy red and green banner spanning the front of the wooden stage, covering up the rough boards and temporary scaffold, it's slogan - 'BIG FIGHT NIGHT - The Ding-a-Ling Brothers'.

They had a routine to nurture them through ten performances a day - a formula. Danny was the Master of Ceremonies, armed with a megaphone, not that he needed one - you could easily hear his voice sweeping the showground. He interspersed the repartee with stories and jokes, creating an 'edge'. Once a few punters amassed, more would congregate, and then he had them - animal instinct. They were ready for a scrap even before the show had started, but Danny had control, put on a good act. Once a dozen were up on the rostrum, Danny primed them, making them flex their muscles, showing off to their girlfriends and pals. He encouraged them to bare their chests, posing like bodybuilders. Girls shrieked and men bayed, the contestants strutted as soon as a hint of limelight shone in their direction.

As this played out, Philip and Raymond disappeared, slipping

193

through the slit curtain at the rear of the platform, which backed directly into the tent containing the Boxing Booth. They readied themselves for the ordeal, jumping on the grass, knees up to their chests, and shadow boxing. They were very fit, jogging and training for the daily slog. Philip pulled away; it was time. Wiping the sweat from his forehead with his boxing glove he would start their 'lucky-charm' mantra.

"Be good Bruv'."

"Be good Bruv'," replied Raymond.

A man took money by the side of the stage. Customers flooded into the tent, filling plank benches. Vivid bare down-lighters illuminated the rough-and-ready ring, a set of boards nailed together each night, buffed to a shine by the increasing army of aggressors' clogs, boots, and hobnails, and surrounded by a thick rope on four sides, a post hammered into the ground at each corner. Danny lined up the potential protagonists on the front bench. He memorised their names, calling them out in-between the rounds, so they could not 'bottle out'[40], sustaining the interest, eliciting squeals of approval from their supporters, skilfully manipulating the drama. Phil and Ray deftly played their parts, swift changeovers - one brother staying out-of-sight, as the other jumped in the ring. Between fights Danny and the doorman (the Boxing Booth owner), would remove the contestant's gloves, quickly lacing them on the next man, take off his shirt, placing it on his stool in the ring corner in an animated flourish, acted out with great panache.

Philip or Raymond would dance round the ring, building the room into frenzy. They had to work at it, stringing out the performance, as two women went round selling refreshments, and a man took penny bets. One woman had small greaseproof bags twisted at the top, filled with salted nuts (but mostly salt), for half a penny. The other balanced beer, mainly froth, a couple of pence for a pint. She constantly refilled 'Dixie Cups' or paper cups, (usually robbed from local hospitals), pint-pots being too dangerous. She took them on a huge tray, nimbly making the transaction. It was tough work, but it paid well for gypsy

---

[40] bottle out - fail to perform a promised or planned action due to lack of courage

194

girls. Thousands and thousands of pennies rolled in every week, many landing up with the brothers, who were courting most of the girls working in the tents, and using the 'Brem-Wilson' charm to make sure they received a cut of everything in the Booth shows. The owner turned a blind eye; it was 'par for the course'[41], an unwritten perk. Salty nuts, raucousness, and the sauna conditions of the marquee made the patrons drink more, guaranteeing the travellers had plenty of money coming in through these favourable months.

"Laydiieezz, and gentlemen."

Danny strung it out, the hailer up to his sweaty lips, wiping his face with a trademark spotted handkerchief in a flamboyant flurry, elongating every word and each action becoming a grand gesture.

"Miisstteerrr Phileepp Brrr..emm-Wiilllsssoonn!"

He slid his voice down and back up, savouring every morsel.

"He's the dancer, the prancer, the Lamber of Lambeth, the Destroyer of Deptffooorrd, all the way from London tooowwwn."

Philip bounced into the ring, arms raised, facing the audience on every side of the ropes, posturing, African drums coming from somewhere at the back, a fairground girl had put on a gramophone. The doorman kept the rival on his stool making a big deal of massaging his shoulders, and prepping him up. Danny collected him, holding up the fighter's arms in the centre of the ring and bellowing.

"Keep it clean, no kicking, nothing below the belt, secooonds outeeer, roundeeeerrr one!"

The doorman clanging the bell. They started, Philip instantly bouncing backwards, the thick-necked thug on the offensive. Philip scanned his opponent, shimmied the length of the ring, ending up behind the ruffian. He spun and lurched against the rope both arms punching the air, baiting the unruly horde. They booed they were livid. The ruffian jabbed away at Philip, who reversed as fast as the man could attack. The adversary was puffing, his aimless blows raining down on an empty space where Philip's face should have been. The audience was on their feet, even women howling expletives. Philip was the 'boxer', fast and lithe, he virtually never needed to throw a punch,

---

[41] par for the course - to be expected; normal; common; usual

as he jiggled round the podium, more often than not facing the spectators, waving, his fists machine-gunning an imaginary challenger. He tippy-toed, he danced, slid, rocked from side to side, choreographed to drive the opponent to distraction and whip up the boisterous thirsty throng.

'Ding! Ding!' came the bell, the challenger was red in the face, breathless, frustrated, the doorman sympathetically positioning him to his corner, giving encouragement, and using his shirt taken from the stool to wipe his sweating body. The Boxing Booth manager would not afford the challenger the luxury of a towel or drink. Danny picked up the pace.

"Place you Bets! Place your Bets! One more round to go, the Bermondzzeee Batteerrrrerrr, the Ilfooord Anniiaaalaatooor, Mmmiisssttterrrr, Raayyyymuuuaanndddd, Brrremmm-Wiiillllsssooonn!" Again the protracted vibration of his larynx stretching the announcements, eking out the words, extending the break.

Philip Brem-Wilson 1935

Raymond was up, and the competitor jettisoned from his corner. Ray juxtaposed Philip, no dancing, he hailed down blows - the man did not have a hope. The spectators whooped and bawled, directing the victim to throw more punches, return the tirade, to lessen the impact by moving out of the way in a direction of their instruction, but he could not hear, his ears were ringing from the cauliflowers that had been placed there by Raymond's searing leather mitts.

The players' bench should have emptied, the likely challengers realising their fate, should have cut their losses at this point, seeing the game unfurl in front of them. They were too busy thinking how much better *they* could do. This was the show. Philip setting them up with his gyrations, quashing any skill the challengers thought they possessed in the fighting department with his compliment of 'ducking and diving'. Then Ray the fighter, coming in for the 'clean up'[42]. The Sunday-best shirt sitting on the ringside stool mopped the bloodied noses. Wherever they pitched up, Joe Bloggs[43] would fall for the same tricks, almost appreciating being fleeced for a few moments, taken out of the 'humdrum'[44], and the 'Brem-Wilsons' obliged.

They grew up as showmen, athletes, fighters, musicians, singers, dancers, comedians, storytellers, and orators. Their father had given everything away, and it was their desire to claw something back. They were sassy, uninhibited, vibrant... they were renaissance men... Soul-Survivors[45].

Autumn, October 1940, was to be a different homecoming from the Fair. The boys return to Downham was to be the last as they knew it, their disorganised formative years permanently interrupted. They got home via a day-out in the West End, a visit to Savile Row to buy themselves handmade suits, and winter coats at Harrods. Astrakhan with cream mink collars, and a pair of boots each, shining patent leather and pointed toes. They kept a little something back for their

---

[42] clean up – to win easily, make 'a killing'
[43] Joe Bloggs – as John Doe: a hypothetical average man
[44] humdrum - lacking excitement or variety; dull; monotonous
[45] Soul Survivor – (Urban) one who is down on his luck for whatever reason; one who is ready to die, be able to make it through in the street and in constant scuffles with the law, and succeeds in living the lavish life that everybody wants - as described in Young Jeezy's track 'Soul Survivor'

mother, but hardly enough, Danny, Ray and Phil were never thinking about tomorrow. They had style and that is what counted. Ettie was overjoyed to see them grateful for the few pounds they put in the pot on the table. Sharing hugs and kisses, they sat round their father's old wooden table (the only item left from their first house at Hither Green), and recounted their fairground tales to Ettie, who was more than pleased to listen to their anecdotes. She too had glorious stories from her own promising theatre career, but was happy to indulge them. Two pots of tea and some Garibaldi biscuits later, Ettie pulled three letters from her apron front pocket.

"I'm sorry these have arrived," she said, and handed the envelopes over.

Each had the Home Office seal. It was their conscription. They had kept the War to the back of their minds. Ettie was crushed by the news, now they were here in the flesh, the boys re-assuring her.

"Mum, we'll be ok. You know us, we can look after ourselves."

Such words being recited in thousands of homes up and down the country. Ettie felt heartened by their warmth, embracing each of her sons in turn. They had dinner. That night, the three young men were ready to go dancing - the 'call up' forgotten for now.

In three weeks they attended the medical and signing up induction at Rochester Town Hall. The orders had said to 'bring a small case with essential items, you may be asked for immediate service to the United Kingdom Armed Forces'. Danny, Raymond, and Philip turned up empty-handed, being of the opinion that the Government should supply them with everything. Danny was retained, sent straight off to Aldershot Barracks for two weeks training, then France. The medical was quick, a test for venereal disease, questions about anal intercourse and sexual preferences, basic eyesight, flat feet, so on. Philip exaggerated his limp with a stick, along with a dodgy letter from the doctor confirming an accident when he was fourteen years old, invalided by being run over by a taxicab. He was sent to a row of seats up against the stage to wait for his orders.

Raymond had produced a letter stating that he was a 'Conscientious Objector', which he had got off a lawyer in Lewisham for five guineas, apparently the mark of a notary was required to validate the reason for abstaining from military service. As soon as he presented it to the stern looking official at the recruitment desk, the Sergeant blared.

"Yellow, take him out and give him his feather!"

The Officer in charge beckoned with his stick, and blasted.

"Coward coming through!" Ray was escorted to a side room and beaten by Corporals, two tough Military Police laid into him, battering his body, and nothing about the face.

"That's what you get for being a nigger coward!"

Insults were thrown in. He knew better than to retaliate, realising this type of punishment (which he'd had from his Dad), would only get worse if any action was taken. He kept his head down and his arms in his lap, to cover his balls. Philip could hear the commotion as did the recruits in the hall, and could do nothing for his brother. When Raymond emerged, he was shoved over to sit in the same row as Philip. Philip made a place for him pushing up a little, and putting his arm round Raymond as he sat down. Raymond bent over clutching his abdomen and coughed up some blood into a hanky that Philip had given him.

"C'mon bruv', we'll be all right." whispered Philip.

"I'm not sure," came the reply.

Both of them were conscripted to civilian roles, the Non-Combatant Corps, cleaning up after bomb strikes on London, driving the heavy plant to clear roads, moving hardcore and debris left by nightly raids. Raymond had to attend a tribunal hearing three weeks after the submission of his letter to confirm his objection to military service. Once a jailable offence, by the Second World War restrictions had been relaxed and Ray was told to work with his brother on the excavators. There had been a small huddle outside the Court hearing. A single magistrate, a circuit judge at Southwark Crown Court, heard statements. A couple of reporters, from the South London Times were taking photographs of the dissenters, the few onlookers yelling cowards, scum, 'Conscies'[46]. When Raymond came out they switched

---

[46] Conscies - conscientious objectors simply did not want to fight in World War One - known as 'conscies' or C.Os they were a sign that not everybody was as enthusiastic about the war as the government would have liked

to racist taunts. He lowered his head and shoved off to Bermondsey, toward the Old Kent Road, where he could get a bus out to Kent, and Downham. He ran, navigating Jamaica Road, cutting through Rotherhithe New Road. Though familiar with the turf he felt uncomfortable, it being notorious for 'toughs', he drew a few 'looks'. Raymond could look after himself but felt vulnerable after the Court Hearing.

Philip and Raymond learnt to drive in a day's training on a site in Silvertown. They were issued heavy-duty overalls, tin hats, gas masks (which restricted normal breathing, and were rendered hopeless when threatened with gas), and standard issue leather lace up boots. They had to go to the corner of Downham Way and Old Bromley Road at nine o'clock every night; to be picked up by an officer in charge of the South East London area, in an old green army issue ambulance, that had been converted with thick solid rubber tyres, and a huge diesel engine, which allowed it to get in and out of the danger areas. They sat in a hut on wasteland at Vauxhall, just off Kennington Park Road, waiting for the overhead hum of Hitler's strikes, a terrifying silence followed by a dull thud somewhere, where a bomb had hit. The phone rang, the Officer answered 'Airressu', the words 'Heavy Rescue' compacted into one continuous phrase from repetition. He replaced the receiver, affixing a magnetic dot on a big board map of London on the wall, and gave the orders.

"Coons to Plumstead."

Typically, Philip and Raymond would get theirs early on, with the road, and the equipment they were to take. The twenty in the hut were gradually deployed through the night until the whole shebang[47] was out. The team covered an expanse, right out to the suburbs, equipped with heavy machinery, diggers, earthmovers, pneumatic jackhammers, barrows, and spades. It was grim, digging bodies out, dead, often in pieces, blown apart, contrary to the publicity that sustained the country's morale. They worked with ambulance crews and firemen to get London mobile after the relentless hammering from the nightly

---

[47] shebang – a situation, organization, contrivance, or set of facts or things: organized and ran the whole shebang

doodlebugs. The racial slurs did not bother the brothers, they were used to it. They mucked in together, and the co-workers knew no different, it was standard 'fare', the teasing that lightened the harrowing duty. Philip and Raymond were glad to be out of the front line war, judging by the infrequent letters from Danny, it was not a place anyone would want to be.

In 1940 the lines in France were pounded by heavy artillery and Danny was involved in bloody skirmishes with the advancing Germans. There was no prejudice here, the soldiers levelled by terror. Danny was temporarily sectioned; 'shell-shock' from the constant battering of enemy missiles landed him in hospital. He was sent back to the front, injured, and then an American doctor botched his operation in the field by severing his jugular vein. Danny died in France. As a black man he received no medals, and no posthumous service Award. Britain classified him as 'persona non grata'.

Philip and Raymond sat on the doorstep at Downham, shoulder's bent, one with his arm round the other. They had lost a part of themselves. Ettie exhibited little grief in front of her sons, holding strong, she did not cry or show emotion like Phil or Ray. Danny's body was taken out to Brookwood Cemetery in Surrey, on the Necropolis Railway line at night, straight from France carried with the other dead from Europe via a discrete terminus at Waterloo. The family attended the short service that was amongst dozens of others that day. It was a chink in the boys' armour, as Danny had been a guardian, the clever one.

Any lost confidence was regained in bravado. Life resumed, the pounding bombs, music, girls, and a scam where they could. Philip and Raymond continued their 'tealeaf'[48] activities, grabbing an opportunity with a scheme in the Heavy Rescue Service. They had a reputation as the hardest working pair and were invariably first on the scene, where houses were annihilated by German bombs, they were able to scramble through the rubble with their torches and ransack possessions, food, and money, before the ambulance or fire crews arrived. They hoiked

---

[48] tea-leaf – (rhyming slang) - thief

out the dead, and took ration books, later to be sold on to a 'fence'[49], who altered the names and cashed in the stamps for provisions. They did not think of it as wrong, but as a public service. The newspapers were reporting a rosy home front but they never found anyone alive on a bombsite. With shifts of seven nights on and four days off, they had plenty of opportunity to spend the extra money they were earning. They were able to go out, to the dancehalls. Philip had his eyes firmly set on a new lady, and started courting. A lot of provisions ended up at home, Ettie benefiting, so there were incremental improvements to their daily existence.

Philip Brem-Wilson and children, Nina right, 1940

The War had given Raymond and Philip driving licenses, regular work, extra income and brought them into mainstream society. They suffered isolated pockets of racism but it had no effect, as they were popular with a mix of friends, and had almost finally thrown off the

---

[49] fence – a dealer in stolen property

shackles of their lunatic father. The Box was inert, firmly closed, hidden under Ettie's small brass bed at the 'two-up-two-down' at Downham. They never saw it nor had any desire to delve into it. They made their own luck, not constricted by traits of the past, or their father, his legacy was dormant, they lived outside of the jurisdiction of the Box. They had no thoughts of Africa, or ancestry; unburdened, free, black men in Great Britain. Their brother had died for the preservation of democracy, that which allowed them *their* liberty. The puzzles and questions of the Box were unwanted and it sat collecting dust for a generation.

❀

We went back to Orlando, had another week in the sun. Jimmy couldn't use the credit card, so we settled in cash and travellers cheques. We departed without a glitch. We'd arrived at the airport early, returning the car to the Hertz lot, but we weren't detained, and our bags weren't searched. Perhaps the Zion Police department had lost interest over such a minor incident.

It was 13th August 1985, we were glad to get home; collecting the old Daihatsu from the long-term car park on the outskirts of Heathrow Airport, a particularly dingy looking industrial estate on the perimeter road, surrounded by hangars, catering firms and logistics company warehouses that service the vast straggling London Air terminus. It was a slate grey afternoon, three o'clock, a little bit of autumn rain, but I was grateful to get out in the fresh air after the eight-hour flight. Jim dropped Mel at her house in Godstone on the way back. We took the A21 road off the M25 motorway; it felt dainty after the breadth of American freeways and took a while to adjust to the compactness of our car and the limited road space. When we pulled in to our drive we bumped down the potholes of the un-made country lane that led up to our house.

"Weather's got them, I'll have to drop a few bricks in them next year," said Jim.

"Yeah, yeah!" I replied, and before I could say get anything else my jaw dropped. There was a posse of cars and people at the end of the lane, outside our metal gates.

"What the hell's this?" said Jim, slowing down.

He stopped a little distance from them. I picked up the Box; the old leather attaché had been sitting next to me, my first instinct, to make sure I had hold of it. We both got out, cameras flashed, everyone clamouring like a pack of hyenas. I still had sunglasses stuck on my head, they hadn't really moved since Orlando becoming buried in my hair, and I hoisted them down over my eyes, the flares blinding.

"What's happening with the court case Nina?"

"Anything to say about the impending court case?"

"C'mon Nina, do you have a reaction? Aren't you guilty of your cousin's murder? How do you feel about a trial in Britain?"

"Are you a murderer?"

"Are you a murderer?!"

"Are you a murderer?!!"

The interrogations were babble, a roar, Jim was shouting and pushing. I held the Box up to protect myself. Jim was in front, pushing paparazzi out of the way. Microphones were stuffed in front of my mouth, questions booming in my ears. I was empty, floating, back in my Mum and Dad's kitchen, feeling the wallpaper again, the sheen against my finger ends, and I seemed to blot out the din and fly through. Jim was tugging my arm and we were at the gates, facing the grey metal railings, I looked down and saw him fumbling with his keys for the lock.

"What the f***!" came Jim's voice came above everyone else's eliciting a momentary silence amongst the rabble.

There was a fat chain and padlock through the railings and an official looking warrant that had been laminated in plastic and tied on with wire. I looked at it and read: 'A Charging Order made against Ms Brem-Wilson, 13 August 1985, by order of Rother District Council, the property reference…' and on it went. Jim shook the metal chain with such velocity I thought for a second that he *could* break it. He was blazing. I don't think I'd ever seen him so angry. He looked up and screamed.

"F*****' c***!"

The melee went crazy, flashes repeating, demanding, more quizzing.

With some effort I pulled Jim off the gate, his fists remained clenched. He looked upward, face green in the fading afternoon rain, mottled skin sparkling from the continuous sulphuric illuminations. It was the straw that broke the camel's back. I dragged him away, a sick sensation of guilt engulfing me. I hadn't driven in ten years, not since I'd met Jim. He was the driver, the driving force, the man who took the wheel. Nothing subsided. This must be how The Beatles and Rolling Stones must have felt at the height of hysteria, trapped. I literally had to push Jim in to the passenger seat, and grab the keys off him. I was on autopilot Jim slumped in his seat, the life drained out of him.

"F*****' 'ell."

I muttered and hit reverse, not even looking behind to see if there was anyone there. I bashed something, I didn't care, the bulbs still popping, and I wrestled the control into forward, spun round and sped off down the lane. There was no concern for the suspension. No one came after us.

"All the sixes, sixty six, two fat ladies, eighty eight."

The cigarette smoke hung in the air. They said that when London smog had been at its worse during the Industrial Revolution, it would seep into homes, penetrating any gap, dangerous particles impeding breathing, bringing London to a standstill. So bad you couldn't see your arm in front of your eyes. I invariably thought my Dad's Bingo nights at the Rivoli Ballroom were a bit like that. Impossible to escape the dozens of ladies with fags in hand, smoke billowing, they knew no better, they'd puffed since teens. First, a crafty one behind the bike sheds to impress the boys then, decades on, coughing up soot in the mornings, trying to scrub the blot off their fingers at the sink, carbolic, cold water and forty a day. Sometimes I looked out across the Rivoli, red velveteen and thick bouncy carpets, conditioned by years of spilt beer and daily hoovering, and thought it kept them in one piece, puffing on and on. Lives, so blighted by work, poor lifestyle, poor housing, and drudgery, the fags ramshackled them like a rotting shed held up with creeping ivy. Cigarettes were special oxygen that kept them breathing. It's what the National Health Service was invented for. Middle-aged women in plastic see-through scarves (to protect their grey and pink perms from the almost permanent South London drizzle); they'd paid weekly, a new fangled National Insurance deducted directly from their factory wage slips. Little did they know they'd need it when they were sixty years old, to pay for a painful death, cancer eating away at the larynx.

I must admit my mind did wander sometimes when I was helping my Dad! Five hundred sandwiches to make for the breaks, I had to get through it somehow. I always had a rich imagination, and liked a story. The Bingo Hall had a story worth telling, and needed no embellishments. It had been a few years since the very last London smog. You could see the thick tobacco fumes hanging over the roof-space like a liquid ready to pour down, at least they had their plastic hats at the ready, and I laughed out loud.

"What you laughin' at Nina, get those bloody sandwiches made will ya!" Came the ringing sound of my Mum's voice.

"That's going to be on my gravestone." I mumbled.

As the glutinous warmed-up butter splayed across six slices at once, I had a method, no hanging around in the buttering department, I said to myself, 'here lies Nina Brem-Wilson, died aged one hundred and twenty, expert sandwicher, and fantastically successful business woman to boot', visualising the enormous marble gravestone and sniggering.

My Dad, Philip Brem-Wilson started up Bingo nights at the Rivoli Ballroom, and advertised them around, with posters on hoardings and lamp-posts, leaflets shoved though doors, handed them out outside the Peek Freans biscuit factory at Bermondsey, and the railway station at New Cross. He knew his potential audience. He pumped everything into it. He'd had second-rate jobs since the War, a bit of plastering, casual building work, but mainly the 'fruit and veg' stall at Bellingham. The stall was by no means a proper 'pitch', he had no license with the council to trade there, but he'd been on the spot for so long nobody ever bothered him. It was an expanding stall, it got bigger and bigger over the years, he was taking liberties. It was a good place on the corner of Randlesdown Road and Bellingham Road, outside Reeves & Co. which was a haberdashers that stocked everything, an old fashioned department store. Maybe they'd complained, because my Dad received twenty-pound notices every week from the police, which was coming to a lot of money. The end of the line came when I was working there one Saturday, helping him out. The police arrived in a squad car, and issued another fine. He packed up and never went back. It was the 'last nail in the coffin'.

Philip was jobless with a family to support, and the future looked uncertain. We couldn't survive on my Mum's job as a factory worker at Wray's Optical Works, in Ashgrove Road, off of Bromley Hill. His brother Raymond had been working for a number of years at a small billiard hall at the bottom of Downham Way, where they also had 'Bingo' nights. Ray kept telling Philip how much money the boss was making. Ray also heard on the grapevine that the Rivoli Ballroom at Brockley was being let on Wednesday nights for twenty five pounds and suggested Philip have a go at Bingo there. Philip took the plunge, persuading my husband Alfie to loan him the two hundred pounds deposit needed to put down. Philip rented the rooms, purchased tickets, cards and benches. There was no proper seating in there, only tables round the edges, as it was a dancehall. Don't ask me why Alfie would lend my Dad money; he must have thought there was something in it. The first night they planned refreshments for a couple of dozen potential gamblers, the Hall could hold four hundred and fifty. Seven hundred turned up. As quick as a flash the landlord offered Philip more nights, making it clear that if he didn't take them, his sons would run Bingo on those evenings, in competition. Philip took them and his fate was sealed for the next ten years. This was the first proper money for Philip since the days of the 'Heavy Rescue', and he played it for every penny.

It was a complete craze, as there were virtually no Bingo Halls in 1960. 'Top Ranks', and vast Bingo emporiums were at the starting block. My Dad had the talent, and in no time the Hall was heaving nearly every night of the week. It wasn't just the Bingo, my Dad, as the host, made it a spectacle, entertainment 'bar none'. It was him they came to see. Little old biddies thought he was their best friend, or the boyfriend they might have had. They didn't care what colour he was. Philip Brem-Wilson was pure charisma, and he turned the Hall into a goldmine. He brought in slot machines for the breaks, fixed in his favour, giving limited payouts, essentially creaming hundreds each week. He gave away prizes galore, a dozen or so joints of meat in a raffle, food essentials, numerous winners, each leaving happy, but still a good profit for Philip. He helped local pensioners, organising day trips to Margate and became a celebrity with publicity galore, pictures of him smiling with little old ladies in the dailies. Philip was the prodigal son for hundreds, if not thousands, of women (and fellas), in South London, acquiring the moniker 'Mr Bingo'. It was so busy, the whole family had to help, and he ended up employing fifteen in the business.

I was twenty-four, with a baby on the way, and was glad to get out of my job at C&A department store as payroll clerk at the Oxford Street head offices. The commute cost as much as my wages. The Bingo Hall turned it around for everyone; even my husband was working there after his full day shift at the Royal Albert Docks. When the cry came up 'House'[50] Alfie would wake up from snoozing at the back of the Hall (he was permanently tired from his five a.m. shifts), to run over and check the numbers on the winning card. He'd shout up to the stage the numbers crossed off, and the call would come back from Philip confirming them. His second job was to sell the 'parcels', strange ill-gotten goods that my Dad had come by. They may have fallen 'off the back-of-a-lorry'[51], often bizarre items, such as black Christmas stockings, and a talking doll, that, when you pulled the string on the back, spoke Latvian (or something like it). It didn't matter as it was like Christmas every night for us.

My Mum would be in the Box Office. She liked taking the entry money. As soon as I'd sold the sandwiches in the break, I had to quickly run into the back and change into my glad rags[52], to start working the 'cards' table as the croupier. It was hectic, mad, raking it

---

[50] House - (in Bingo) the cry of "house!" shouted by the winner of a game, probably from full house
[51] off the back of a lorry – also fall off the truck, means stolen goods, articles whose origin is not strictly legal
[52] glad rags – clothes for a special occasion, one's best clothes

in[53]. Along with the sandwiches and acting as croupier, my brother and I had the job of counting and bagging up the pennies from the machines in the back room at closing time. There were mountains it would take us forever.

Dad and Mum bought a spacious five-bedroom detached house in the middle class area of Bromley, and life was very good, with their 'pride and joy' powder blue Mercedes Benz Estate parked outside.

Philip Brem-Wilson found a cheaper 'cash-and-carry' to buy stock, his Bingo raffle prizes. It was run by one Johnny Bradbury; Phil had no idea that he was a 'front man' for the 'Richardson Brothers'. Charlie and Eddie were East End gangsters who ran 'rackets'[54] terrorizing South London. They were permanently locked in a turf war[55] with their counterparts the 'Krays', prolific sadistic gangland bosses during this era. Philip always paid cash, wads of notes, and Johnny Bradbury duly reported this back. The weeks that Philip came buying, Johnny would start up conversation and be chatty with him. They became friendly and he invited Phil to one of the Richardson's clubs, Mr Smith's at Rushey Green, Catford. It was there he met them.

The Richardsons were charming, nothing like crooks. Looking the part, modish, and erudite, they projected an image of successful businessmen, not the sordid torturers that they were. It was vogue for celebrities to 'hob-nob'[56] with villains, and Philip loved this. He went drinking with them, going to West End clubs. Steadily, they ingratiated him, giving him gifts, and taking him out to star studded evenings. Philip liked the attention and felt he was living the 'high life'. He may have known about their darker side and chosen to ignore it, or perhaps he liked the notoriety. Either way it was destined go bad. The blood

---

[53] raking it in – to acquire money in large amounts
[54] rackets – 'protection racket' is an extortion scheme whereby a criminal group or individual coerces other less powerful entities to pay money, allegedly for protection services against external threats (usually violence or property damage)
[55] turf war - an acrimonious dispute between rival groups over territory or a particular sphere of influence
[56] hob-nob – mix socially, especially with those of higher social status

brothers were psychopathic 'users', their minds on one thing.

Predictably, they asked Philip to come in on a business venture. With the fraternising, nights 'on the town', and compliments, Philip was obliged. It was a bogus company and they were using him to 'front' it. They told him it was a bona fide enterprise and they would be 'silent partners'. It was 'Long Firm', that is long-term fraud. A company would be set up with a legitimate businessman at the helm. The company would conduct normal commerce, build lines of credit, and sooner or later place a large order on credit. The goods would be sold, the money pocketed, and the company would suddenly disappear. Philip had final signature on the cheques. Soon the Richardsons were forging his signature and the company was sued for fraud. The police had been after the gang for years, and needed little excuse to delve into the company accounts. Philip was taken in by the police, two CID and four officers arriving at the Bromley house, in two cars, early one morning. They waited an hour whilst Philip shaved and dressed. Nellie was polite as punch to the police, taking them tea and toast on the drive, she trusted Phil because he'd done so well.

"It's a lot of fuss," she told everyone, "be over in a jiff."

Deep down her stomach churned. Philip was in a Catch-22, if he 'snitched'[57] on the Richardsons, they'd kill him, and if he didn't, the police would prosecute him for fraud resulting in a lengthy jail term.

After a day of 'buttering up' from the detectives at Lewisham station, and the promise of police protection, Philip decided to be a witness against the Richardsons, having to take a chance to stay out of jail and keep his livelihood. The police wanted names, the characters involved, and the 'comings-and-goings' of the gangland bosses. They knew my Dad was a hapless pawn in the whole affair, took pity on him and made an amnesty if he would help send 'The Torture Gang' down. The police escorts were needed straight away, as that Sunday afternoon there was a phone call, a threat. From then on in, he was put under protective custody until the trial. We were scared, but that's how life was. If truth were told we were terrified. There was constant police

---

[57] snitched – informed on someone

security day and night, two plain-clothed 'coppers'[58] went everywhere with him, even to the Bingo Hall. Both policemen became well known fixtures with the customers.

You couldn't escape the prevailing cloud of syndicated crime and corruption if you were working in gaming, or making as much money as my Dad in South London in the 1960s. When I conjure up the episode it's through a filtered lens, as I prefer the idea that Dad was looking out for the business by becoming linked to the Richardsons. He would be aware that one of the fraternities would rear their ugly head and come calling for their slice of the pie, to cream off the slots, protection money, with a couple of heavies collecting their due each week. Why would he get involved with a gang like that? He must have known, everybody knew them. If he mingled in their circle, perhaps he'd be left alone, immune, protected. An endearing perspective, but the fact was that he was probably as shallow as the next man, his star shining for a few moments. I still like to think that Dad came out of it with his self-respect intact, that he was upstanding, and I didn't doubt his integrity. The Richardsons weren't exactly folk heroes and their reign was short-lived. My Dad *was* a 'player' and they were nothing, he had a respectable business, he worked hard and built up a reputation. It rubbed off on me, made me determined to create something, to make my own way, be independent, a 'going concern'. I wanted to engender that in my family - a Brem-Wilson trait.

It wasn't often Dad talked about times with his father, except to spin a tale, or make a joke of it but I knew it had been difficult, a rough upbringing, his incarceration at an early age. He was resilient and this wasn't going to beat him. I'd never seen him with the Box. He thought I didn't know about it, but of course, I'd rifled through it as a girl, taking the keys down from the parlour wall, hung from a nail, having to stand on a chair to get them.

The weekend before the final trial the Box was on the pullout oak parlour table. I walked in on him. I'd visit in the afternoon for tea, before the Saturday stint at the Rivoli.

---

[58] coppers – police officers

Nina Brem-Wilson, monkey! Philip Brem-Wilson, Brighton, 1956

Philip Brem-Wilson, Brighton, 1956

Nina & Philip Brem-Wilson, Brighton, 1956

Philip Brem-Wilson and son, working the Bingo Hall, from the Kentish
Mercury newspaper, 1961

Left to right; B-movie & TV Star (name unknown), Joe Copeland (car dealer),
Frankie Howard (comedian) and Philip Brem-Wilson
(others unknown), circa 1962

Philip Brem-Wilson 'Bingo King', Lewisham Borough News, with the winner of Bingo Bonus (lady called Christine the German!) 1962

Left to right - Jack Solomons the fight promoter (of Henry Cooper) and boxing manager, Joe Copeland (car dealer), Philip Brem-Wilson, 1962

Left – right: (blonde unknown), Janet Whatmore, (man unknown),
Philip Brem-Wilson, Freddy Whatmore, Nina Brem-Wilson, Maureen and
Les Elkins, party - Bromley Court Hotel, 1962

Left – right: (1st man unknown), Freddy Whatmore, Philip Brem-Wilson
and son, (man unknown) party - Bromley Court Hotel, 1962

Nina Brem-Wilson (right) with mother Nellie at her 50th birthday party, 1964

Philip Brem-Wilson (right) with Police C.I.D detectives guarding him during
the trial of East End gangsters 'The Richardsons' where Philip acted as a
witness - attending a dinner function, 1967

Philip and Nellie Brem-Wilson, C.I.D Police guard detective 'Chick' Fowler
and wife attending a dinner/dance at Bromley Court Hotel, 1967

The two bluebottles[59] sat out the front, one on a chair by the door, the other in the car, door open and facing each other, smoking. They knew my routine.

"All right Nina, ready for work?"

The same-old-same-old. I wandered in; Mum was out shopping with a friend at Lewisham market. I think my Dad expected me to walk through, as he didn't say hello, and no cuddle.

"Hello Dad, what's going on?" but he gazed down at the Box.

"Nina, don't tell your Mum, she doesn't like me getting this out," he said.

Then he breathed a long breath, and slid out his gold cigarette lighter, ready to light a cigarette, holding it in mid-air, but neglecting to take the cigarette packet out, standing motionless. I could tell he was thinking about his father, and I had that empty wrenching feeling in my gut that became more familiar as I got older.

"If it all goes rotten next week, take this, it's locked in the cupboard under the stairs, left in some boxes at the back."

I didn't need to know where the key was as it had always been in the same place. He stood, more morose than I'd ever seen him (he was virtually always good humoured), looking down, the limp afternoon sun filtering in through the net curtains on to his dark skin. Philip was always smart, a suit and tie, and buttoned waistcoat. He touched the Box a bit, training his finger along the little space where the jewel used to be for the elephant's eye, the carving on the top.

"It's got diaries and whatnot, about the family, my Dad, land, I've put my deeds in there too."

He walked over to me, ruffling my hair, which he'd done since I was a baby, and left the room.

"Put it back for me doll."

Even though it wasn't the first occasion I'd lifted the lid, I could smell it's history as it creaked, the gold hinges worn. I flitted around inside, fascinated as I'd been when I was a small child. It was like a box

---

[59] bluebottles - a derogatory British term for policeman that may have derived from Cockney rhyming slang and from the action of police when responding to a serious incident, as "swarming like Bluebottle's", or blowflies

of irresistible sweets, or delving into a secret world. I'd been charmed, as soon as I laid eyes on it. I could hear ladies' voices in the kitchen. I closed it, took the keys lying next to it, and went and locked it back under the stairs.

We were with our lawyer, Mr Morley, sat in the warren of barristers' chambers, and briefs' cubbyholes at Lincoln's Inn Fields. You couldn't park anywhere near the place, so we'd got the train to Charing Cross from Mel's house in Godstone, Surrey and walked from Aldgate. It was the only property that didn't have a charging order on it, since I'd put it in her name. After the disastrous night we stayed there. Our credit cards had been stopped and we couldn't check in to a hotel. We were down, back at the bottom rung of the ladder, living with my daughter.

Luke Brem-Wilson, Will's son had wangled a Judge to freeze my assets pending the Civil case, and of course the tabloids had got hold of it. 'She-Devil Killer Embezzlement Family Shame' and 'Ice Queen Steals Family Millions' ran the headlines in the press - what I'd expected, but devastating. Jim was still reeling; he never got over the house being taken. He wanted to go and cut the chain with an angle grinder one night to get the van back, but I insisted it would make things worse.

Mr Morley's certificates and qualifications hung framed from the mahogany picture rail, honoured member of associations, Law Society affiliated. Morley, ironically originally recommended by Lord Allens, erudite and florid as ever.

"Oh Nina, Nina, how are we going to get you out of this mess?" he asked, as if it was a small spillage in a supermarket checkout aisle that needed mopping up.

"I want to know how you're going to get us out of this, and how much it's going to cost Mr Morley?" was my reply.

I was particularly bolshy[60]. I had no reason to be stroppy, as I

---

[60] bolshy – as Bolshevik - emotionally charged term used to refer to extreme radicals or revolutionaries

couldn't really afford Morley at the moment and he knew it, so in a way he was working for free based on my past earning power. Also, I hadn't paid the last few bills, so he would have to invest some more time to get his money back. Maybe he knew something I didn't, my mind was working ten to the penny as I sat looking up at the panelled ceiling and expensive gold detail painted in the alcoves.

"Oh Nina, Nina," he said again and sighed a considerable sigh. "There are two issues. One of the claims from Will's son, getting your assets released, the forthcoming court case, for which I have been preparing a defence. Two, this very interesting document," and he held up the contract from the Zion Church.

"I need to kill two birds with one stone Mr Morley," I said, "I need to get Luke Brem-Wilson off my back, if he wants my assets he can have them and I'll start again from fresh, and then I need to get my share of the money from Zion without giving any to Luke, or his clan."

Jim looked straight at me, startled I'd offered up the house to Luke, but I'd only this minute thought of it.

"Hmmmm, interesting," said Morley.

Swivelling in his leather chair, contemplating the racks of legal books from floor to ceiling, he got up, his voluminousness no longer hidden by the huge veneered desk. He removed a book from about half way up the shelves, and started reading, murmuring, not addressing us. I could tell Jim was thoroughly hacked off. He would have voted to go home, albeit Mel's home, he'd prefer to be in front of the television watching the rugby. It had been getting too much for him, but he wouldn't leave my side whatever happened.

"You have to ensure you have the ownership for the lands at Tuasi and Assor Brompon wrapped up, but I can't see you getting anywhere with Stamnex and B.W.P's current occupation there, and with the lawsuit from Luke Brem-Wilson. Our chance would be to lay Luke off the scent by giving up your assets to him. We'll need an excuse, otherwise they'll be suspicious." said Morley.

"Tell them it's too stressful, we want a fresh start," I said, "its sort of true."

"I'll give the Judge a call this afternoon. See if we can set up an out-of-court settlement. Then he's disarmed, and you can get on with the matter in hand of the getting the lands in your name," replied Morley.

"How's that possible?" said Jim rather un-encouragingly.

"Class Lawsuit," he said. He looked down at the book, and continued, "You only have a chance if there are three or more members of the family willing to take on B.W.P and Stamnex. We'll need them on-board, all signatories to a partnership. Willing to go to court if necessary. A hurdle being, we will have to take action in the UK and America. The cost will be astronomical."

I winced, and Jim let out a slow gasp of air.

"I can get Jason, my brother," I said, "I *was* paying him, he'll help out, but there's no-one else."

"What about this Kenneth fellow? What's his allegiance?" Morley replied.

"He's too thick to have allegiances," said Jim.

"Well go and see him, and get him interested!" said Morley, his words becoming more fervent.

"There has to be something in it for him." I said.

"Tell him it'll come up roses if he goes with you. He's not getting much from Stamnex now is he?" Morley said.

"I doubt it, I don't think they ever got much anyway, that's why they were chasing me for my money."

"So what's the financial aspect?" said Jim.

"You won't get any change from a million," Morley replied.

"What!" Jim got up, "I'm going back on the road, let's go Nina, we have to get our old lives back - this is cloud-cuckoo-land."

"Jim. No! Let's just hear the details, then we can decide," I raised my voice, the first time I'd ever opposed Jim and he stopped on the spot in shock. Placing my arm on his, I wasn't one for outward displays of affection in public, but I had to stop a scene.

"Come along now Nina, Jim, we can resolve this," said Morley, "I have some influential friends. I'll take a third of the Zion income, in return for arranging the legal costs, in perpetuity of course. Sets us up for a nice little pension, does it not Jimmy?"

Jim had sat back down but I could see he wasn't happy. I knew it was unethical, but I wasn't going to telltale.

"You sort out Jason and Ken. I'll speak with the Judge get your house signed over to Luke. Get the ball rolling on the injunction to Stamnex and B.W.P," said Morley.

"OK, this one last thing, then that's it, but I want my van back, Luke can't have the Merc'," Jim replied abrasively.

"Okey dokey, lemon smoky," Morley smoothing Jim's prickliness, "I doubt if he's bothered about an old van when he lands on that little plot in Sussex Jimmy."

Later on at Mel's house after leaving Morley's office.

"We're going back to Africa," I said.

"Oh no," said Jim, "I can't go."

"That's where Ken is, we have to go, I'll speak to Morley, see if he can smooth the way," I replied.

Ken hadn't come back after the court case, he liked it out there, a little bit of money coming in from Stamnex, not enough to pay his bills in the UK, but he preferred the pace of life, and he'd moved his family out. He could be comfortable there, 'top-of-the-range', with a couple of staff and a cook. Will had always domineered the relationship.

We sat round the table in Mel's small kitchen.

"We've got no money Nina," Jim pleaded.

The cars hummed by outside. She was on the outer edges of an estate on the bypass, tiny rooms, a modern home, wafer-thin walls but that's what she'd wanted. I wish now I'd put *my* house in her name, then we'd be sitting pretty, but you live and learn. As it was, the three of us were wedged into her shoebox home. Mel was easy going, but it was sending Jim crazy. He liked a set pattern and Mel coming and going, although perfectly normal, didn't fit with him. She'd enthusiastically taken her old waitressing job back, jumped in her old Volkswagen Polo every morning to the Pizza Palace up the road in Croydon, 11 til 11 shifts, with two hours off in the afternoon. By the time she got home, gone for a run, had a sleep it was time for the evening session. Her money was keeping us afloat at the moment, but Mel didn't care either way, she liked to help out.

"We gotta go back to work Nina, let's get the van and get out there, we need the money, we can't go on like this!" said Jim.

"I'm not f*****' goin' back out there on the streets, I've been doin' it since I was twelve years old, I want what's mine, what my Granddad

223

left, and what my Dad should have had comin' to 'im," I spat out.

"C'mon, calm down, I'll put the kettle on, we can sort it out," said Mel.

"We haven't got the money Nina, we need at least three grand to get out to Africa, what with the hotels, an' the rest," said Jim.

"I've asked Jason," I said, "he's comin' in, he's agreed… the class action thingy."

"Jason hasn't got the bloody money Nina, it's spent, puttin' it down 'is neck!" Jim replied, frustrated and sounding gagged.

"He's borrowin' it, borrowin' it off his boys, they've both got good jobs, he's gettin' it off them." I said.

"And when did you ask 'im?" said Jim.

"I called when we got home," I said.

"You didn't tell me" he replied and he got up, pushed out his chair, and walked out the back door.

"Jim, Jim?!" lobbied Mel.

"Oh, he'll come round, he likes an adventure, it'll be like a holiday," I said.

"Mum, he might be right, maybe it's time to drop this. Hasn't it been too much with the court case and everything?"

The phone rung and Mel got up and answered it.

"It's Mr Morley, Mum."

I went over taking the receiver. The line clicked as his secretary connected us.

"Nina," came the long cool voice, "everything's on. Will's boy has agreed. They're taking the house as a one-off final payment for the money owed. There was no talk of Stamnex or B.W.P. The Judge thought the house was sufficient. Tell Jim he can collect the van at ten a.m. tomorrow. It'll be outside with the keys in it. I'll send you the agreement for the property transfer. What's your current address?"

I gave him Mel's, asking to get Jim and me a visa for Ghana, and to scratch some backs to get Jim back in the country.

"One last thing Nina. There's nothing wrong with these Zion, Dr. Dowie materials is there, you obtained them in a legitimate way did you not?" asked Morley.

"Yes, yes that's all right." I said, and put the phone down as Jim came back in. He had a grin on his face and a Daily Mail stuck under his arm, he'd been to the corner shop.

"All right Nin'?" he said, embracing me, and we never spoke about it again. The following morning Jim and Mel got up at five, she dropped him at East Croydon station, and he caught the train down to East Sussex, getting a cab to the house. The van was there, a bit mucky, but Jim soon had it sparkling again dropping in at a jet wash. I cried a bit as he came round the corner of the estate in it, but I didn't let him see, my eyes dried before he pulled in.

"Lookin' nice Nina, I'm off to see Sahid tomorrow, get a bit of gear, see if I can get a pitch for this Bank Holiday, Brighton racecourse, get a few quid in eh?"

"We can't do that Jim, I've booked our flights, we're going Monday, Jas' came by with the cash."

"Ha ha ha!" Jim laughed, "let's have lunch then, I picked up a lovely bit of salmon on the way back."

<hr />

July 21st 1968, I can remember very well, although not in sepia tone this time. The mood was sombre, my Mum didn't speak, they were both dressed in dark clothes. She was in a charcoal suit; it may as well have been a funeral.

"C'mon Sir, you're going to be all right," said the officer.

The two guards were replaced by a squad who'd arrived early in an unmarked car, a temporary Belisha beacon stuck to the roof, Mancunian, at least not Londoners. The assurances did not convince us. They took Dad and Mum in the their car, an executive emerald green Rover 3500 V8.

"Nice motor," Alfie said.

We piled into his MG Midget, which I hated because I could barely get inside. The weather was good, but I wished it was inclement, to reflect my mood. It was unfair of the weather to be nice when we were filled with such trepidation and worry. I shuddered inside.

"He'll be OK, ol' Phil has the gift-of-the-gab, you know," Alfie said.

"Shut up Alfie, I can't listen to you now, I feel ill," I said.

225

We remained silent, I fiddled with my hat, don't know why I'd worn it. As soon as we got to the steps of Southwark Crown Court, beside Tower Bridge the havoc hit us. There were more police there than could be imagined, and an army of press. We'd been following Philip's police car, they had their blues flashing, and siren, and Alfie kept right behind, the traffic parting as it sliced into the morning rush hour. Up through Deptford, New Cross, the Old Kent Road, the buildings, the souls, the shops, houses, the huge pre-fab blocks of flats they were constructing splurged amidst Peckham and Bermondsey, my whole life was here, gaping. I saw myself from above, as if I were a tremulous giant lying on my back, taking up the whole of South East London, staring back up at me, green, as in the advert for the Jolly Green Giant. I couldn't release it, and it was giving me a headache, which I never usually experienced. Like a bad dream you can't control, and that won't leave, even after you've gotten up, been to the toilet, and come back to bed, it hung on.

The scenery was a blur, I had a pang, a familiar knot below, 'this is it', I thought to myself, 'I have to get away from this, I have to get my family out of this, this can't be what it's about, there must be more'. I thought of my Dad, he'd shown me love. My Mum wasn't unkind but not the 'cuddling' type. You'd never hear a 'hello' or 'how are you today?' from my Mum, she'd be straight into a tirade, setting me on edge, stating what *she* was doing. I could have been ill, spurting blood, and she'd be recounting a happening from the grocers that morning. That was Mum. Hers was a hard life, rejected by her family for the pregnancy to a black man, and the racism that was the daily grind. It had toughened her, becoming oblivious to the idiosyncrasies of affection. My Dad had done the best with his lot, progressing unimaginably from his origins, he'd instilled in me something, and in that twenty minutes sat in the MG, I determined to move on, to something, I didn't know what yet, but when the opportunity came, I would be ready to seize it, put it through the wringer and hang it on the line in a fresh Monday wash day wind.

"I call Philip Brem-Wilson."

It was madness in the court as my Dad stood up and made it up to the witness box. The court building was modern, a sixties concrete block on the exterior, built for the purpose. It could easily house two hundred, and was at capacity. I didn't know what the criterion was to enter the arena, but everyone and their brother was here. You could have sold tickets. Lots of South London petty hounds that wanted to be somebody, their slutty girlfriends, relatives, sidekicks, cohorts, and reporters, anyone who was no one. Where I was sitting you could easily recognise the whiff of cheap Woollies[61] perfume, and Brut aftershave, molten into a gagging tang of Neanderthal. The sooner I was out of this the better. The ushers and police got order, the room quietened.

The Richardsons were flanked by police two each side and three in front, officers placed so they wouldn't be able to jump over the dock in a last bid for a Spanish hotspot. I tried to keep my head lowered and not draw their attention, but as soon as I looked up at my Dad, Charlie caught my eye, pulling his finger across his throat, indicating a blade. Alfie took off out of the seat and went for him, the police bulldozing in before he could get anywhere near. Bellows flew from the public benches.

"Snitch!"

"Dirty Snitch!"

The police picked off the rotters, tussling them out, girlfriends in tow. Mini-skirts and kitten heels, a flotsam of bleached hair, and protestations:

"Gerroff!"

"All right guv!"

Alfie would have killed Charlie there and then, had the police not intervened. We regarded the Richardsons as ponces, but it hadn't stopped Alfie obtaining a gun and keeping it under his pillow since the threats.

The Judge repetitively bashed his hammer against the sounding block; the percussion drill that still drums out a beat in my nightmares. He did establish order, the gallery hushed, no one else wishing to be ejected. Charlie and Eddie had slight smirks on their faces, as if it were their moment of glory. The sycophants watched, and were ready for

---

[61] Woollies – reference to the former high street retail outlet called Woolworth

227

the two minutes of fame. Somehow, they had shed the prison garb and were 'suited up', skinny ties, small collars, thin lapels. With their arms crossed, and brown suits they were like twins, fey, not at all 'hard-man'. My Dad was rooted, fixed on them, black knuckles wringing the chrome rail that surrounded the witness stand. He was as cool as cool could be. He knew pressure he knew the public the boxing booths had that covered. This wasn't going to faze him. The Richardsons kept their eyes on him, knowing why he was here, the gallery waited, I felt the whole building breathe and the ceiling was coming down, the white faux detail surrounding large cream globe shades were tumbling.

"Mr Brem-Wilson," a voice called and I snapped out of it.

The Crown Prosecution lawyer had started.

"Evidence, item three."

I wondered where are items one and two, why begin with three? An usher raised the clear bag that contained a cheque.

"Is this is your signature Sir?" said the lawyer, "show the witness please."

The usher walked over to Dad, holding it up between the tips of his fingers. Dad crimpled the bag to see and it was tugged away.

"Don't know." he answered.

The Judge slammed his hammer.

"Either it is, or it is not Mr Wilson, answer the question."

"Don't know, can't tell, your honour." Dad repeated, drawing a collective snigger from the plebs.

More from the gavel, the Crown lawyer standing in front of the witness box, a world-weary look on his face that said 'this is a good start'.

"Mr Brem-Wilson, once again, did you sign this company cheque, do you recognise this as your signature?" the lawyer asked, referring to the bag, which now sat on the evidence table, along with a number of other similar objects.

"Don't know, not sure Sir." he replied.

"One more time, and you'll be in contempt Mr Wilson, you've been warned," said the Judge.

I was more interested in the CID officers sat at the Crown lawyer's desk, two of the northerners, about five yards from the Richardsons' lawyers. They weren't in the least bit niggled by Philip's obtuseness. They were pleased with themselves. A bead went across my brow; there was something amiss.

"Answer the question, yes or no, Mr Wilson," said the Judge, "one last time, is it your signature on the cheque you have been shown as evidence item three?"

"Don't know Sir, difficult to say," said my dad.

"One week in custody, £200 fine. Contempt of court, take him away."

There was an eruption, two policemen took my Dad out, it happening so quick I barely had time to catch his eye. A bag of flour was thrown, and two eggs toward my Dad, which missed, the reporters let their cameras rip, though they weren't allowed in court.

"A waste of good eggs," I whispered, aghast at the bedlam.

"What?" said Alfie.

"Clear the court, clear the court, I won't stand for this, clear the court," said the Judge.

More police came in and the place was emptied, with Mum, Alfie and me escorted to an anteroom. A tray of teas arrived. I sat with my head in my hands, my Mum at the window, her hankie taken from the stiff leather handbag now clamped tightly shut, staring across at Tower Bridge.

"What in God's name is going on?" said Alfie.

No one answered.

"This is unbearable," said my Mum.

I'd never heard a scrap of emotion from her, and never heard anything like it since. In thirty minutes we were taken back through. It had been cleared bar a handful of reporters, the Richardsons, and people I knew to be their relatives. The police still sat with the Crown lawyer, they were all as 'happy as Larry'[62], indifferent to the uncooperativeness of the star witness.

"We shall continue please, notwithstanding the waste of public funds from the prosecution, we'll carry on and see if there is a case to answer... please Mr Prosecutor," the Judge drawing his view toward

---

[62] happy as Larry – extremely happy and carefree

the stenographer tapping at the recording machine, "make a record, that I am continuing."

I viewed the Richardsons. Same stance but now they were chuckling, nodding their heads, satisfied the main witness was gone. I shook my head in disbelief. I was confused.

"Call the witness, Johnny Bradbury," requested the prosecutor. Charlie stood up incredulous, not fast, the policeman beside him laying his hand on his shoulder before Charlie could stretch to his full height. He lowered himself back down, but slowly, staring directly at Bradbury who had his hands out in front, handcuffed, striding sheepishly through the court doors and the mock Roman portico, and up to the witness stand, sandwiched between four bobbies[63]. We all turned and trailed his progress across the floor. He didn't look over to the Richardsons. He wore prison regulation, which looked like a sack. A postbag styled jacket, four pockets at the front, and baggy trousers, that had most of their shape defined by a thick leather belt.

I knew Bradbury he was a fixture round the Old Kent Road, and the Thomas A Beckett pub, where half a dozen of the gangsters trained upstairs in the boxing gym. He was a hard man, a scar right across his face, cropped prison haircut, yellow teeth, a Dickensian caricature who could have been marched in shackles from a derelict detention ship moored in a mud-flat near Chatham. He was the Richardsons' gofer, undertaking the tortures. Bradbury swore the oath, assisted by the court official, I could see his hand trembling on the bible, a course South London growl saturating the room.

"Continue," said the Judge, not looking up from his papers.

The Crown lawyer rose and deliberately took the five steps over to Bradbury, who tried to catch the lawyer's eye, so as not to be captured like a rabbit in the Richardsons' headlights. The barrister took a breath, hesitating before he began, as if he already knew the result of his questioning.

"Do you know, and have you been associated with the Richardson brothers, who are sitting in the dock to my right Mr Bradbury?"

"Yes." he replied.

---

[63] bobbies – as 'coppers' – unformed police constables

I watched the Richardsons. They weren't giving anything away, but I sensed they were not so comfortable. Not a sound in court, the lights buzzed overhead, their capacitors drawing energy from the scene below.

"Would you..." and the lawyer looked down at his notes, "would you say, that you were a member of their gang, Mr Bradbury, from 1965 to 1967?"

"Yes," said Bradbury.

"Objection!" The defence lawyer intervened, stumbling over his words, kicking his chair back, not quite pulling himself up, aware he would only get halfway up before being asked to sit down again. "Objection Sir, this witness is unreliable, a fugitive in Britain, a convicted criminal."

"Overruled Sir. I'll decide on the credibility of the witness," said the Judge.

The questions were fired straight; Bradbury was part of the Richardsons' inner core. The defence lawyer had little chance. The Richardsons sat here, their grins gone, the relatives schtum[64] in the gallery. Bradbury spurted on about the rackets, the long firms, the tortures, thefts, scams and protection; apparently the more the lawyer asked the more he wanted to confess, like a wave of relief. I had to leave; the nailing of someone's feet to the floor of a docklands warehouse and being urinated on for four days was one statement too many. I took Mum with me. It was pointless us being there, we had no association with these people. Alfie stayed.

The Richardsons had sent Bradbury to Australia, to carry out a contract killing on a business associate called Waldeck who'd absconded with their money. Bradbury was caught there, and sentenced to hang. He offered to turn Queen's Evidence in exchange for a pardon and a new identity, and was returned to Britain. So my Dad was a decoy. Corruption, endemic in the Metropolitan Police, meant the real witness was being handled by another force altogether, in Manchester, so that he couldn't be 'nobbled'[65] by the Richardsons or

---

[64] schtum – (German origin) to keep quiet
[65] nobbled - to influence or thwart by underhanded or unfair methods

their associates. Over seventy percent of the Met' were found to be corrupt. The Minister at the time, Roy Jenkins, alleviating them of their posts, retiring them off, and a lot got prosecuted. Many of them were 'in the pocket'[66], and being bribed by criminal gangs. They were drinking buddies. Dad didn't tell anyone, it was all arranged; he had to keep it hidden. They had enough on the Richardsons without my Dad, and with Bradbury. The brothers were sentenced to twenty-five years. They were made an example of and it was a way of clearing out the crooked coppers in London. The police got their result, by the time Eddie and Charlie were out[67] my Dad was forgotten, and the sidekicks[68] disappeared. Dad got off of his minor charge in return for his contribution, and could get back to work. It had been an unprecedented year. I was exhausted.

A week later the champagne corks were popping at the Rivoli.

Mel was the taxi, our cases and us squashed into the Volkswagen Polo. It was Summer Bank Holiday 1985, the airport brimming with travellers. We had a heat wave, it felt hot, but would be a lot hotter when we got to Ghana. Jim already had his shorts on, I don't know why he'd worn them, as we had ten hours of air-conditioned plane ride, but he insisted. I had the African Box, also now containing the contracts that Morley had drawn up, which my brother Jason had signed. He'd taken little persuading, appreciating the extra money from before, it had put his two boys through University, he'd been keen to re-enlist in how 'the other half lived' as he called it. As he said, I'd done it once '…you can do it again Nina.'

It was Gatwick Airport, on the southern perimeter of London, more convenient. When we'd gone to Ghana originally there was no choice, but now there were regular flights. We'd called C.P from Mel's to stay at his hotel. We'd kept in touch, and he was happy to have us,

---

[66] (put) 'in the pocket' - having a good thing happen to you
[67] out – released from prison
[68] sidekicks - a person's close associate, especially one who has less authority

not dragging up the past. Frankly that was down to Jimmy, he was the 'salt of the earth'[69] and you could easily forgive him any misdemeanor. Faysal was picking us up from the airport; he'd been overjoyed to hear we were on our way back. It was 'spick and span'[70] when we got there. Accra airport had completely changed. Cooled corridors, tidy plastic seating, new toilets, you could feel the money.

"Well this is different," I said to Jim.

We then alighted a moving walkway to deliver us from the plane to immigration control. We were both feeling okay. We had the luxury of a film on the flight, which we'd never experienced, and Jim had fallen asleep after dinner, a blanket over his knees. Three security guards in blue uniforms quickly joined us, complete with holsters. We were expecting the lengthy waits, questions, checking of our visas and 'the greasing of palms'. They didn't exactly take us physically, but we could feel them right beside us, ensuring there was no escape route (not that we could have gone anywhere).

"Bloody 'ell, we're in for it now." said Jim.

"It's OK, Morley sorted it out." I replied.

"Well he's not here now is he?" Jim was agitated.

"What you up to?" Jim kept saying.

"This way sir," they ignored him and coaxed us along.

We continued via the busy arrivals terminal into the luggage hall. Our cases had already been off-loaded onto a trolley, being held by a newly arrived security man. They signalled and he went in front. The six of us proceeded through the baggage area then on to passport control. People were looking now. Once at immigration the four attendants parted the queues, pushed past the gawping lines waiting for papers to be checked and cases ransacked. Suddenly we were on the opposite side of the barriers having gone through a side gate opened by an officer. We were past the Customs Control and outside. Our security companions turned, and disappeared back inside. We hadn't even shown our passports. Jim looked around in every direction completely baffled.

---

[69] salt of the earth - thoroughly good type of person
[70] spick and span - spotlessly clean, neat and tidy

"What?"

"Morley" I said.

"Yeah, OK." laughed Jim.

"Jim, Jim, Nina!!" Faysal was waving.

He stood next to his car, a new gold Nissan. I missed the jostling 'luggage boys', it was civilised, there were a half a dozen baggage attendants, with badges on and blue rimmed caps.

"I didn't think I'd see you back here," Faysal said, elated by our arrival.

"Neither did we," said Jim, "good to see you."

We had hugs, and left for C.P's hotel. It was 'welcomings', dinner and drinks with Faysal, C.P, and their families for the next couple of days, and then we got down to the business of finding Kenny, and attempting to get him in on the Zion plan. We had his address, which was on the coast near Accra. We took a hire car that C.P had arranged and got going early. Jim had a notion that if all this didn't work out, at least we should return home with something, so he wanted to take advantage of the locally crafted basketware on sale.

"We can buy a couple of pallets, ship them to England, if they're cheap enough we can earn a good profit on them Nina."

He kept on about it. We'd seen them before in the markets plenty of times, and I conceded, appeasing Jim for the moment, but it wasn't exactly in the forefront of my mind. We went by the biggest market in central Accra, and found two basket makers who could do the job, taking their cards and factory telephone numbers. Jim bartered on two pallet loads, which was quite an amount, about four hundred baskets, assorted sizes that could be loaded inside each-other like Russian dolls. I was beginning to see his reasoning. We paid a small deposit and would be back in one week to carton them up and take the load to the shipping office at Dixcove. Jim enjoyed bargaining. We were very cheerful, I liked the wheeling-and-dealing[71] and the townsfolk were always smiling, willing, and amiable. Jim enjoyed bargaining, but it gave me a feeling of reticence over the shenanigans[72] and discontent my pre-

---

[71] wheeling and dealing - buying and selling things to make a profit
[72] shenanigans - secret or dishonest activity or manoeuvering

occupation with the Box was causing. I said to myself, 'this one last attempt', as we secured the basket samples the salesman had given us, driving off in the direction of the coast.

The Cape Coast Road from Accra ran west towards Takoradi, a familiar route, now smoother, sections of it like dual carriageway. We arrived at the little post of Elmina. Easy to find, there was only one turn off, and Ken's house was a couple of miles beyond the village, near the beach. As we drew up we found him on the porch.

"What the 'ell, Nina?!"

I couldn't help laughing when I saw him, a familiar face in a far-away place, and he broke in to laughter with me.

"Thank God," he said, embracing us both, which was our first surprise.

"F*****' miles from anyone here Jim, got to get home, it's so lonely, me and some f*****' fisherman. Drink?"

"Yes OK," replied Jim, "two beers."

"That's all there is to do here, f*****' drink."

The house was impressive, a massively spacious bungalow built on stilts, a wooden porch extending the whole length of the house, and a jetty that ran right out over the beach.

"Yeah, I go up to the ol' mines, see how they're gettin' on, but it's not the same as when Will was 'ere."

"I'm sorry." I said, starting to feel a tear in my eye.

"C'mon Nina darlin', you can't go back."

I could see Jim welling up too. We ended up crying and laughing together, sat on the porch all afternoon, watching the sun go down over the sea. It was a stunning place, the wild South Atlantic Ocean waves relentlessly rolling in against the endless sands, kicking the driftwood around, darters whooping, diving into the sea for snacks. Familiar swifts, like daytime bats, carried out aerial manoeuvres from their nests perched in the cracks of old fisherman's huts dotted along the shoreline, picking off insects in the warm damp air that nestled amongst the bush that met the sand. Paradise.

Ken's wife and older boy had lasted six months, going home, but Ken's money was wrapped up in a building project in Takoradi, started with Will, and he had to sit it out, waiting months on end to get any work finished, with the laissez faire attitude of the workforce eating into to his capital and his life. The cheques from Stamnex diminished every month, he thought they were ripping him off, but didn't have the means to prove it. The situation was the exact opposite to how I'd imagined and Ken bore no grudge. He was the type to 'latch on' and Jim and I had found him at a vulnerable moment. We had the contracts signed by ten o'clock that night. Ken couldn't wait to get out of there, even came with us to Faysal's, and then to the hotel for a week, so he could hear us talk about rain, dodgy British politicians, and fish and chips. Jim and Ken were amusing themselves at the hotel, by the pool and in the bar. I was happy with the plot, I had two relatives on board, Ken didn't care about Stamnex, and couldn't wait to get his money and escape from Ghana. He didn't understand the contractual parts much, but wasn't bothered.

I looked out at Ken and Jim lounging poolside, on recliners, the old style wooden ones with white cushions, towels behind their heads. Jimmy recounted stories from the 'good old days' at Downham, Ken chuckling out loud at one of Jim's jokes. I'd first caught sight of Jim, when I was a girl, at the Boy's Club there, which doubled as a kids' youth dance every month. I'd gone on to marry Alfie and only properly met Jim after the divorce, but we soon hooked up and started doing the 'markets' together. We had a lot in common, Jim had come up from the rough Downham estates, a poor working class district; he'd worked hard to move on, buy his own place. We had a good life, making money on the stall, until I'd got us in to all this. It was great to see him relaxing. Ken was easygoing and amicable, not too clever, but he didn't bring any 'issues to the table'.

The assignment for Mr Morley was time-consuming and I was faxing back and forth from the hotel whilst Jim did his own thing. He went with Ken to the factory to check on the basketware, and had a 'mosey' up to see Faysal. Morley gave me a list of chores, he wanted details of the lands mentioned in the Zion contract, and so I had to keep going to the Land Registry, wading through the monolithic bureaucracy to get the maps and confirmations. Morley helped, but I had to do the legwork. It wasn't often Jimmy and I spent any time apart but these things had to be done, and he deserved some breathing space. Morley had kicked off the legal rigmarole, issuing an action through his American associate. He told me to 'stay pretty'[73] in Ghana, as he didn't want us in the UK when the press caught wind of what I was doing. The stay dragged on, and he started wiring us money every week and paid C.P direct, his 'investor friends' covering our accommodation and per diems.

Four weeks in and we took up Ken's offer staying at his beach house, after realising that the hotel costs would be subtracted from anything we might earn. It was very luxurious by African standards, quiet, and we felt we were on a mini holiday. Jim wanted to see Ken's building site, the embryonic flats, and Ken offered to take him round Tuasi and Assor Brompon. They would say hello to the Chiefs and locals who Ken had got to know. He had a friend with a pick-up truck, so they could also collect the basketware and safely deliver to the docks. Jim was looking forward to it, he loved having a 'drive out', an adventure, plus he could double-check the pallets were well packaged up, reminiscing about his old 'loading days' on the lorries.

I was having trouble speaking each day with Morley from Ken's house, the phone lines were terrible so they dropped me back at the hotel where I stayed on my own for a few days. It was a little disconcerting, being solo, as we usually did everything together. Even with C.P, staff, and the hotel guests, it was lonely.

I had plenty to do what with Morley calling several times a day to discuss the civil suite in the USA that was accelerating apace. The papers had been lodged and the trustees of the estate had responded with an offer to keep it out of the media. They didn't want anyone knowing the full earning power of Zion. I was relieved as it would soon be over, and it looked like none of us had to attend court. Morley was negotiating an arrangement and I was closer to realising my Granddad's legacy. The time difference allowed me some respite, so in the mornings I laid in the sun by the pool, relaxed, yet disconnected. Before breakfast I swam, I could blank my mind until late afternoon, and sit at the water's edge, wallowing in my thoughts. C.P would come out at intervals, filling me in on the latest guest arrivals and his newest

---

[73] stay pretty - to leave alone or let be; to wait

business venture, a drainage contract for roads and bridges the government had commissioned. He was talkative and for once, I simply listened.

Perhaps the sun was softening me up, caressing my contemplations into malleable play dough. I'd probably been unfair to Jim, it dawned on me that if he hadn't been around I wouldn't have got any of this done. His organisation, talking to each and every one, his pleasant demeanour, and his skill got everyone on our side. I could be gregarious, but without Jim I was quieter, taciturn, even insular. Together we were a rollercoaster bulldozing through life. My first husband had said I was pushy, actually he said a lot more than that! The day he stayed behind in court at Dad's trial was the beginning of the end. Jim and I were suited. With Jim not around a perpetual nervousness permeated my stomach. It was a feeling I was used to, one of guilt, a personal demon, which he helped me conquer. It was a panic attack that never quite materialised into a full-blown stroke, a neurosis. Jim always had something positive to say, a joke, something affectionate, it kept me cheerful. I could feel the small demon, the butterflies of insecurity, the nervous twitch at the starting line of the sports day race, the worrying nag that you'll be late for your first job interview, a hollow despair that your Mum may not love you. The anxiety carried on, and sometimes I was so acquainted with it I would savour, go along, and use it like a calming pet, the enemy pitted against the aggressor - so much going on in my gut! I dozed off in the sun, only to be woken by the receptionist calling me.

The fax had come through Morley had a final offer. There was a lot of legal language. I needed Ken's signature to fax back the following day. I asked C.P to drive me down to Elmina and he was happy to oblige. I'd been trying the phone to Ken's house but it was just crackles on the line. They were due at the hotel the next day, but I wanted to surprise them with the fantastic news. I knew Jim would be elated and would be missing me. It was over; we would have money coming in from Zion and could find a house. Morley had mentioned some figures, but it was mind-blowing. He also said the tenants could be evicted from Tuasi and Assor Brompon, he'd exerted influence with friends and Stamnex, and B.W.P agreed to a pay-off out of the Zion profits, rather than have endless years of litigation over who got to mine the 'lands'. I wanted to get the agreement signed and faxed to Morley ASAP.

The drive would be about an hour. I chatted to C.P along the way about our adventures of when we first came to Africa. He said how much things had changed, with investment and a stable government. He'd expanded his business with civil engineering contracts. He enjoyed this subject, I'm sure he never discussed it with his wife or anyone, as every detail was waiting to be spilled out. C.P had always been enterprising.

We got to Elmina quite late, having stopped at a restaurant that C.P recommended for lunch. It was hard to keep calm with such good news. I was looking forward to seeing Jim, even though it had only been less than a week. I couldn't make C.P go any faster; he had his own pace, talking and eating, the motoring felt like days. It was a hot Cape Coast afternoon. I could feel the sea air wafting in the car window as we pulled down the lane. Until now I'd had to keep them shut because of the filth thrown up by passing lorries on the main road and the omnipresent heat. C.P pulled up at the grove, which was at the farthest point after the village had ended. We got out and could hear music. Jim loved his music, they had a Frank Sinatra tape on, blaring out of the house.

"Nice sound," said C.P, grinning.

He knew Jim was fond of a 'sing song', and his voice was soaring above the recording, belting out 'New York, New York'. He would take to the microphone whenever a band had been booked at the hotel. C.P leaned in to the car and tooted the horn, but they didn't appear.

"Jim, Jim!" I called out, and got the Box out of the car.

We walked the few yards to the house and went up the steps into the side of the bungalow, pushing open the screen door; the main door behind it was ajar for the breeze to come in. This side entrance went directly into the kitchen, there was a pile of washing up, and empty beer bottles on the table. The music was louder and I heard Ken and Jim's voices in the din. I shouted excitedly again. We went through the living room door, which was also partially open.

239

"Jim I'm back…!"

C.P and I stopped in our tracks. Jim swivelled round, all I could see was his erect member, behind him two native girls on the sofa with Ken, he had an arm round each, all nude. The music kept battering out of the huge speakers either side of the stone fireplace, 'top of the list, head of the heap, king of the hill…' I looked at the hearth, thinking, 'I wonder if that fire will ever get lit, surely it's never cold enough, maybe for effect?' I looked round at C.P, his mouth agape, his permanent smile ever cheery wiped from his face, replaced by a look of utter fear. They were waiting for me to speak, but I didn't. I looked again and Jim's penis was flaccid. I moved six steps in a second, and wacked him so hard with the Box the side cracked a bit, and blood immediately poured from above his forehead. He was on the floor. I turned to Ken, throwing the whole Box at him, he ducked and it missed, landing behind the sofa.

"Sign the f*****' contract and make sure I have it by nine a.m. tomorrow or the same will happen to you!"

The girls were hysterical, Jim was pushing himself up off the floor on one arm the other holding the wound.

"Nina, darlin' Nina, c'mon, it was just a bit of a laugh, there's nothin'…"

I span round, grabbed C.P who was motionless, panicked by the whole thing, and tugged him out.

"Let's go C.P there's nothing more for us here."

We sat at the kitchen table at Bromley, it was two years after the court case and Dad was back to his usual self, the Bingo carried on, with us all still working there. I had branched out with my own market stall, buying lots of clothing, and anything I could get cheap for the pitch in Deptford. We were forever working and a visit to my Dad's was entertaining, better than anything on TV. He had a close call with the Richardsons and it brought the family together. Nothing was said about him being a witness, how he had kept it a secret from us. He'd got off, and the Richardsons were gone, that was all that mattered. My daughter Mel was ten years old and fascinated by the house, rifling through her granny and granddad's mementoes, ornaments and photographs, but best of all, like me, she loved the outlandish tales that my Dad spun.

Philip: "We had a knock at the door one morning at Downham. It was the milkman."

Milkman: "My mate's got a round and he's seen one of your lot, down the road, in Bromley."

Ray: (standing at the door, with Philip behind him) "What you mean, one of your lot?"

Milkman: "You know, a eerrr 'spade'."

Ray laughed, slammed the door. The milkman knocked again. Philip opened the door.

Milkman: "He's a 'Brem-Wilson', like you lot."

Philip: "Is that right?"

Milkman: "No, on me life, here's the address." He passed a small scruffy receipt with some scribbling - an address on the back.

Philip: "The three of us brothers got the bus that morning, and found they had the old man in a nursing home. He was called (lowering his voice) Ebenezer Brem-Wilson. He'd come all the way from Africa when he'd heard of his brother's death, our Dad, your great Granddad (pointing at Mel), Thomas. It was my Uncle Ebenezer from Africa! He'd been to Penrose Street, thinking that's where we still lived, but was hospitalised with a terrible stomach complaint. When he didn't recover properly they sent him to an old folks place, not knowing what else to do with him. He was going to go back to Africa, but was too ill. When we turned up, there was this crazy fellow, mumbling. He smelled, residents sitting as far away as possible on the other side of the room. The nurses didn't want to go near him. His hair was up all over the place, a great big grey balloon, un-shaven, and an African gown like a big dress, legs spread so you could see his pants."

Mel giggled.

"He kept muttering they were robbing him, and now and then was delirious. He was a ringer[74] for our Dad, we couldn't leave him, he was

---

[74] ringer – as in dead-ringer, a look-alike

241

family. All his gear was locked in a bulky wooden chest, it was so heavy we could barely get it home even between the three of us. Mum, (he pointed at Mel), *your* Great Grandmother went berserk, she didn't want any of her ex-husband's African relatives, it reminded her of the time when she had a full house with Thomas' hangers on. Ebenezer wanted bathing everyday, treated us like servants, it was rotten, we'd made a right booboo. We didn't have any money, and the ol' boy had a taste for fresh fruit, you know, foreign type, which cost 'an-arm-and-a-leg' in those days. I was given the job, as the eldest, to confront him, tell him that he'd have to go that we weren't a charity. So I went up to his room one day, knocked, and was given permission to enter. He was lying in the bed in his dressing gown, I tried to explain, but he looked agitated, I got nervous, and couldn't get to the point. He was looking more and more annoyed, when he raised his finger to his lips and told me to hush, 'ssshhhhhh'. Ebenezer put his hand under the bed cover, took a key out of his pocket, rose gently, went over to the chest, slid back the lid, and took out a bar of twenty-four carat gold. I sneaked a peek over his shoulder into the chest whilst he had his back to me, and my eyes popped out because I'd seen a massive pile of solid gold nuggets.

When he turned I was back by the bed. He gave me this one piece, and told me to go shopping to get his groceries, and extra things. I gave it to Mum, she got fifty pounds for it in London, paying the bills, and keeping him in plenty of fresh fruit. After a month we were back to square one, the money gone, Ebenezer increasingly demanding, and he didn't offer again. We decided the gold belonged to the family so we waited until he'd gone for a walk one morning. Danny kept watch, Ray and me forced the lock with a hairpin - Ebenezer had taken the key with him. We took a few nuggets out of the chest. There were so many he'd never miss them. When he went for a walk we'd take a bar. They were evidently going down, and we were evidently becoming better dressed(!) spending it on clothes, and giving a bit to our Mum.

Ebenezer was getting sicker by the day, and stopped his walks. He got very irritable, haranguing us, wanting this-and-that. The doctor didn't have a diagnosis, and Mum couldn't stand it any more. Every time the doc' came out Mum had to pay. Ebenezer blamed the climate, said he wished he could go home to Africa where he would get better.

I got lumbered with going up town to get the boat ticket for him to go back to Africa, only glitch was it went from Liverpool, so I had to take him up there. We'd cleared out his chest, but he was too ill to notice. He insisted on a bag of fresh fruit for the trip. We got the ten a.m. train from Kings Cross. He was ranting, all the passengers were looking, I tried to keep him quiet, but he wasn't well, there wasn't much I could do for the poor ol' sod. We were stuck in this carriage, Ebenezer sandwiched between a stout lady in a lovely fur coat, and me. Businessmen sat opposite, the train was crammed, we couldn't move. He ate the whole bag of fruit, and his belly started grumbling, the smell in the carriage turned rotten, a right STINKER!"

Mel was so amused she was shaking.

"I apologised, but before I knew it, he'd thrown up all over the woman and the seat. She ran out of the carriage with her coat covered in puke, followed by the other fellas, and I was left to clear up the mess, which was already 'honking' and looked like scrambled egg. Luckily, Ebenezer fell asleep for the rest of the way.

At Liverpool I could hardly move him, he weighed a ton, and I couldn't wake him up properly. I tipped a porter a couple of bob to help me, we managed to get him off the train and I took a cab to the docks for the voyage. Typical, the boat was delayed until the following day so I found him a room in a Bed and Breakfast. He was 'half-a-kip' still and I struggled with him. I needed to use my return train ticket, so I was forced to leave him in his room, telling the owner to put him in a cab in the morning. I grabbed a taxi, and headed straight for the station with minutes to spare. We never heard a thing about it, and presumed he'd got home OK. It was only years later we got a letter from Africa saying he never returned. We found out he'd died in Liverpool, they had no details for him, so was buried in a pauper's grave! And that's the end of that!!"

"No! That's terrible Dad!"

"Yes, but it's the way I tell 'em!"

As he grew older, my Dad developed a taste for fruit, often consuming too much for his own good. Even when Mum and Dad divorced, she still kept going round to his flat, taking him his shopping, with bags of cherries and kiwi fruits. The separation came as no surprise, Dad had an affair with a young girl who'd been working at the Bingo Hall when he was sixty-five, and fathered her child. It was galling that he now had a daughter younger than my own. But that's what he was like; something of Thomas had rubbed off.

My Mum was up against it from the outset. Thrown out by her staunchly Catholic father because she was pregnant (by a black man) with my brother, the only place to go was to Downham with Ettie. It didn't last, as the house was too small for five adults, and a baby. It was an impossible slog trying to find somewhere to live in London when there was still a great deal of prejudice against mixed race couples. They got married, and devised a plan, which worked for a while. A white friend would meet the landlord, and put the deposit on a flat. They'd sneak in and out, and it helped if the landlord didn't live on the premises. Sometimes they'd have a month or two, and sometimes only one night. It kept going like this for a while, until at last a lucky break, a suitable flat came up over a shop, at 21 Bromley Road, Bellingham.

Both my Dad's brothers were wed. Raymond married Rose, had a son William, and Danny married Lillian, who was widowed, raising their son, Kenneth. Ettie had six grandchildren in total including me! She became a gently eccentric character. There was an infinite supply of provisions from her carpetbag, produced at will, a sandwich, pie, or piece of cake. She moved to a bungalow in Keston, Kent, often visiting her doting family, keeping everyone amused for hours with theatrical stories, spontaneously bursting in to choruses of music hall songs, where we all joined in, 'A Little of What You Fancy...'

In 1970 my father had a letter from the Gaming Control Board, he had to apply for an official license for the Bingo Hall, as they were now being regulated under the same jurisdiction that controlled gambling. It was a burgeoning industry, the Top Rank's taking over. Dad's week in custody for contempt of court could not be struck off the record. A minor offence, but it was a criminal act in the committee's eyes. Moreover his association with the Richardsons was a thorn. The Gaming Board wouldn't grant his license. Petitions were raised, signed by thousands of supporters, but it made no difference to them. Three hundred uniformed police officers had retired early, including four hundred C.I.D, and many senior officers were sent to prison. They wanted a clean sweep of anything linked to this sleazy period. It was the end of the Bingo at the Rivoli, and my Dad, at sixty-two, had no contingency plan, no retirement fund. Dad's philosophy was 'spend-spend-spend', never thinking ahead.

He started up Bingo in Lewisham, putting the license in his son's name, but luck was not on his side. Building work commenced outside, the street dug up for months, traffic diverted, and pavements rendered almost impassable. He complained and fought the council but trade dried up before anything was done. The original success could never be rekindled and he shut up shop. Mum divorced him when she heard about the pregnancy and Dad moved in with his young girlfriend, who soon threw him out, realising that his collection of expensive Savile Row suits weren't going to pay the bills. He lost the house, as he'd taken a loan against its equity to launch the Lewisham venture, and ended up in a local authority 'council flat'. So that year spelt the death knell for any Brem-Wilson legacy, the fortune my Dad had built up whittled as quickly as it had amassed. When you're at the top, there's a lot further to fall, and you land with a harder thud. It's something I've never forgotten.

Philip carried on working with a series of 'get by' jobs. He ran a pool shop in Brixton, then a snooker Hall in Deptford, which he enjoyed. He was a character, and the young clientele came to know him affectionately as 'Pops'. He maintained his 'look', suited, well turned out in indispensable ties, colourful waistcoats and trilby hats. This lifestyle, augmented by some minor 'wheeling and dealing' continued until his health deteriorated in 1998. He died in hospital at ninety years of age. It marked the end of an era, the offspring of an original African migrant, a newcomer who'd started afresh. They'd integrated and I was the result - a quadroon[75], lighter skinned, all three Brem-Wilson brothers having married local women. There was nothing left of the money my Grandfather, or my father had obtained. The Box remained, but not much to show for an extraordinary life - a cupboard full of old suits, some photographs and our memories.

---

[75] quadroon - a person whose parents are a mulatto and a white, and who is therefore one-quarter black

Tunnel vision. That's how I trundled along for the next few days, weeks, and months. I laughed a bit louder than I had before, made jokes, struck up conversations, and busied myself in every way, ensuring there was no time to think or contemplate. The television sent me to sleep and got me up. I called Mel each day, and constantly got Morley on the phone.

C.P was silent, awkward, I'd chattered away as if nothing had happened. We'd stopped for petrol, C.P got something to eat but I couldn't look at food. As soon as we got back I ordered a cab, and checked into a hotel near the airport, staying there for the remainder of the trip. I didn't tell C.P where I was so he wouldn't tell Jim. I left Jim's passport and ticket with C.P and instructions to fax the contract to Morley. Morley got it the following morning at eight thirty, so Ken and Jim must have returned to the Liberty Court immediately.

The airport hotel was bland, expensive, but modern and air-conditioned. I was at a loss, not having been alone before, so I walked over to the terminal, which unlike UK airports was invitingly approachable and bought a ticket with what cash I had. I went home early. Once on the plane I was relieved, liberated. I'd accomplished my ambition and it struck a vital chord. I flicked through the in-flight magazine, the usual watch and aftershave adverts, and city guides. I started reading about London's Tate Gallery, an art article. I knew nothing about the arts but I knew they'd got it made. They've found the core of 'what it is', the 'meaning of life', and something permanent, leaving their 'mark'. I fancied a bit of that, for someone, somewhere, to say 'Brem-Wilson' and the back of my neck to bristle. There had to be a point to life. My achievement, the restoration of the Brem-Wilson legacy overpowered my shock, the betrayal and infidelity. Mel picked me up from Gatwick, she was crying, but I was all smiles. I wasn't going to let it get us down. At Mel's house the postman had been, with dozens of telexes and letters, all from Africa, in Jim's handwriting. The answer-phone was blinking, full up.

"I'll get them later Mum, don't worry about it."

I took the post, ripped it up without looking and threw it in the bin.

246

"Cuppa tea Mum?"

I met someone else. I had the honey pot of wealth, and the flies swarmed. I welcomed the distractions, upping my lunches out, shopping trips, dinners, theatre, golf, hairdressers, anything. I had eyes for an Estate Agent who showed me round a spacious mock Georgian house on the prestigious Keston Park Estate. In my new circle he was considered 'upmarket', my old market buddies would have phrased it differently, but we hooked up anyway. He was a gentleman, treating me well. I bought the house, but made sure I put it in Mel's name. Mel told me that Jim had come to collect the van one day. Jason said he'd gone back on the lorries, renewing his Heavy Goods Vehicle license, getting a job on the skips - two hundred pounds a day, delivering as many rubbish skips as humanly possible, which with Jim's experience, he probably could.

I got Mel out of her two-up-two-down[76], up-graded, round the corner from the old place. She didn't want to move off the estate. Mel missed Jim, she had her own Dad, but had taken a liking to Jim's relaxed outlook, his animated interest in folk and everything going on. I wanted to believe that this naïve keenness led him into that fateful situation with Ken in Elmina. Jim wasn't gullible, but he was too easy going. Had I bullied him? In the back of my mind I knew I could be a bit 'mouthy', and sent him crazy with my preoccupations. Ken had 'acquaintances', they had a few drinks too many, it went a little too far, but 'it-was-what-it-was', there was no going back. The letters and calls subsided.

In 1995 my estate agent friend Roger upped and left, saying I was too pushy. I knew my anecdotes were becoming stinging instead of witty. I liked my own way, and sometimes his presence niggled me. I had friends but I was on my own, they were no substitute for Jim. I took cruises, holidays, met people, but it wasn't 'me'. What was I to do? Start up a market-stall again? So I could build up a new stable? The old market pals had jumped ship after the 'Will thing', anyway, who could blame them? Mel met a chap and had gone to Australia for a

---

[76] two-up-two-down - a dwelling house, semi-detached or terraced, with only four basic rooms

247

'career change'. I don't know why she couldn't pursue it at home but she was single minded like me. Occasionally my brother Jason popped round when he was sober enough to drive, his increase in income in direct correlation to the amount of time spent propping up the bar at the local pub. I didn't speak with Ken again; he'd gone back to his wife, who didn't seem to mind about his extra marital activity, because she had the money. The gagging order from Zion curbed any possible broadcast of the Brem-Wilson history. I had the cash without the recognition. It became a bitter pill. I felt like I'd let everyone down and I was alone. It hadn't turned out how I thought.

There was a time in British history when the post came at a reasonable hour, well, before eight in the morning. Post was sorted through the night then delivered at a useful time. Now it seemed that the postman sorted it as he went, no doubt part of a vast money saving initiative aimed at costing businesses thousands everyday, chasing late cheques and payments. It came so late I often wondered if they might as well wait until the next day to bring it. I had a post lady, or perhaps a 'post-person', since they were determined to modernise my postal service, I should honour it by using the correct terminology. She pulled up at her eleven slot, but there was going to be nothing regular about *this* morning.

The metal gates at the top of the drive were permanently trapped open, the electrical circuitry defunct, and I lacked the inclination to get another workman to tinker. Jim had always headed up this department. Nobody was trying to break in, and if they did I might welcome it as 'change-is-as-good-as-a-rest'. So the post lady drove up, I heard her on the stones. I was by the swimming pool having some breakfast, which invariably lasted from about eleven through to three in the afternoon. It would be bills and junk mail, but I went to the front door to scoop up the pile, past the burbling television (which was angled so I could glimpse it from the pool), and the prerequisite detritus that amassed prior to the visit from the cleaner every week. An audience participation chat show was on, made exciting by some testy argument.

There was one letter, I recognised the franking mark, 'Lincoln's Inn Chambers'. I hadn't heard from Morley for years, the royalties came directly into my bank account from the USA. I looked at the date 25

July 1995. I stood for about twenty minutes in the hall turning it round in my fingers, raised conqueror envelope, the feel of money, officialdom, disaster. The old feeling came, stomach down in my bowel, shaking, jitters, churning. I knew what it was. I expected this day. I returned to the pool, the letter remaining un-opened. At midday the phone rang. It was Morley.

I arranged lunch with a golfing pal, and went to a favourite boutique in Croydon, buying a new outfit. It rained that night, the letter irrefutably ruined, but the franked date and tactility of the paper loitered in my half-sleep. I'd employed an avoidance tactic, but like a panning nature television camera shot swooping in on a polar bear across an ice-field, my eyesight whizzed over the sodden communication in a perpetual three-D slow-motion all night.

The phone kept ringing the next day, the answer-phone filled-up, I didn't listen. The panic mode didn't disappear altogether but I did manage to suppress it by ignoring the impending news, throwing myself into tedium, watching television, eating, trying to sleep, and trips to the shops. More letters came during that week, recorded post, and registered post by courier.

Finally I had a knock at the door and it was Morley himself, the Bentley parked up on the drive. I nodded at him without speaking.

"Nina, we have to talk."

I backed away and turned so as not to face him. He followed; I tied the dressing gown higher, not being properly dressed, even though it was around two thirty. I knew what was coming so I sat, silent. He sat down opposite, uninvited, on the huge puffy cream leather settee, his mass significantly denting the stuffing. He spoke, slightly breathless.

"Nina, you stole the contract didn't you?"

I waited.

"I didn't steal it, we paid seventy dollars for it, I've got a receipt."

"I hope that's the case Nina. Your money, my money, my investor's money, it will dry up if it's found you took the contract without consent… then we'll be sued for our underwear."

"I didn't."

"The police in Zion are reinstating the investigation. They've emailed me Jim's statement. You've got to make amends with Jim and get him to be a witness at a trial for you, and us."

There was no delay in my thinking.

"I won't do that."

"You have to Nina. Whatever's happened is water under the bridge. You'll have to swallow it and get Jim back as an independent witness to corroborate your story."

"What about Mel?"

"She's too close, she won't be credible."

"No," I said

I was shaking, a slight compression in my chest, on the right topside. If I'd been a smoker I would have lit up.

"Nina, I organised investors, how do you think I got Stamnex and B.W.P out of the frame? These things don't just happen!"

He raised his voice, sweating, reminding me of the Chief at Assor Brompon, asserting power over his troupe; an over-the-top ostrich feather headdress and the picture would be complete. I dug my heels in. I wasn't going to speak to Jim. They all called me. Even Ken came round. The court case went ahead. Jim had said he would go to America, they'd contacted him, but he wouldn't do it unless I approached him. There was nothing in it for him, except to get back together with me, and that wasn't going to happen. I was forced to fly out by subpoena, a court order in Britain made by Zion. It was the worst journey I'd ever had to make, the sojourns with Jim, a lark in comparison, messing around in the bush. It was serious, the prospect of jail, theft, fraud, corruption. They were throwing everything in the book at me. The flight was interminable, checking my watch every five minutes, constantly annoying the attendant over the ETA. I thought of how my Dad would cope. I wish I'd inherited his confidence but that attribute wanted to skip a generation, except when I could muster a kind of paranoid belligerence. I'd been preparing, don't get me wrong, Morley had put up a fight, holding them off for months, breathing space to prepare my answers, speeches, lies. I wasn't exactly escorted out of England, but they were definitely keeping an eye on me, same at O'Hare. I was politely met by police officers that escorted me to the hotel.

My experience proved beneficial as the familiar court atmosphere afforded me a second wind. I was calm and steely and ready for the probing. Morley didn't attend. He had a representative who wasn't officially my defence, but advised and briefed me on the protocol, as I was representing myself. Morley was staying at arm's length, so as not to be associated. I got some good answers in, told the story about how we paid for the contract, and showed the receipt. It had some 'legs' and I avoided jail.

"What difference does it make? A contact's a contract," I said, "it's the same either way, it shows the deal between my Granddad and Zion… whatever the receipt says?!"

The Judge upheld Zion's claim, using some bizarre piece of legislation, a legal grey area. Zion could stop paying me. The contract was not considered binding between us, because my receipt was 'not legible'. That night at the hotel I lay on the bed watching the un-changed continuous advertisements for fat in the form of biscuits, cakes, ice cream, and toppings, thinking about a faulty kettle I'd returned to a Curry's electrical goods store at home. They refused a refund because the receipt wasn't clear. It annoyed me more than what I'd just been through. The tension rose in my chest, a slight tightening.

"Is this what they mean when they say your blood's boiling?" I muttered to myself.

The smarmy assistant wouldn't back down.

"Sorry Madam, you'll need the receipt, no returns, without a receipt. Sorry Madam, please keep the receipt next time."

"Receipt this, receipt f*****' that!" I carped on, with the response I should have made at the time.

I flew back. The house was empty when I got home, some messages from Mel on the machine. I had to pick myself up, put things in order. I called Roger and he found a buyer for the house. Mel agreed the sale, the money quickly transferred to her in Australia. Morley knew money was invested in the house, he'd find it, but not before I'd let Mel spend it. Letters had piled up again at the front door, bills, a financial claim from Morley, which I answered, as I knew it would stall him whilst I squirreled the cash abroad. The investors were after me. I stayed at Mel's old place, which I'd kept on with some sporadic rentals, taking a suitcase with me, and the Box from the display cabinet in the hall. I'd lost the key, and broke the glass with a brick from outside the front door covered in a tea towel. I should have binned it by now. I hated the sight of it. I'd done everything, everything within my means, moved the earth, and look where it had got me. Sitting in Mel's living room.

I had no money. Morley commandeered what remained after Mel had bought an expensive car and jewellery. She didn't wear jewellery but I recommended it - 'portable' was my motto when it came to investments. I was signing on, on the dole, 'on the rock 'n' roll', as Jimmy used to call it, nearly at retirement age, when my pension would start. Moneyed friends vanished, with the posh house and gaudy lifestyle. The cars went by on the bypass, my scintillating view, the net curtains getting progressively muckier. Never a conscientious housekeeper, I had nothing left to tidy for. Jason visited, he had no 'agenda', 'comme ci comme ça', the philosophy of a boozer, and 'what's wrong with that' I would think to myself, 'what's f*****' wrong with that'.

"C'mon Nina, come round, see the boys, see the grandchildren, you got to get out, do something," he kept at me.

I would say okay, but it would be forgotten the moment he'd gone. The Box rested by my chair, with loads of knick-knacks precariously piled-up on it, press snippets about the court cases, the national papers going on about the bingo, and my Dad's photographs. I sat there pretty well for a year, maybe two, the television bleating away in the corner, and Mel paying my bills from Australia, money going out of her account for electric, gas, television licence, so on. I would walk down to the parade of shops, get some breakfast cereal (about all I could eat with the stomach cramps I was getting regularly now), and sit and have a bowl of milky mulch. The telephone had stopped, and the post ceased when it was established I had no money left.

One Saturday Jason brought his grandchildren. I perked up, both of them bouncing around the living room in their bright trendy clothes. He'd been babysitting for the day and taken them out, calling in on the way back from an adventure park at Chertsey, Surrey. They were excitable. I made tea, gave them orange juice. Jason sat talking about the old times, Downham, Bromley, jazz, like Ella Fitzgerald, and what his sons were doing. One of the boys, Michael, pulled out the Box, the rubbish on it toppling.

"C'mon boys," said Jason, "don't be naughty."

"That's all right, let them look," I said, "what's it matter now?"

They played with it on the floor, pulling out all the photos, the diary, running their little fingers across the leather, and the jungle scene engravings. Jason and I sat watching them, me commenting on all the photos and bits 'n' bobs.

When they'd gone the Box was left open on the floor, Thomas Brem-Wilson's diary opened. I picked it up, looked at it for a few minutes, and bent down grabbing a piece of scrap paper one of the children had been scribbling on with crayons that they'd brought with them. I wrote, in red crayon, 'Linen and lace fluttered in the air. Thomas pulled out a fresh white hanky to join in the flurry, and as he did so, he customarily felt the small bible that he always carried in his inside jacket pocket'.

THE END

CLIVE PARKER-SHARP

About The Author

Clive Parker-Sharp, from rock star to dole queue and back again.

"It felt like I'd been kicked out of the limo onto the street corner, and they were pointing at me through the smoked glass windows as they slowly pulled away. In reality it's not as simple as that, but when you've been 'on-top' and it all comes crashing down, it leaves a mark," said Clive.

Envisaged as a 'rock 'n' roll' travelogue charting the ridiculous ins-and-outs of a 'pop' career, Clive's scribblings and taught observations took on another guise, as his first intended book metamorphosed into something completely different. The Box came about after he started restoring his mother-in-law's family recordings in his small studio, and then further researching the diaries of her grandfather Thomas.

"You need that 'push' to organise yourself, and starting on the tapes and diaries was a catalyst. Such a wealth of content, it inspired me. Perhaps this is just Volume One!"

Clive Parker-Sharp started his career at the age of nine, treading the boards in local workingmen's clubs in South East England, and then punk acts in and around London. As a teenager he joined what became the biggest independent band of all time, and was at the forefront of creativity in the new wave movement of the 1970s and 80s. He then became a founding member of the super group Big Country, and has graced stages with The Clash, The Human League, The Only Ones, Siouxsie & The Banshees, Alice Cooper, and numerous others in a career spanning three decades. Not content with life as a musician, Clive has gone on to produce, and make his own folk and electronic guitar music, with eclectic and stunning effect. As a composer and producer Clive made a 90s dance hit, as well as running his own mini record label, undertaking all the press, PR, promotion, videos, tours, art and editorial content.

It was inevitable that Clive would eventually turn his creative talent to writing; his poignant observations and ambient narrative continuously honed in composing, productions, jots, blogs, and notes. Unconventional, occasionally outspoken, Clive has a refreshing approach to his writing. As a maverick musician, pushing boundaries, he also plays with pace and rhythm in language. His results are an unorthodox blend, colourful and sometimes shocking - a unique experience.

Nina Brem-Wilson is a major contributor to The Box with fascinating anecdotes and stories about her family history. Nina started work on her father's fruit and veg stall in the 1950s, then onto her own stall in Deptford and South London. She spent time looking for her 'family gold' on the Ivory Coast in the 1970s and 80s. Nina instigated the archiving of her grandfather's diaries, which influenced the book. Nina worked alongside her father in his Bingo Emporiums in the 1960s, keeping all the news clippings. She had a successful boutique in Bromley called 'Weeds' in the 1970s selling designer hippy clothing. Nina has strived in a man's world, an independent businesswoman with an unconventional outlook, and irrepressible sense of humour. Nina is now a prolific artist making ceramic pottery and painting.

Join us on Facebook: http://facebook.com/parker.clive

ALSO AVAILABLE FROM
STRAND PUBLISHING UK LTD

- *The Challenge of Reality* by Sultan Bashir Mahmood
- *The Path Of The Gods* by Joseph Geraci
- *The First Casualty* by John Adam and MA Akbar
- *The Strand Book of International Poets 2010*
- *The Strand Book of International Short Stories*
- *The Assassins Code 1* by Christopher Chance
- *Tragedy Of Deception* by Humayun Niaz
- *The Misunderstood Ally* by Faraz Inam
- *Marie Antoinette, Diana & Alexandra: The Third I* by Alexandra Levin
- *Faceless Enemy - A True Story From Waziristan, The Last Outpost* by Ghulam Qadir Khan Daur

All titles are available to order online from Amazon.co.uk and Amazon.com, Kalahari.com, Play.com, Tesco.com, WH Smiths, Waterstones, Blackwells, Ingrams, Gardeners, from all good booksellers and direct from Strand.

For more information about our books and services, visit our website: http://www.strandpublishing.co.uk

Strand Publishing UK Ltd
Golden Cross House
8 Duncannon Street
Strand, London
WC2N 4JF
+44(0)207-1-833-121
email: info@stranddpublishing.co.uk
http://www.strandpublishing.co.uk
Strand Facebook page: http://www.facebook.com/pages/Strand-Publishing-UK-Ltd/294372581198?ref=sgm
Follow Strand on Twitter: http://twitter.com/#!@strandpublishuk

Lightning Source UK Ltd.
Milton Keynes UK
UKOW040756220612

194881UK00005B/35/P